THE UNPRINCIPLED

THE UNPRINCIPLED

DAVID CROYDON

First published in Great Britain in 2012 by
Hilltop Publishing, Brill, Bucks. HP18 9TQ
Hilltop Publishing Limited Reg. No. 3998266

Cover design by Peter Mays at white space, Oxford

A CIP catalogue record for this book is available from the British Library.

ISBN 9780953685066

Typeset in Minion by Avocet Typeset, Chilton, Bucks
Printed and bound in Great Britain by Biddles Limited, Kings Lynn, Norfolk

For Catherine,
who put up with all this.

Foreword

Or as Frankie Howerd would have put it, "The Prologue."

STARTED MAKING THIS RECORD of events because, when it was all over, and indeed during the long roller-coaster ride that was the relatively short life of the sales promotion (and subsequently direct marketing) agency, Marketing Principles, which I co-founded, I was aware that so much had happened to us – Harold Macmillan's "Events, dear boy, events" – that it really was worth committing to paper. I've written it in the present tense, largely because I felt it made it flow better and come alive; but because it was composed retrospectively – eight years after the endgame and more than double that after the start of it all, I am acutely aware that, while everything here did actually happen (there is no fictional over-writing to pep it up), it almost certainly didn't happen all in quite the order it has tumbled out of my defective memory.

As I progressed with it – having started and aborted it three times because I couldn't get the shape and feel of it right – I'm also aware that my recent activities as small business coach/ mentor/non-executive chairman have coloured some of the later contents: while its primary purpose was never didactic, I increasingly felt it worth commenting on lessons learned, in case it benefits any future entrepreneurs who feel like giving it a go.

If the people involved in this saga get into this, I have changed many of the names to protect the guilty; the innocent largely, though not exclusively, appear as they are/were. Anyone who knew us will easily be able to work out who's who, in any event. If you don't like the way you are portrayed, tough: write your own record of events as a rebuttal. If you worked for us and don't appear – either at all or very much, compared to your contribution to the business – take it as a compliment. I have very much concentrated on the big events in the 12-year history which shaped it (and sometimes shook it to its core), and that means focusing on the heroes and villains in the piece. If I'd written this contemporaneously and included all the bit-part players along the way, and there were many who contributed hugely to our success, it would have ended up twice as long and far too rambling.

If you get into it and enjoy it, let me know: dave@ hilltoppublishing.co.uk/blog

If you dislike it, for whatever reason, keep it to yourself. I did it for me, not for you, and as I complete the last sentence before editing and publishing begins, the catharsis is complete.

David Croydon
9/10/11

One

Palm-Tree Head and the art of conspiracy

W HEN YOU DECIDE TO SET up a business in competition with your current employer, you are by definition entering into a conspiracy. The beginnings of any business, like any enterprise, require considerable planning, and so you begin a cycle of secret squirrel meetings, at which all possibilities are aired.

There are three of us at the outset, soon to become four (we realise we need a creative geezer, so recruiting the agency's studio Head is logical – but I'm getting ahead of myself). We all like a drink, so the idea of using one of the town's many pubs for meetings is hardly unusual. And in the unlikely event that one of the senior managers stumbles across us, it will hardly ring alarm bells.

So the Abingdon Arms – aka the Abo's Armpit – becomes for six months or more our planning headquarters. It is also a youth pub, so there is the added bonus of being able to eye up fit totty while conspiring. We are all in our mid-twenties to thirties, so the idea of pulling isn't a total fantasy. Not that it actually happens, mind.

Three of us: me, because our head of department, Jimbo, is becoming Managing Director, and it becomes immediately obvious that they are going to try and recruit a heavy hitter from outside to replace him, and are only going through the motions of interviewing me for the job (and when the small organisation

9

that you've joined originally to enjoy the fruits of its planned rapid growth starts to grow above you, it's time to get out); the Cat, who is 10 years younger than me, has no family ties and has only just taken on his first mortgage on a little house for one, and is therefore open to and up for any adventure, especially if there is the potential promise of riches; and his partner in crime (at the time), who for the purposes of anonymity (even though everyone involved knows exactly who he is) will be called Stid – married, mortgage and ambitions.

I have mentioned in passing that I have been pretty pissed off with the way things are going and am seriously thinking of jumping ship; the two of them have been talking about doing something independently, and out of that conversation, the conspiracy is born.

The premise on which our putative enterprise takes shape is that many of our existing clients have a closer relationship with us than with senior management (or Jimbo, put simply; none of the others have anything to do with them and wouldn't recognise them without a detailed introduction), and therefore are more or less likely to transfer their business to us if we set up shop ourselves.

Much of our early discussion revolves round who would and who wouldn't come with us. The only way to be sure, of course, is to ask them, but it would only require one of them to tip off Jimbo, for the whole gaffe to be blown. Any business plan will inevitably be based on informed guesswork and a dose of wishful thinking, which is probably the formula for a large proportion of start-ups – those that bother with a business plan at all, of course. Many just start trading without the first idea whether they have a viable business model, which is also no doubt why so many start-ups fail. At least we can say we got that bit of our enterprise right.

Between us, we have maybe half a dozen probables and possibles on the list of potential client defections. The Cat and I work together on one group of clients, and four of the possibles belong to us, possibly because, as the senior operator in the department, I've probably engendered a degree of trust that enables me/us to operate more autonomously. Stid's two, though, include one that he has already labelled as a copper-bottomed certainty and on which we can plan with more than a degree of confidence.

This kind of conviction is pretty typical of Stid in general, and does not diminish as time goes by. I guess he's arrived at middle-aged man syndrome* as my wife put it, earlier than most. To be fair to him, though, his prediction is borne out by events.

So the major conspiracy lies in us planning to feather our own nest at the expense of our current employers, by enticing away half a million pounds of business from them. Some among you may consider this is amoral, if not absolutely immoral; others may shrug their shoulders and say, "That's business." What it most certainly is not is illegal: not even in the civil courts because, amazingly, none of us has proper contracts of employment (a serious error of management that we all vow will not occur in our new enterprise). Even if discovered before the evil deed is done, the worst that could happen to us would be to be sent on gardening leave for the duration of our notice period, which is only a single paltry month anyway.

We have, however, determined that the element of surprise is fundamental to the success of the enterprise, and as the months go by, everyone becomes increasingly paranoid about the possibility of being discovered, with one hand on the lighted taper and a trail of gunpowder leading to the barrels of explosive in the

---

* Middle aged man syndrome: occurs when men reach an age at which they magically become unqualified experts on every subject under the sun, regardless of the actual levels of knowledge (or more often ignorance) on the subject.

cellar. We begin our conversations in late Spring. The plan is to resign en masse on New Year's Eve, and to have our new agency operational on 2nd January.

All we need for complete success is:

- A creative facility
- A company name
- Motor cars to replace the company cars we all drive now
- An office with telephones, desks, etc
- A client list to deliver income, ideally from day one.

Doesn't sound much, does it? Rolls off the tongue quite easily, really. Each one of them presents difficulties and challenges though, and the foundations for what could become the company motto are laid even at this very early stage: "What can go wrong will go wrong." All this is with the benefit of hindsight. At the time, they are just the expected difficulties associated with running your own business, of which of course we have zero experience. When we finally get round to doing the dirty, this is exactly what Jimbo accuses us of: not the anticipated treachery, but the fact that we know nothing about running a business, which I think is a bit rich, coming from someone who has omitted to issue watertight (or indeed any) employment contracts to his own staff, complete with non-compete clauses.

Let's take each of those headings in turn, and remember the "challenges" (god, I hate that word) that they throw up.

The creative facility

All three original conspirators are account handlers – what in advertising circles would be called bag carriers, though in sales promotion circles, the ideas often come from marketing-literate account people and then are creatively executed by design teams.

We can come up with the ideas OK, but we will need someone to handle design and artwork.

Prime candidate is Michaelmas, our nickname for the ex-studio head, who has in the last few months left to set up his own free-lance operation. We're all mates; we'll all get on; and Michaelmas is a dab-hand with the magic markers, to turn ideas into reality. He's a cheeky Cockney character from Reading – never been near Bow Bells – but talks as if he's the original east-end geezer. So it's another session in The Abo's Armpit to tap him up.

It turns out his freelancing has been particularly successful, and while he's flattered to be asked, feels he needs to give his own operation a full chance to succeed in its own right. We tell him this is an opportunity to be part of something bigger – with a huge potential future upside financially – whereas, as a one-man band, there is a limit to what he can earn. And every time he takes a holiday, or gets sick, he stops earning. All pretty obvious stuff, but he's unmoved and adamant: it's the bird in the hand argument for him. So we have to think again.

Our alternatives now are severely limited. The new studio head at our employer has only been in situ for less than a year. He's as camp as a row of tents, even though he's married with kids, (hence his nickname, Gaylord), corpulent, and patently not 'one of us', but there isn't anyone else who comes close to fitting the bill. At least we know he can do the work. And we guess that he hasn't been with us long enough to develop an enormous loyalty to the new regime – a loyalty that, to their credit, they do engender in their staff through good man management. Paranoia rules, though, so when we approach him (back to the Abo's again), it's with all sorts of scarcely veiled threats about what might happen to him if he breaks confidences, none of which, it turns out, are necessary, because he more or less rips our arms off with enthusiasm to be part of it.

So the gang of three has become a gang of four. We have a viable management team and we can plan our prosperous future with a degree of confidence.

It is at this point that I make the next big mistake. As the senior operator, I am going to be Managing Director, but in the interests of fairness and ongoing motivation, I propose that we should all have equal shares in the equity of our new venture – 25% each. This is accepted without issue, and it is fair to say that if I had proposed having a bigger share myself, there probably wouldn't have been a vigorous debate about it at the time. In hindsight, of course, it doesn't take a genius to spot the potential problems in gestation for board decisions that are split down the middle – or worse, the other three ganging up on me and forcing me out. Such cracks are papered over by a general agreement that we won't proceed with any initiative without unanimity. The likelihood of this creating major problems at some point in the future sits like a dark cloud on the horizon, but as with so many things, it is put to one side in order not to prejudice present progress. It will of course come back to haunt us, but by the time it does, much more water will have flowed under the bridge, so let's get on with the key planning issues.

The name

Surely the easy bit. Jesus, that's what we do for a living: create ideas, identities, memorable catch-phrases. But of course there are four of us, so that means four opinions on everything, including every possible name in the known universe. We actually have the cheek to run a brain-storming concept meeting to come up with a name in one of the secondary meeting rooms of our current employer. With a cover story of course, in case anyone barges in on us. After what seems like several hours of pulling teeth, but probably is no more than an hour and a half, we have a name we can finally all agree on: Marketing Profile. The one thing we have a reasonable level of agreement on is that the word 'marketing' should appear somewhere, on the grounds that "it does what it says on the tin."

A few days later and Gaylord has turned the name into a logo, incorporating four triangles – one for each of us – all with a different primary colour (because we're all different, even though patently I'm not). All very creative. And then the cost implications of four- or five-colour printing on all our stationery sinks in. Perhaps not such a good idea.

Before alternatives can be discussed, however, another bombshell: someone else already owns Marketing Profile. Well, what a complete bastard, as Vivian on 'The Young Ones' would say. So it's back to the drawing board. We discover that Marketing Profile is a dormant company, having ceased trading, and briefly consider whether it could be acquired from its existing owners. The potential for delays, uncertainty and cost conspire to convince us to start afresh with a new name, and after more lengthy concept meetings, we come up with Marketing Principles. Actually we're all glad that Marketing Profile is already taken, because the new name is a lot better – indeed, we all think it's the dog's bollocks. A little older and wiser, however, we don't feel too self-satisfied until someone has been dispatched to check that it is in fact available. There is a discernible sense of relief when that someone returns with good news. So now we have a name – and a logo, but not in four or five colours: Gaylord is sent off to come up with a creative compromise (we're just like all our clients really) which turns out to be silver foil blocking. Ruinously expensive to produce, naturally, but don't we want all our communications to shout quality?

For a start-up with no track record, it really shouts delusions of grandeur, but we stand for it. It won't last much beyond the first reprint, but at this stage it's one less thing to think about.

Motor cars

Surely to god this can't be a big deal. We're going to need wheels. Our current employer will want theirs back. We're talking about a time, in the mid-80's, when the company car isn't just in vogue and a genuine tax advantage – it's a status symbol and statement about how successful you are. That's why I'm driving a red Alfa Romeo GTV (adding another inch to my knob in the process), and the others are driving Vauxhall Astras, apart from Gaylord who has a black BMW 3-series. Anyone who ever has to deal with the vexed question of year-on-year salary reviews will tell you that more discussion goes (or used to go) into the make and model of motor car the employee aspires to than their actual salary. With the gradual removal of the tax breaks, this is much diminished, but we're in the middle of the 1980's – Thatcher's Britain.

Magnanimously, I agree to equality: we'll all drive the same vehicle (alright, the same make and model). Sadly, we won't be affording Alfa GTV's all round, just yet. At the same time, everyone has aspirations to something a bit sportier than a Ford Fiesta (which in all honesty would have been perfectly fit for the purpose). Anyway, we're all 20/30-somethings with more testosterone than you can shake a stick at, so it's got to be something with a bit of grunt, as Jeremy Clarkson would no doubt inelegantly put it.

After much debate – at least as much as the name issue – and deep study of 0 – 60 performance over several more pints at the Abo's (drink driving is still barely on the agenda: our previous studio head, Michaelmas, used to get home from particularly beery do's by putting a hand over one eye to prevent him from seeing double, and didn't mind everyone knowing), we eventually agree on Vauxhall Astra GTE's – the classic hot hatch at the time for Jack the Lads. This choice will backfire (no pun intended) over the years, as the local Oxford youths purloin them on a regular basis for "hotting" purposes, though mine escapes the general trend and doesn't even have its radio/cassette nicked – another common occurrence.

We'll lease them over three years, and rather than get them from the local dealership – where we know the owner quite well – we'll go to the next town, on the paranoid grounds that word might get out to our superiors. When we finally take delivery, in the first week of the New Year, we have sequential number plates: C546 – 549 GBM – two red ones, one white and one black. The Cat has the white one; Stid the black one; and Gaylord and I have selected red. Driving in convoy, we look like a second-rate rally-cross team.

An office

For the first time, we start to get an appreciation of the difficulties of starting a business from scratch. It's relatively easy to decide on the basics: how big – big enough for half a dozen people initially, ideally with room for another half dozen, as we (hopefully) start to grow; style – as a creative marketing agency, we can't afford to look shit, so there does have to be a degree of style to our business address, and we'll need a proper meeting/presentation room; location – we're all agreed on Oxford: it's far enough away from our present employer to avoid the risk of bumping into them in the street, it has the ring of class, quality and excellence about it, and there's no other comparable organisation in residence, to our knowledge.

So off we go for a tour of business premises estate agents, where we discover two unpalatable facts:

1. There is a dearth of good office accommodation generally

around the city, though there are quite a few crap-holes that we wouldn't be seen dead in. And parking – or the lack of it – is a major issue.

2. We are not ideal clients, because as a start-up we have no track record and are therefore high-risk. This is a theme which will recur with any supplier arrangement we try to establish in the next 12 months.

After several weeks' fruitless searching, we finally see something that appeals: the top floor of a 3-storey office building on the edge of the city centre, where access and on-street parking is reasonable, and with all the necessary space for business operations, meetings, storage, etc. We offer the asking price and are beaten to it by an existing company with a track record. Bugger.

Back to square one. With two months to go before we supposedly open the shop, we still don't actually have a shop, but a new development in Cowley looks like it could be a candidate. It has a few drawbacks, but beggars can't be choosers, so we express an interest, only to discover it won't be finished in time. Do we want to put back our start date? Do we hell. On the other hand, we are still homeless, with only weeks to go.

It is at this moment of desperation that we finally get a break. We've been introduced to a local accountant (about whom, more later) to help us set up the company and do the necessary registrations and paper-work. He wears a cardigan and slippers in his office, which is a clutter of little box-rooms and corridors over a shop in Headington. In spite of his sartorial inadequacies, however, he does have his ear to the ground (actually, if he did that in Headington, his ear would be full of dog shit, but I digress), and he understands that there is an air conditioning and cooling business in offices over the Midland Bank with spare capacity, and they might be interested in sub-letting some space on a cheap and flexible basis. He also reveals that his own organization is planning to move into a new building, currently on the drawing board, about 200 metres away, and could probably let us have a floor to ourselves, sometime in the next twelve months.

We go to view our prospective new home. The bank is on a busy main road in a secondary shopping centre, and the offices on the top floor are up a lung-busting three flights of stairs (lift not supplied): a wide open space with a half-glazed meeting room in the middle; there are two or three individual offices down each side to about half way, being used by our putative landlord's management and staff. In truth it is a pretty depressing spectacle – most offices without furniture that are over two years old are. Dingy and atmosphere-less, with obligatory strip-lighting to add a veneer of institutionalism, it nevertheless has as much space as we could possibly want, albeit all in open plan, with a separate meeting room; shared kitchen and toilets with the landlord – there are only half a dozen people employed here – and they will let us use (and pay for) other office services, like photocopying and telex (yes, telex: the facsimile machine is still a year or two away from regular everyday business use).

It's hardly ideal in image terms, and someone immediately coins the term 'camping out' for how our few desks and office possessions will look, perched in an enormous open-plan square footage, but we are between a rock and a hard place, and if we want to start on schedule – and we desperately do –this is probably our best, if not only, bet. It's cheap, flexible in terms of sublease term, and we quickly talk ourselves into it.

At last we have a base from which to start operations. Without it, you cannot order phone lines, produce stationery, or do much at all in a practical sense. Once you have premises, you can start to plan the rest of the detail.

Clients

Having offices, cars, stationery, and all the rest of the paraphernalia is all very well, but without the clients to pay for it, we'll be in and out of business in six months flat.

Here's a walk through the financial realities, all formulated on a delicious irony: the reason we're (I'm) doing this is because Jimbo is becoming Managing Director (and I'm not getting his Head of Department's job, complete with Directorship); the reason he's becoming MD is because the company is being floated on the AIM market, and presumably the merchant bankers have decreed it would be better to split the Chairman/CEO/MD role, which the company's owner and 60% shareholder has traditionally held – not unusually in a growing small business; as a result of that flotation, each of us is being given shares in the new listed business, and we are planning to liquidate them as soon as we need to, to give the new business a start-up, cash-flow breathing space (essentially knowing we can pay ourselves for a few months, while we kick-start some business income); so in effect, our employer's stock-market flotation is funding our own start-up, which will (we like to think) have an adverse effect on its own share price. Does this count as insider trading? Discuss.

Whatever, we have all agreed, at some stage in the discussions, to put five grand in the pot, so we open for business with twenty grand sitting in the bank account. Our proposed salary bill is £20,000 a year for me (as senior bod) and £15,000 for the others. We all have mortgages and – apart from the Cat – other mouths to feed, so we can't afford to be greedy (yet). Our seed-corn funding might sound like a decent wedge, but in practice, by the time we've added in start-up and office costs, it'll last less than two months, so we'd better be confident we can persuade some clients to give us some business pretty sharpish.

It is at this point that the subject of this chapter heading enters the story. It's funny how relatively tiny incidents and personalities can intrude on proceedings and lend a colour to your memory of events out of all proportion to their actual significance. As well as getting together at my place for conspiracy sessions, we've also been meeting at the Abo's on a fairly regular basis in early evenings, discussing which clients are going to keep us in the manner to which we'd like to become accustomed, and we're used to the young student crowd from the local furniture college who frequent the place. Indeed, we're familiar enough to be on speaking terms with a group of them, one of whom one night turns up with this ridiculous haircut. Heavens knows where he (for it is a he) went to have it done or what possessed him, but it looks like something one of the more outré brothers in Jamaica might sport – a sort of top-knot sticking up from his head. His mates have obviously been giving him stick about it, so are over-joyed when we join in: "Blimey, what have you been doing with your hair? It looks like there's a palm tree growing out of your head." And from this throwaway line sprang the nick-name "Palm-tree Head", a moniker he will be stuck with in perpetuity in my mind, and long after he's reverted to a less eye-catching confection. And, moreover, an image that will forever represent for me the many conspiratorial meetings that took place in that establishment.

Having ribbed Palm-tree Head mercilessly for a quarter of an hour, however, we eventually remember why we're here, other than to sink a few pints, which is always the sub-plot in any event, while ogling the odd fit bird who strolls by. Who can we count on to switch their business to us and in what timescale? If everyone sits on the fence, waiting till our current employer fucks up (which they will, because we are taking all the experience out of the department, and they'll never be able to replace us in the kind of timescale they'll need to), we'll be broke before they give us a chance. So we write a list of clients we hope to persuade, in order of apparent likelihood to switch their business to us most quickly, and the likely annual turnover value that we could reasonably expect to generate. This is that list, with the prime client contact from among our number:

CLIENT	CONTACT	BUSINESS	BUDGET	LIKELIHOOD
Lease Plan	Stid	Car leasing	£100K	100%
Hall's Brewery	Cat	Beer/pubs	£50K	85%
DRG Stationery	Me	Paper	£50K	80%
Harp Lager	Cat/me	Lager	£100K	70%
Lyons Coffee	Cat/me	Coffee	£150K	60%

There are others we are less confident of, because of their familiarity with and ties to the Directors and the other (auxiliary merchandising) side of the business:

Burton's Biscuits	Stid/me	Biscuits	£100K	20%
Meat Promotion Exec	Me	British Meat	£50K	10%
Hasbro	Stid	Toys	£400K	5%
Bulldog Tools	Cat	Garden tools	£250K	5%

We determine we will definitely not approach these prior to our defection, because of the high risk of their senior management blowing the gaff to our senior management. There is one possible misjudgement here, because after the event, one of the clients at the Meat Promotion Executive sounds quite hurt that we haven't taken him into our confidence, and maybe there would have been a chance if we had, but you can't rewrite history (even though that is exactly what I'm doing here). On balance, I still think the risks probably outweighed the potential benefits, given the importance we attached to the element of surprise. Sorry, Keith!

There are one or two "gleams in the eye" too, but these represent no more than the usual new business hopefuls, that we may be able to subvert, if we can land them at all.

We indulge in endless speculation about the likelihood quotient, and how and when to approach them with the news of our defection.

Apart from Stid's Lease Plan client, whom he will tell very soon because he's confident of his trustworthiness and pliability, we decide that the best course of action is to entertain them to a fine Christmas lunch sometime in December at our current employer's expense (if you're thinking 'How immoral', much worse is to follow), and break the news to them of our new venture during the course of it.

What do we expect them to say? Well, we're hoping it will be a bit more than, "Good luck, chaps." The perfect response would be their agreement to bring their business with us on the spot. Realistically, however, the most likely scenario is that at some point in the next couple of months, they will either give us a project, to see how we get on with it, or put us in a pitch against our current employer (and maybe others) for a longer-term or bigger project.

The reality at this point in time is that sales promotion generally is treated with all the loyalty of a brothel. It is dealt with on a tactical basis (probably because it is largely a tactical activity) by relatively junior Brand and Product Managers, rather than Marketing Managers or Directors, with little or no strategic vision. You are vulnerable, at the best of times, to the siren approaches of other agencies offering free initial ideas to get through the door. The risk is that, while we are slugging it out with our current employer for the client rights, someone else will slip in the back door and sneak off with the spoils. On the other hand, as a new agency, we have the opportunity to do the same thing to our competitors: new agency, fresh thinking, wouldn't it be worth at least seeing us, etc?

Essentially we are counting on the personal relationships we have built with our key client prospects being strong enough to bridge the transition from agency employees to agency owner/managers. But once we have determined how, when and where to let them in on our little secret, there is little we can do, apart from speculate idly and endlessly – which we do – particularly as we are all effectively gambling the roofs over our heads on the success of our enterprise.

*   *   *   *

Which brings me neatly to the next obstacle (and I use the word advisedly) to free enterprise: the banks.

Watching the slickly produced commercials of any of the major players, you get the impression that they understand business, are supportive of it, helpful to the ends of the earth. I particularly remember one (not from this era) in which the subject was new business start-ups and the strap-line, "I went to WankBank and everything just seemed simple." Needless to say, the ASA never forced them to withdraw or amend the copy, but all I will say, based not just on my experience, but that of nearly every other business owner I've ever had a conversation with, is that this is so far removed from actual experience as to constitute corporate mendacity of epic proportions. The only thing that banks understand is, guess what… money. They are like that Monty Python spoof on BBC's then *Money Programme*: "Tonight on the *Money Programme*, we're going to be talking about … money: lots of it, some in crisp bank notes, etc etc."

We, of course, at this stage are delightfully naïve in our hopes and assumptions. I've written a business plan, with 5-year profit and loss projections, cash-flow forecasts, a clear explanation of where the business will come from and how we will make our money. We shall naturally need a bank account for all the basic transactions of everyday life, but it is probable, certainly in the first 6 – 12 months, that we shall also need an overdraft facility for short-term cash-flow needs. Incidentally, for those of you not of a commercial disposition, the bank makes money (that word again) whatever the state of your finances, right up to and (very often after) your bankruptcy. If you have money in the account, they use it in the money markets to make money for themselves (and you only get to join in this cash fest once you've got enough filthy lucre in your account – and the know-how – to justify doing the overnight money markets yourself.) If you don't have money in the account, they charge you interest on the overdraft. But I digress.

The only way the bank can lose money is if your business goes bust with a large overdraft in place, so obviously, being the entirely risk-averse characters they are, they can't have that. The only way you can get a bank to give (for give, read loan) you an overdraft facility is if you have something of value that they can cash in and get their money back, in the sad (but not for them) eventuality of you defaulting on your responsibilities. Your house, say. Don't own a house – with some equity in it: first-time buyers need not apply – or some other valuable asset? Don't waste your breath even asking. Let's face it, the only valuable asset most ordinary people have that could raise more than a few thousand in a fire-sale is their house. We all have houses. Apart from the Cat, who's only just got on the bottom rung of the property ladder, the rest of us could probably raise a couple of hundred thousand between us, if they were all sold and the proceeds put into a central pot.

We're going to set up in Oxford, so we might as well do the rounds of the big four there – except for Barclays: they left me high and dry in Paris for two weeks as a student, through their administrative inefficiencies, and the difficulties and embarrassments they put me through as a result (without ever a word of regret or apology) mean I still wouldn't piss in their corporate ear if their corporate brain were on fire. So we rock up to the first one – let's call it NatWest, because that's who it is – and present our credentials, our business plan and our relatively meager requirements: cheque transactions and a maximum overdraft facility of, say, £50,000, with a projected first-year turn-over of £400,000 leading to a break-even scenario.

For those of you who know nothing of the marketing services industry, the business model is delightfully simple. We charge our clients fees for devising and implementing promotional campaigns – typically 10–15% of the budget – so a budget of £50,000 might yield £5-7,500 in fees. Then we generally make a commission on bought-in products and services, so if we buy 10,000 T-shirts at £2 each, we might charge £2.50 for them and hoover up another £5,000. And if we have all the design and artwork under our own roof, the margins are in the 60-70% area, even after paying salaries and establishment costs. So on a £50,000 budget (peanuts these days), we might clear £15,000 gross profit. We're only planning to pay ourselves £15-20,000 in year one, so a couple of these for each of us and we're in the clear. If you add half as much again to salary costs for all the other overheads (office rent, rates, etc) – a rough rule of thumb that works for pretty much all service organizations – you'll soon find how much money you need to make to break even.

For those of you who aren't ahead of me here, in our case this means salaries at £65K + 50% = around £100K. Add in a Secretary/PA and one or two other unforeseen costs, and it's never going to be more than £130,000. If we can turn over £400,000, can we anticipate a gross profit of 33%? Answer: yes (and this isn't wishful thinking, it's reality). In fact we expect to outperform these figures.

Now here's the thing: our first bank manager looks through all this and he can't understand how we're going to make money. It's not that he doesn't understand our optimism. It would be easy to counter that turning over £400K rolls off the tongue very easily but who's to say we're going to achieve it? That would at least be a fair point. All we're really bringing to the table, in truth, is a good gut feeling and the optimism of youth. But he actually cannot understand the business model. He turns us down flat. Doesn't want to discuss it any further. It's just a 'No'.

Which brings us up a bit short. It has not occurred to us that acquiring banking facilities will be anything other than us making the choice of who we go to from the best of the bunch we present our wares to. We have an attractive business proposition. We can't fail (can we?) They'll surely be ripping our arms off for a chance of our business. Or not.

When we pay a visit to the second one on our list, therefore, it is with a lot less confidence and a bit more trepidation. This time it is the Midland (now HSBC), whom I've personally banked with since the student Barclays debacle. Incidentally, going to the bank you have a personal account with may help you get the facility you need, but it may not be a particularly smart idea long term. Banks have a nasty habit of knocking down the walls between personal and business accounts, in the unfortunate circumstances of the shit hitting the fan, and playing fast and loose with whatever meager resources you still (think you) have, in order to recover debt. What's yours is basically theirs, unless you can persuade them that maybe a bit of it could be yours, if you're really nice to them.

This time, at least, we get someone who is a bit more business savvy. I'm not convinced he understands the business plan much more than the first one, to be honest, but he can see we're confident of making a profit, so he's prepared to let us have a run at it. Strictly on a no-risk basis to him of course. He wants all our houses (not just one of them) assigned to the bank on a joint and several basis, so that if the worst should happen, he gets his money back and we end up, jointly and severally, on the street. So what he's really saying is, "If you boys want to risk losing it all, then be my guest. I'm not losing anything." What he actually says is, "You do realize, don't you, that 80% of all start-ups fail in the first year or two of operation?" There's nothing like positive thinking, is there? And this is nothing like…etc etc.

At the end of it all, we decide we may as well go with them and not bother talking to anyone else – it's such a dispiriting exercise. Lloyds, Royal Bank of Scotland – will they be any different? Answer, based on a conversation we eventually have with RBS many years later about a potential new business venture we are considering, is probably not. Mainly it's about the luck of the draw in terms of the individual you get to see and whether there's any personal chemistry between you (just like every other business relationship), rather than which actual bank they work for.

*   *   *   *

OK. We have a name, a bank account, an office (finally), a creative facility (aka Gaylord), wheels (on order), a start date, a business plan and a list of potential clients.

In the intervening six months, my decision to try to go it alone (which is the subject of a TV commercial for Renault cars right at this moment spookily) is fully justified by events at the current employer. Having been interviewed for my boss's job, though never in my opinion ever seriously in the running, they have appointed an outsider – an alleged heavy hitter from the London agency scene – to come and breathe life into their little provincial establishment. I've been wondering what I would do, in the unlikely event of them actually offering me the job, given the advanced preparations for our own little show, and I know my co-conspirators have fretted a bit too on this front. If I were to be offered it, and greed and safety-first attitudes prompted me to accept it, I would necessarily know all about the conspiracy and be duty bound to scupper it, as far as I could. It's a situation that the word 'invidious' was made for.

Luckily the decision is made for me, as my gut instinct has always told me it would be. Even luckier for us, having announced their new signing to the staff, the new guy gets a better offer by his existing employer and withdraws his verbal acceptance of their offer. This is brilliant for three reasons:

1. Schadenfreude: no one likes being passed over, and the joy at watching them fuck up is exquisite.
2. It flushes out the reality of the situation. In going back to the drawing board, there is no longer any pretence that I am under the slightest consideration for the job. They want an outsider.
3. It buys us another three months. By the time they finally do have someone in place, it's going to be the New Year, by which time we'll be up, up and away.

It is in fact absolutely brilliant timing. A new guy arriving in October would have wanted to meet the clients, get involved, do all sorts of things that might impinge on our ability to feather our own nest. Now we can plan, safe in the knowledge that we'll almost certainly never meet the new man (who eventually turns out to be a big tobacco company Marketing Director, with no experience of running an agency; it gives me particular personal pleasure to watch from afar as he fails to make any sort of impact and is eventually dispensed with).

*　　*　　*　　*

And so we hit December. (Naughty December: don't do it again). Three weeks of fevered client entertainment, long festive lunches stretching into the late afternoon, when we thank them for their business, announce – with a little fanfare of trumpets: "We have a bit of news" – our new business plans and hope for a positive response. All this new business entertainment is generously provided, needless to say, at our current employer's expense. Immoral? Guilty as charged. Anyway, they can afford it: they're all millionaires, on paper at least, since the company was floated on the stock market.

I think it's fair to say that everyone is supportive, in the sense that they genuinely wish us well. Equally, I don't think that anyone commits there and then to coming with us, apart from Lease Plan (who, Stid claims, is so fully behind us, they've put back the print of their corporate brochure, so we can do it for them in January and get it in our first month's accounts: now that's what I call supportive). You probably wouldn't expect it of the others, particularly during a boozy lunch, when the news has just been dropped on them. In some cases there are other people in their business who may have a say in things. In any event, in their position I would want to think through the implications.

Mostly, our likelihood quotient doesn't change. We get

comments ranging from, "I'm sure we'll be able to give you a shot at something" to, "We'll have to see how your current employer continues to service our business, but do keep in touch and let us know how things are going." (Oh we will, we will). There's nothing to be disheartened about. They probably feel morally bound to continue with the current arrangements until such time as they are given good reason to reconsider. But if they fail to get the quality of service they are used to, there would be every reason to look elsewhere, and why not in our direction, where previous good service has come from? Plus, with the defection of the three top account handlers, and the studio head, plus the arrival of a new number one with no knowledge of running an agency and no relationship with any of the clients, we have every reason to hope, expect even, that with resources stretched to breaking point, they will fuck up and let us in.

As Christmas approaches, we've done just about all we can. There is now only the question of how, when and where we tender our resignations. At the department Christmas bash, in Europe's biggest sauna allegedly, in Stock's at Tring, I finally tell my secretary what we're up to – the noise prevents anyone else from hearing – and it's obvious she's already smelled a rat, unsurprisingly; she agrees to come with us there and then. Her husband subsequently suggests she asks for a stake in it herself, which is what you'd expect from the MD of another successful business, but the other guys are not keen. Actually she ends up deserving it far more than some others I could (and will) name, but that's for the future. For the moment the gang of four has become a gang of five, and we have determined to resign en masse on New Year's Eve. The days when Christmas and New Year blend into one long holiday are still in the future; Jimbo is a workaholic, whose family life seems a mixed blessing and, we discover, will be in the office on December 31st. Actually the Cat has to work that day too, having run out of annual leave. Astonishingly, in hindsight, given what we are about to do, he is planning to go in and work as if nothing is up, and be matey-boy with Jimbo into the bargain. To no one's surprise, he finds the two-faced reality of it just a bit on the tense side.

And so, shortly before lunch on New Year's Eve, we meet up at the Abo's for a last shot of Dutch courage and set off in convoy for the office. I have phoned earlier in the morning to check that Jimbo is actually in as planned (in the unlikely event that he's been unexpectedly whisked off to the January sales, we don't have a plan 'B', but predictably enough, he's there, warbling into his Dictaphone), and to ask if I can pop in and discuss something with him.

The office is, as anticipated, deathly quiet. Who'd want to work, apart from Jimbo? Sitting in his goldfish-bowl of an office, it doesn't take long for me to outline what we're doing. He takes it on the chin, but I can see for sure that he's had absolutely no inkling of what was coming. Once he knows the others are in the building – the Board Room as it happens – we all retire there, including of course the Cat, who has been in the office all morning, allegedly working, but skulking sheepishly round the corner for the last five minutes.

Finally getting all this out in the open is a relief, to say the least. Our triumph at being able to drop a bombshell on the current management is only slightly tarnished by Gaylord's inability to keep his mouth shut. He can't resist having to say something to show how clever he is, which inevitably just shows what a twat he is actually. "We've got a proper company formed, and everything". "Yes, Michael," (for that is his real name), "I'm sure you have," is Jimbo's withering reply.

Of course the thing we've been most concerned about is how he treats our notice period. It may be only a month, but if he can keep us out of action for that period, a lot of spanners might be inserted in various works. We have speculated that he might try to get us to actually work our notice period, in the warehouse perhaps, doing manual labour, just to keep us out of general circulation. Or "gardening leave", though in fact the likelihood of his being able to control what we do in that month, in hindsight, is somewhere between tiny and nil. In the event, his concerns are of a much more pragmatic, and easily satisfied, nature. Because he has so little direct contact with the day-to-day client business, it dawns on him that once we walk out the door, he won't have a clue what precise work we've done for the clients or what moneys are due to be billed. When you think of it, it's an astonishing lack of process, almost on a par with the lack of employment contracts, but there you are. Anyway, the simple deal is: if we agree to come in tomorrow (New Year's Day – ugh!) and get all our invoicing up to date, he'll let us all go quietly. Result.

The cars of course will have to come back – shall we say by the end of the week? There may be a slight hiatus in handing in the old and picking up the new, but what's a day or two in the grand scheme of things? We've all got partners with cars, except the Cat, and we can sort something out. Only Gaylord demurs. "We've got the right to keep them for a month. It's in our contract." Technically, he may be correct, but looking at the bigger picture and given what we've just done, we're on shaky ground. On the whole we've got off pretty lightly (especially as he doesn't have to write any invoices tomorrow), so we tell him to shut up.

And that's that. There's a ritual of hand-shaking and good-byes. Jimbo's only barbed comment is about our lack of knowl-edge of running a company (which, as I've already said, is a bit rich, given the lack of process and employment contracts in his own company), and we're off back to the Abo's for a relieved refreshment or three and de-brief. It is the last time all four of us will ever drink together in that establishment: it has served its purpose – the conspiracy is over.

The next day, we go back to our (ex) office and together we write invoices for, as I remember, the thick end of £100,000, thus ensuring Jimbo has a spectacular year-end on paper, even if his resources to repeat the feat in the next few months are seriously depleted.

Tomorrow, January 2nd 1986, the journey begins in earnest.

Two

Dodgy accountants: Pit Pony, Cardy Coxy and The Bookie's Friend

WHEN YOU SET UP IN BUSINESS, chances are the last thing you think about is accountancy (unless you're an accountant of course). You've worked for someone else, probably quite a big outfit, and accountancy just happens, as if by osmosis. OK, you know there's an accounts department where all the bean counting goes on, but essentially it's "over there", someone else's domain, and largely to be avoided at all costs if at all possible.

Of course there is no "over there" now. All the numbers to be produced by and for your business are going to be produced by you, or someone you employ to do it. We have a firm of accountants – introduced to us by the bank (or was it the other way round?) – to set up the business, but they're not going to do our day-to-day accounts, not at their rates, they're not. The choices are pretty simple: do it yourself, or find someone (probably retired or semi-retired) to do it on a part-time basis – a day a week, say, to begin with. Nowadays, and knowing what I now know, and with the computer hardware and software available, I'd definitely do it myself. This is the eighties though, computers are still in their infancy and my knowledge of accountancy is of the 'O' level maths variety.

As time goes by, and the business grows, as it undoubtedly will (it had better, or you'll be in the gutter, old son), you will eventually find yourself employing someone full-time to count the beans and ensure there's enough cash in the bank to pay the wages and the panoply of other debtors you owe money to. In reality, of course, it's *your* job, but a good accountant can juggle the cash so it seems like you've got more – or to put it another way, to make what you've got work harder and go further.

I don't know about you, but I always assumed that accountancy as a profession, by definition, attracted people who are dull but the soul of probity. Monty Python's "Why Accountancy Is Not Boring", a copy of which hung in my toilet for several years (don't ask), has a lot to answer for. Recently though, Radio 4 (where else?) has announced research has enabled them to profile the type of person most likely to commit company fraud, and guess what? Male, aged 36 – 55, working in middle to senior management in the *finance* department. Didn't women commit fraud, the interviewer asked? Yes, but 80% of them are men. 80% of accountants are probably men. Anyway we will return to this theme a little later.

For the moment, any such thoughts are simply non-existent. Arriving on day one of our new venture to the bareness of what must have been about 1500 square feet of empty office space, with a goldfish bowl in the middle which passes as a meeting room, our cars full of flat-pack furniture from Habitat that need assembling before we can create any sort of office atmosphere, it is astonishing that no one expresses any negative vibes about the wisdom of the whole enterprise. By the end of the day though, the enormity of what we've taken on sinks in, and initial elation has dissipated considerably.

Gaylord has acquired the desks by nefariously having our regular photo studio inflate a few invoices on a recent DRG shoot with "Props" (such as office desks). None of the rest of us are very comfortable with this, given that it's basically fraud, but he's done it anyway, and we're stuck with it. They're not exactly expensive, but more to the point, they're not exactly complete either. They're supposed to consist of a 3-drawer unit and a cupboard unit, with a big plank of wood, aka desk-top, straddling the two, with little plastic suckers to stop slippage. In black ash, naturally, this being the eighties. Unfortunately only one half of the units has arrived for some of them – the traditional 'out-of-stocks' afflicting our nearest branch. Luckily our new office has a shelf running along the furthest wall at about the right height, so three of the desks have to be set up at right angles to it, with one end balanced on the shelf. How crap is that? It's called mend and make do.

Naturally we don't have any phones. They've been organised all right, but anyone who has ever had any dealings with BT will be unsurprised to learn that they have not turned up to do what they promised. Does anyone have a good word to say about BT? They must be the most inefficient, irritating organisation (and I use that word in its loosest sense) to deal with in the known universe – and 20 years later, I have no reason to amend that view: if anything, they're even worse now. Mobile phones as we know them do not yet exist, so we throw ourselves on the mercy of our new landlord.

The company with the main lease on the premises is a cooling and air conditioning business whose manufacturing and distribution is located somewhere in Bedfordshire. For reasons unknown (the MD probably lives nearby), they have set up a Head Office function here. It's miles too big for them and doesn't do much for their image – not that many small businesses give an owl's hoot about that – being up three flights of stairs at the back of an unprepossessing sixties building (ground floor a Midland Bank) in a secondary shopping centre's busy main road. Head man looks a bit like ex-Tory Minister, Douglas Hurd, so we immediately christen him the Home Secretary. An avuncular chap, he's friendly and helpful. His second-in-command is called Clive – he does all the work, by the look of it – and has spent time on the sub-continent, we learn, so naturally is referred to as Clive of India. There are a couple of secretaries, who no doubt do most of Clive of India's work and who don't merit a second glance once they've shown us how to use the photocopier and telex, which we're being allowed to share on a pay-as-you-go basis. Yes, telex. A sort of cross between a telegram machine and a fax, which is still in its infancy and few businesses yet have.

We send out an announcement about our existence and new contact details to all our clients and prospects by telex. Hard to believe, I know, but there it is.

It takes me about two hours to put together my desk. The others seem to manage it in about half the time. Years later, my desk will still be robust, however. Those that were chucked together in a hurry gradually loosen up and deteriorate.

Gaylord is busy setting up the "Creative Department" in the L-shaped area at the far end of the space, so it looks like a vaguely separate unit, or as Stid puts it, he's nesting. One of his freelance contacts comes in to say hello and wanders in to our camping out area, also known as our new office. Gaylord invites him to come in. It's open plan; he's already in; so he exaggeratedly opens an imaginary door, walks through it and closes it behind him. When you're having a bad day, it doesn't take much.

Creativity at this point in time does not involve any technology, as we know it today. Designs are hand-drawn using Magic Marker pens. The only meaningful piece of machinery used is something that resembles a Punch & Judy show, which enables graphic designers who can't draw (most of them) to trace objects from source material that is bigger or smaller than they need, by projecting the image via magnifying mirrors on to a glass plate, under a black hood to keep out the light.

By the end of the day, we've created a small officey encampment in the middle of this vast floor, extracted a firm promise from BT (yeah, right) that they'll definitely install our phones tomorrow, sent messages (by telex) to clients, and er… that's it. Feeling exhausted and depressed in equal measures, reality has sunk in, after the initial excitement. We don't even have the energy to go for a beer – a state of affairs that will be rectified over the coming months.

The rest of the week is all about the things we didn't think of. The phones arrive, eventually, at which point you start to feel you might actually have a business. What pisses me off most about BT is that they know that a business without a phone isn't a business at all, and yet they still leave you in limbo without a hint of regret or apology, never mind compensation. How much business might you have lost because those fuckers left you up shit creek without a paddle? They don't give a toss. The mobile revolution's changed all that of course, and I hope it eventually drives BT into the ground, where it belongs.

We know my secretary, Jools, who has agreed to come with us, can't arrive till the end of the month: there was little chance of Jimbo letting her go immediately, so she has to work her month's notice. We have, however, negotiated with a couple of my wife's friends to do a job-share on the secretarial and admin front to get us through the first month, working 2½ days a week each. So Jenny turns up for her first day, and it dawns on us that we may have created a mini office, but we haven't acquired any means of producing correspondence. In these days, dear reader, word processors are still in their infancy: we're talking typewriters, and we haven't thought to get one. Someone is deputed to go into town and buy an electric typewriter from the office equipment shop – Ryman's, if memory serves. Office World and their ilk are still a distant gleam in someone's eye.

Finally, by about Wednesday lunchtime, we're actually in a position to do some work (if only we had some to do). The Home Secretary then returns us neatly to the subject of the chapter heading, by enquiring what we're doing about accountancy.

I think our inability to string together any sort of coherent response rather gives the game away: yet another thing we hadn't thought of (or, if we had, had clearly put to one side again, sharpish). Anyway, you don't need bean counters if you haven't got any beans to count. However, the Home Secretary has a suggestion: he knows someone who is retired, does a bit of book-keeping for them, might be interested in doing a bit for us, etc. Maybe a day or so a week. Would we be interested? Frankly, since we haven't given the matter a single moment's thought, and since we are less interested in the subject than the price of fish in Hindustan, anything that allows us to think no more about it, happy in the knowledge that we've got this particularly dull issue covered off, is of interest.

Enter Hopalong, the Pit Pony. Four feet ten in his stockinged feet, if he's an inch, looks about 70, bald with straggly grey hair around the edges, glasses (natch – he is an accountant), dressed like some out-of-touch college professor – as Basil Fawlty put it, "It's called style, you wouldn't understand" – and with a pronounced limp when he walks. Obviously born and bred locally because he has that soft Oxfordshire burr to his voice. He's an extremely nice chap, and about as far removed from the agency image we're trying to project as it's possible to be. So obviously we sign him up immediately on a casual basis, until such time as we decide what sort of accountancy service we want or need. His name is Pitkeathly, which is where the "broken down pit pony" epithet comes from, and which evolves into our inevitable nickname for him. Nearly everyone we ever come across gets a nickname, unless they are so mind-numbingly dull that we can't be bothered to think of one. It helps us get through our puerile day. Stid takes the piss by giving him a proper yokel accent: "Yer see, what yer do is wroit it down in scratchy, spindly wroiting, so's no one can unnerstarnd it."

Anyway old Pit Pony inevitably wants to talk accountancy. This is all very well for him. He's interested in it. He purports to understand it (I bloody hope he does). We, on the other hand, wouldn't know – or care – what a nominal ledger was, if it came up and slapped us on the arse – an unlikely scenario, I grant you. He sets about telling me what he's going to do for us in some detail, what with purchase ledgers and sales ledgers and nominal ledgers and … I'm not sure if he's noticed my eyes glazing over or whether it's me pouring petrol over myself and starting to light matches, but he eventually stops, and it's my turn to comment.

Given that I've switched off after a couple of minutes and only understood a third of what he was wittering on about when I was listening, I have little option but to agree to all his suggestions and let him get on with it. Any accounts he does will be manual anyway – little more than double-entry book-keeping (whatever that is, oo-er, missus), so he can't do much damage in the short term. Money in; money out; hopefully more of the former than the latter, so that the last number at the bottom is black, not red. Accountancy at that level is that simple, and most small businesses are at that level. Amazingly, many do not even do the basics, I've since discovered. More businesses go bust through their inability to manage cash-flow than do because of a flawed product or service. At this stage, though, we're still learning the ropes. Pit Pony's crash course in basic accountancy is a shock to the system, highlighting our utter ignorance. There are many other areas where our ignorance is also bliss for the moment, but they will emerge as we proceed.

It's not all doom and gloom though. Stid's been down to see his

Lease Plan client and comes back with confirmation of the brochure reprint, on which we'll make a decent margin. And DRG have called to ask us to buy the prizes (travel weekends in Paris) in the incentive scheme we've been running for them; they obviously don't have much confidence in the rump of our old place getting things done. They're probably not seen as a particularly attractive or high-profile client by the new guy, who's come from international tobacco marketing and likely doesn't understand the value of a few rock-solid, if dull, bread-and-butter clients, who are loyal through thick and thin. His loss.

So in the space of a couple of weeks, we've got a start, got a foot in the door at two of our hot-prospect clients and have ensured we'll bill a decent wedge in our first month. OK, there won't be that much margin in it, but it's still a decent start, and when our bank manager arrives to see how we're getting on, it is a real pleasure to be able to counter his "Most start-ups fold in the first year" pessimism with the information that we'll have billed £30,000 in our first month. That shuts him up. So much so, that I'm not sure we see him again till the end of the year. Which is about par for the course for the banks: all over you like a rash if you have a problem, and not in a helpful way; otherwise invisible.

So in spite of early hiccoughs, we are up and running, with some real causes for optimism. And as always, after a sticky moment or two which seem to last ages, time just flies by once you get into a new routine.

Within six months we've picked up business from Hall's Brewery, more from DRG, who seem to have just come with us without ever saying so, and we've even picked up a new client from some mailing we've done: Stag Furniture. Not only that, but Cardy Coxy's accountancy unit are taking over brand new-build offices across the road in September and offer us a floor to ourselves if we're interested. OK, it's over a video hire shop, but it's modern, nicely designed, the perfect size for our needs, and no onerous lease for us to worry about – three months rolling, so we can move on any time we like. We can create a small, separate studio, meeting-room and informal discussion area (comfy chairs – no, not the comfy chairs) and still have loads of room for half a dozen desks or more. And its arched windows look out over the outré arthouse cinema, Not The Moulin Rouge (now sadly defunct) with its giant chorus-line girl's leg sticking out at 90° over the entrance: much more the sort of outlook a cutting-edge agency aspires to. We look forward to the move with anticipation. Indeed within a few months of moving in, the guy opposite the cinema (and its then owner, I believe), local radio presenter Bill Heine, has installed a giant shark in the roof of his terraced house – a protest against nuclear proliferation, apparently (no, really). All of a sudden, it's part of the tourist circuit, as national news gets hold of it and over subsequent months the local council spends a fortune trying unsuccessfully trying to make him take it down: planning, health & safety, all the usual bureaucratic pedants hell-bent on stopping anyone expressing themselves and having a bit of fun. Not sure how I'd have felt if I were his neighbour, mind. It's still there to this day, or was last time I looked.

We move in during the last quarter and can finally say that we have a proper business with proper offices, with its own door that people have to knock before they come in. Alright, I made that last bit up. No one ever knocks before they come to see us, unless they're being deliberately ironic.

We run far too easy-going a ship, which we continue to do throughout our existence and which may be why so much shit happens along the way.

During that quarter we pick up a brief from Harp Lager. It's for all of £10,000 but we celebrate as if we've won the pools (the lottery doesn't exist yet, remember). We've acquired a couple of junior account executives along the way, Michelle and Carolyn (who will feature throughout as it turns out) and we all repair to our local French restaurateur's local outlet, Café Noir, where we consume the entire profit margin on the new job in champagne, drinking through the afternoon and leaving the offices entirely unattended in case of client need (mobile phones still not invented!) You may debate at leisure the strengths and weaknesses of this approach: great team spirit and work hard/play hard mentality versus unprofessional behaviour leading to unknown opportunities lost. Discuss.

We will remain a hard-drinking agency throughout our existence. It is well known that businesses recruit from the top down in their own image, so inevitably we end up with an alcohol-fuelled staff too. As long as work doesn't suffer because of it, that's alright by us, but there's no doubt that we're serial drink/drivers, and as the noose tightens on such anti-social behaviour (remember, we all started in the 60's and 70's when it was perfectly acceptable – a bit of a jape even), we have to become more circumspect and our local taxi account goes through the ceiling.

Café Noir is the only vaguely quality bistro in the area. All the rest are rough boozers – all gentrified now, but at the time, you needed tattoos before it was safe to go in. We frequent them, nevertheless, because they are within walking distance. One of them, the Britannia, has a large car park at the rear, which never seems to have any cars on it.

We're currently parking on the street and it's the usual shrinking story, as the council designates more and more space as residents only – thus making it virtually impossible for people working in the area to park anywhere, other than at the extortionate rates at the one municipal park a quarter of a mile away. When you have to be in and out of the office, going to client meetings and the rest, you don't want a ½-mile walk there and back each time you go out. So we decide to talk to the landlord of the pub about whether he might rent us spaces on a long-term basis, Monday to Friday. We might work late quite often – most days actually – but we don't work weekends, or only very rarely. On that, we are as one. Anyway, the landlord's a bit of a shadowy character, never knowingly over-worked, indeed never spotted actually behind the bar at all, so when the three of us march in after work – ties, suits, overcoats, briefcases, the full monty – for a spot of liquid sustenance and to enquire about parking rights, we're not sure if the geezer behind the bar (for he is definitely a geezer) is the man himself or just a hired help. "We'd like to speak with the Manager, please." "Who wants him?" he enquires, in true geezer fashion. You couldn't make this dialogue up, unless you were scripting a crap cops and robbers movie for the British film industry. Any minute, I'm expecting the phone to ring, and him to answer it, "Yeah, bloody yeah."

The Manager finally makes an appearance. We've never seen him before, in spite of the fact that we've been in a couple of dozen times. Apparently he owns more than one pub, has a manager in each and spends much of his time at his villa in Spain. Nice work if you can get it. He's the anticipated rough diamond. Anticipated, on the basis of organisations recruiting from the top down in their own image. If we owned the place, we'd have it staffed with fit totty flashing their body parts. But I digress, again. Yes we can have four parking spaces and he names a figure. It is a figure which explains why he spends so little time behind the bar. We thank him and retire to consider his offer. For about a nanosecond. Playing cat and mouse with the wardens it is, then.

So we stagger to the end of our first year, with a team photo-graph (including Hopalong) on the steps of the office. There are now eight of us, and by December 24th 1986, we've turned over just over £400,000 at more or less break-even, which matches almost exactly the business plan what I wrote for the bank. Spooky, brilliant, or just luck: you decide. Maybe we did know what we were doing after all.

There have inevitably been a few moments of negative sentiment. The Stag Furniture promotion was a great idea – free Dartington Crystal glasses with furniture purchases: the more you buy, the more you get; but in retrospect it's hard to believe we accepted at face value, without testing first, the supplier's confidence that the product would travel perfectly safely by post in its existing packaging. (You could argue that they should know). Nevertheless, we've had two months of boxes being returned to us that sound like a rain-stick, when shaken. Even after introducing bubble-wrap to every one, we under-estimate the skill of postal workers in spotting a fragile package at ten paces and knowing the force required to throw them from A to B, via various delivery vehicles, to reduce the contents to bits. I still have one pint mug as a memento of that promotion, but I'm afraid that my abiding memory is one of broken glass. God knows what the client felt. I think we kept the worst of it from him.

In spite of this, though, our business is growing, and so we return to the subject of the chapter heading: accountancy (oy, you over there, stifle that yawn).

By the time we get to compete for the Lyons Coffee business and win it, the three of us who look after the clients have an account executive each (enter Pauline, in my case – not literally), revenues show every sign of doubling in year two, and we decide we need a finance man on the staff, rather than outsourcing, which is all the rage now. Sorry, Hopalong. Even in these outsourcing times, I'd always want to have the facility in house where it can be interrogated personally any time you like. To get anyone who's any good, we'll have to pay someone pretty much what we're paying ourselves, but if we want to take this business where we want it to go, we need someone who's going to be fully part of the management team – one of us; in it for the long haul; can see the potential benefits a few years down the track. We won't be appointing a Finance Director just yet. For one thing, salary costs would be prohibitive; for another, anyone coming in will have to earn that moniker (and the privileges it will bring) over time. We start by considering asking a couple of the guys in the finance department at our old place – the two second-in-commands – if they'd be interested in taking a punt on a career change as our number one. One of them actually shows lots of interest and agrees verbally to join us, but then inexplicably changes his mind and sends us back to square one. His loss. And a considerable loss it will eventually be. So we advertise for a Financial Controller.

We get half a dozen decent replies and go through the interview process, which everyone knows is a flawed affair. You decide whether you like someone within about 10 seconds of them walking in, and then spend the next hour trying to confirm the prejudice. There is one woman who looks a good candidate, but she is a bit pushy and the other guys are horribly sexist about the whole thing: given our tendency to blokey nights out and general bad behaviour, how would she fit in with all that? The idea that we might moderate our behaviour doesn't even get a mention.

In the end we settle for Steve because he is overtly one of us. A bit outré for an accountant, maybe (ear-ring, long-ish curly hair), but we're in a creative "profession" and he is/will be unarguably one of the lads. He seems to know his onions, though how we can tell is anyone's guess. It doesn't occur to us to put the two short-listed ones in front of a proper accountant as a back-check. References? Sure, but we never bothered to take them up. They wouldn't give them, if they were dodgy, would they?

And now you're going to have to stick with me as I jump a few fences, because this isn't a linear diary about what happens next (unless it happens to suit me), but what happens in various areas of the business, which might be next, but might be – as in this case – two or three years down the track. The theme of this chapter is accountancy, and our experience of this dull subject necessarily spreads over the lifetime of the business, but events in the first three or four years are particularly noteworthy.

First up is a spectacular falling out with Cardy Coxy, a partner in a growing regional firm of accountants with branches in a number of locations around the Oxford area. He is also our landlord, you will recall, which, on closer inspection when things start to go seriously pear-shaped, turns out to be not just a bad idea generally, but against the chartered accountants' code of practice specifically. It's OK to have sub-tenants, but not to be their auditors too. I suppose there are potential conflict of interest issues at work here, though I doubt we would have given them a second thought when we took up his offer, even if they had been brought to our attention, and to be fair, he was doing us a favour (though I guess he was also doing himself one, offsetting half his rent without the inconvenience of an estate agent middle-man to find him a tenant.) Whatever, it certainly works in our favour when the shit finally hits the fan.

The reason for the ordure in the air conditioning is that, having turned over three-quarters of a million in year two and on target for a million in year three, we suddenly get hit by a back-tax demand from the Revenue which amounts to around £10,000 each. When you're only paying yourselves £25/30K and the mortgage is looking after every spare cent, it is fair to say that none of us has this sort of sum slopping around against a rainy day. But more to the point, what on earth are we paying accountants for, if not to avoid this kind of experience? First of all, how come they didn't see it coming and forewarn/forearm us? Secondly, why can they not mitigate it, once the issue's raised its ugly head? We start by being astonished at the sheer incompetence of it all, but I guess we shouldn't have been so surprised: we've had a fax machine installed, Cardy Coxy's been using it for incoming missives from his own clients from time to time, and we've seen at least one from a disgruntled client complaining he's been hit with a half-million pound unexpected bill. Confidentiality? You must be kidding. We read anything that might give us an advantage: why do you think salesmen teach themselves to read upside down? So they can check what their prospective customer's got on his mind/desk today that might help them make the sale.

We then proceed through various stages of crossness, anger and rage at our new landlord's shrug-of-the-shoulders, well-that's-the-way-life-goes, you'll-just-have-to-pay-it attitude. With Stid, it becomes a bit of a cause célèbre. Given that his favourite phrase is, "Revenge is a dish best tasted cold," perhaps this shouldn't come as too big a surprise, though in this instance, he's definitely looking at a hot dish, not a salad, and preferably a Vindaloo. He writes to the senior partners and receives, eventually, weasel-word expressions of regret, but no redress. So he makes a final complaint to the Chartered Accountants trade association, which at least shakes the senior partners into taking things a bit more seriously, mainly because their own butts are now in the firing line.

Never forget, though, that while a trade association speaks fine words about protecting its members' reputation by weeding out the few bad apples, its essential role is to protect its members' interests and, wherever possible, to pour oil on troubled waters (to mix metaphors) whenever someone is trying to stir up a hornet's nest (there's another one). So we are being gloriously naïve in anticipating that they might take our side, accept our statement of events entirely and come down like the proverbial ton of bricks on the hapless Coxy. (Who pays their wages, after all?) What we actually get back is the usual Sir Humphrey-speak of, "On the one hand" and "On the other hand", and absolutely no action taken whatsoever. It's what the politicians would call a mild rap on the knuckles, if that.

What it all boils down to, however much we huff and puff, is that we've failed to blow his house down, and we're still left with a hefty tax bill. It is indeed fortunate that the business is thriving, because the only apparent solution for us is to pay ourselves a dividend to cover the tax bill. It's a damn good job that there's enough cash in the bank to enable us to do so.

As for Coxy, we fire him as our accountant and appoint Grant Thornton. They may be more expensive, but at least we expect them to give us no horrid shocks – plus, by going to an organisation that is very much part of the establishment, you do send a signal to the tax authorities that you're playing it by the book, and as a result, there is a tendency for them to leave you alone and do the minimum of spot-checks. What you don't get is any meaningful tax avoidance ideas, but that's the price you pay.

By the end of the second year, we're leaving Coxy behind physically too – we've outgrown our second home already and are moving into new offices in the city centre: another twenty minutes drive in, even on a good day, and the parking's crap, but the city centre has a buzz about it that is unachievable in any suburban setting. So Coxy's not our landlord any more either. We say a fond farewell to the shark, with a mental V-sign to the accountants, who will not feature again. Apart from the fact that six months later, we notice that the name of the practice over the door has changed from its original one to Coxy and his partner in crime. We had the impression when dealing with the senior partners that we weren't the only clients complaining about Coxy's incompetence; now we infer that he's been given the order of the boot and is being forced to set up on his own. No idea if we're right, but there is a definite flavour of revenge on the palate for a week or two. It soon passes of course. We have bigger fish to fry.

Indeed, we have an absolute monster to deal with about eighteen months later, in the shape of accountancy misadventure number two. This time, though, it's well and truly self-inflicted. We're up to getting on for £2 million turnover, my PA has moved upstairs to help Steve with the day-to-day accounts, and it all kicks off while Steve's on a fortnight's holiday in the sun. Around the end of the first week, Jools asks me to go to the accounts office and she tells me she has concerns about what seem to be a number of payments that look odd to her. She's being careful with how she phrases this, but what it boils down to is that it looks as if someone has been skimming money out of our account, and the only person in a position to be able to do that is Steve. Bloody hell, that's all we need. So I ask her to spend a couple of days going through all the books and seeing if she can identify any more and how much it might all add up to. Until we've quantified the potential scale of the problem, I tell her I'll not be mentioning it to the other guys. With Steve away for most of the week (due back the following Thursday), we have time to check facts at our leisure before deciding what to do.

A day later and she's back with a list of transactions as long as your arm – £300 here, £500 there, some in petty cash, some a franking machine scam at the Post Office, some in the purchase ledger, unsupported by any invoice or the usual job bag details. It amounts to close to £20,000, and this is just for this financial year. Steve is mates with one or two high-profile jockeys (the champion jockey among them, as it happens), and it emerges later that he's been using our money to bet on tips he's presumably getting from them. Unsuccessfully, by the look of it. It's the classic gambling pattern: start with small amounts; losses build up; bet larger amounts to recoup accumulated losses; lose again, and the cycle spirals in ever-increasing amounts. Except it's our money he's been losing, and concealing, in accounts that, if not awash with cash, are certainly comfortably off as a result of our growing business. We've made decent profits three years in a row, after the first-year break-even, and we've paid the corporation tax on it and left it in the business, not being too greedy about what we take out, so there is plenty of slack in the system, in case we have a bad year, brought on, say, by a recession. Steve's been using that slack to become the Bookie's Friend.

It's time the others should hear the worst. There is a palpable sense of shock, when I give them the bad news, followed by the inevitable string of recriminations and the assorted acts of revenge he can look forward to when they jointly and severally get their hands on him. On mature reflection though, it seems more sensible to take some professional advice. In the last couple of years, we've been introduced to some fancy-dan city-slicker lawyers called Biddle & Co (when we negotiated the lease on our offices, which is another story), but they have a reputation, already, for getting results, so we lay the facts before them. Their advice is simple and unequivocal: trying to negotiate with him (he's bound to offer to re-pay whatever he owes over whatever period) would leave us with a very weak hand if he then subsequently defaults. We need to bring in the Fraud Squad at the outset and let the law take its course, however harsh that may seem. Actually it doesn't seem at all harsh to us. We're not expecting to get our money back any time soon, if ever, so we may as well exact as much revenge (that word again) as possible. The first thing we have to do, in any event, is quantify the total amount of losses, so we can give the filth the full and unexpurgated story, and to that end, we need Grant Thornton, under an oath of silence, to go through the books with Jools and add up the damage. Quickly. Before Steve's back from holiday.

The previous year's books have not yet been audited, and together with the three months that have already elapsed this year, some £25,000 of unauthorised payments are uncovered. In addition, there's another £10,000 from the previous year's books, which *have* been audited. This tells you everything you need to know about the efficiency of the big accountancy firms (or probably any of them) when it comes to cooking (*surely auditing – Ed.*) the books. In fact, the bigger the numbers and the more of them, the greater the scope for maladministration. Usually of course, it's the business owners themselves feathering their nest at somebody else's expense (the tax-payer, say, or the company's pension fund); you'd like to think that the accountants would notice £10,000 of dodgy payments out of a total turnover of less than £2 million, but you obviously can't count on it.

All up, we've been fleeced for somewhere north of £35,000. William Hill's shareholders must be delirious. The police on the other hand play a completely straight bat. They don't get excited – they've seen it all before, and in the grand scheme of things, £35K might seem like a substantial sum but it isn't going to be breaking any records. They take all the details and ask us to call them when he's next in the office, presumably on Thursday morning, so they can come and arrest him.

It's around this time that one or two of the others recall Steve shooting his mouth off at one of our Directors' motivational piss-ups, thinly disguised as the Annual General Meeting (see chapter 5 for gory details), about how crap we all are and how little we know etc etc. And someone else remembers his wife flashing a massive diamond he's given her, at one of our directors' and wives' dinners. In other words flaunting his ill-deeds in our faces, so Thursday morning's events are eagerly anticipated. The thought of giving him a good kicking before Inspector Knacker arrives crosses more than one mind, but on Wednesday afternoon Steve himself puts a spanner in the works.

Late afternoon, he suddenly turns up at the office with his missus, who's on crutches after some misadventure or other. Given what else is going down, we don't enquire too deeply, or to put it another way, we don't give a shit. Who gets off the plane from their holidays and pops in the office on their way home? Answer: a workaholic (which he isn't: I've worked with a few in my time) or someone with a guilty secret who wants to check he hasn't been rumbled. I know which one my money's on – not a great choice of phrase, given the circumstances.

What follows next is like a scene from the Keystone Cops or a Brian Rix farce. Someone phones the police to tell them he's turned up a day early. Steve picks up the vibes that all is not well, and eventually he is given a summary of our investigations while he's been sunning himself. He immediately announces that his first priority is to get his missus home, presumably on the grounds that, if he gets his collar felt, she won't be able to drive herself. We tell him that the police are in fact on their way and he literally runs for the exit, collecting a startled missus (who has no inkling what is transpiring) and drags/pulls/carries her out the courtyard, down the alleyway and into the busy city centre. Two minutes later, in comes Inspector Knacker. "He went that way," we all chorus. Off he goes in pursuit. Alright I made that up. There's no point in him going in pursuit: he hasn't a clue what Steve looks like (though man carrying woman with crutches probably would do the trick). Steve has promised to return once he's delivered his human cargo home, but the law takes his address and goes off to pay him a visit and save him the petrol.

And then it all goes quiet. It's as if there's been a death in the family: one of our number has departed – we all know, never to return – and after the high excitement of the last couple of days, there's a distinct sense of anti-climax. The following day, though, events take another surprising turn, when I receive a call from Steve's father, asking if we can meet. The immediate assumption is that he's trying to mitigate the damage by asking us not to press charges, though anyone who's ever got the law involved will know that, even if you want to, you can't just call them up and stand them down. Once you set the ball rolling, it turns inexorably and takes on a life of its own. He turns out to be an extremely nice man from the old-fashioned school, retired from a senior role at some multi-national with a very comfortable pension. He asks us (Stid's accompanied me in a safety-first out-numbering exercise) why we felt the need to call the police; could we not have dealt with matters without going to such extremes? It is the only time there is a hint of an accusatory tone about the proceedings. Once we explain that it is on the basis of our own highly respected lawyers' unequivocal opinion (and why would we have such an expensive dog and bark ourselves?) he soon realises that, in that respect at least, the game is beyond him.

He does however have a plan B. He is, quite clearly, desperate to try to keep his (only) son out of jail – and the size of the fraud makes the prospect a virtual certainty, we understand. So here is what he is proposing: we give him an audited breakdown of all the money Steve has misappropriated, and he will raid his pension fund (legally) and repay us every penny; and if he does, will we not press charges? This would put us into a moral difficulty: should a miscreant get away with his misdeeds just because he's got a rich(-ish) daddy? Of course, society's full of examples of exactly that, and as Tommy Cooper once put it in a gag about someone owing him half a crown, "It's not the principle, it's the money." Fortunately for us, we are able to wriggle off this particular hook, because it is our understanding that the matter is out of our hands. The decision to prosecute will be taken entirely by Inspector Knacker, and indeed, having provided the evidence, we will probably not be required further – not even in court, if and when the case gets there. It is for precisely scenarios like this that our City lawyers insisted we just call in the fraud squad and be done with it.

We all retire to consider our options, so to speak. Well, he does; we just go off for a beer to discuss the plot. Eventually after a couple of days, he calls to say he's decided he wants to repay all the money anyway, presumably in the hope that either it might persuade the police not to press charges, or if they do, to mitigate the sentence handed down. After a few days of to-ing and fro-ing with the lawyers, a cheque for somewhere in excess of £35,000 arrives, "in full and final settlement" etc. No doubt he doesn't want us returning to the table with our hands open at a later date, with the words, "Guess what else we found he's had away." Given that we weren't expecting to get any of it back after discovering his treachery, we're jolly happy to sign whatever he wants, bank the cheque and put the whole sorry mess behind us.

In the aftermath to all this, we learn that the bank itself would have been liable for the losses: he'd been cashing cheques with forged signatures on – Gaylord's mainly, as it turns out, as the easiest to forge – and that, together with the abnormal amounts being requested, should have at least rung alarm bells and generated enquiries to check their bona fides. Maybe they did, and Steve himself fielded the calls to put them off the scent. Whatever, I'll bet it would have been a lot more difficult and time-consuming wringing compensation out of the bank. As it is, we can draw a line in the sand, as the current saying goes, and get on with the business.

As it turns out, too, we never see or hear from Steve again. It is reported back to us that in the court proceedings six months later he gets a month in jail (a month?) serves about a fortnight and is out so quickly that few people notice his absence, and those who do assume he's been away on business or pleasure (and not her majesty's either). It is also reported that his father gets him a job at some service station to try to get him back on his feet. I have to say I doubt my father would have done half as much, had I been in the dock. All of this is hearsay in any case: there's no prima facie evidence for any of it, and a year later he's just a distant fading memory, like the death of a soap star, erased from the script and all mention within a fortnight.

Indeed a year later we have a new Financial Controller on board, sensible, conservative (in every sense), agency background, altogether a more reassuring presence. Jools tries to carry the burden for a few months, with a day or two support from the accountants, but without any accountancy training it all gets a bit much for her, so we go back to the recruitment table, and in comes Pierre, who will still be with us at the end – or very nearly so, as you will discover. Finally we find someone who is trustworthy, reliable and can be left to get on with the bean counting in confidence, while we go off collecting more beans. The fact that he features so little in our further adventures, relative to his time with us and the contribution that he makes, is the biggest compliment I can pay him.

Three

Sharp practice: creative accounting in the creative department

URING STEVE'S 'REIGN' AS Financial Controller, we have moved offices into the city centre – briefly alluded to in the last chapter – and we are now ensconced in our own dedicated 3-storey building of 3,500 square feet in a courtyard adjoining the Oxford Union, up an alleyway off the main shopping street. Central it is. Accessible it most certainly isn't. So why did we go for it, once we'd outgrown Cardy Coxy's little pied-à-terre? Mainly because it's 1988, and astonishingly now maybe, but there is very little office development going on in Oxford at the time, central or suburban. Of the few options on the market, the rest are either old and grubby, or new and characterless. We eventually go for our present home because we convince ourselves that the buzz of the city centre will (just about) outweigh the inaccessibility and lack of parking, and the office layout is perfect for our medium- to long-term needs. Ground floor: reception, studio, store-room and kitchen; 1st floor: account handlers; 2nd floor: board-room, more account handlers, and a separate lockable office where Steve can cook the books, away from the prying eyes of the fraud squad (not exactly how it was articulated at the time). There's also a bijou meeting room off the first-floor stairs, tucked away for maximum privacy, where all the comfy chairs go – handy for brainstorming sessions, say, or sackings, or a bit of sexual harassment.

All that are needed are a few partitions on the top floor to create a Board Room/meeting room, and a few glass partitions on the ground floor to separate reception from the studio. We have some fancy furniture produced by Neville Johnston to make the meeting-room fit for a king (or at least the Marketing Director of Coca Cola – the sales promotion industry equivalent), with a table big enough to sit a dozen round comfortably.

By now there are around a dozen of us, which is why we have outgrown the view of the shark, but in 3,500 square feet we can all spread out in palatial splendour, everyone marking out territory and creating their own space – more 'nesting', in Stid's words.

Which brings me to the creative department, an entity that for most office workers is an alien concept. What, after all, do they actually do in the Creative Department (a question I've heard from time to time in agencies too)? Quite unfairly. Probably. Most of the time. My desk on the first floor overlooks the entrance, as does the window to the studio below. I'm sitting musing on some issue one day, when I see two local herberts stroll in to the (private) courtyard, having a nose around, and overhear their conversation through a half-open window: "What goes on here then?" "It's one of them yuppie companies: no one knows what they do." I guess that neatly pigeon-holes us. They have of course informed that opinion by their view through the ground-floor window of the creative department. All drawing boards, computer screens and magic markers, we are on the cusp of the transition from old technology (pens, pencils, paper) to new (electronic – Apple Macs), and the studio looks messy.

It is the first rule of all creative departments everywhere that no one looks smart. "The suits" is what they call the account handlers who have to deal with clients and sell their work to them, on a day-to-day basis. With the advent of dress-down Friday (what is the point of that?) which predictably spreads to the rest of the week eventually, a more relaxed dress code, along continental lines, is now replacing the old norms, but in the late 80'/early 90's, we're still in the office in suits and ties (even if no client meetings are scheduled), while the studio turns up in jeans and T-shirt, or whatever. This neatly sums up the conundrum for office workers at the time: most of them have a wardrobe consisting of suits and ties (weekdays) and jeans and T-shirts (evenings and weekends); few spend any money on smart casual wear – when or where would you wear it? Which is why dress-down Friday nearly fails to establish itself. When staff turn up in ripped jeans (contemporary fashion statement) and various anti-establishment T-shirts, senior management starts to stamp its corporate foot and make conservative statements about maintaining standards. All tosh of course. Go into any office today, in most small companies, and there's barely a tie in sight (unless you're an accountant, a solicitor or a banker, who still cleave to the old ways, bless 'em), but it's taken the best part of two decades to get anywhere near the standards of our European neighbours.

But what does the creative department do? In an advertising agency, they devise the ideas and execute them, from a client brief distilled from a multitude of conversations by the suits with their client contacts into an agreed creative brief. Once it is handed over, the suits' job is to shuttle back and forth between the creatives and the clients, trying to sell the fruits of their labour. From the creatives' perspective, the suits have no role to play in criticising or arguing about the ideas or execution; theirs is to sell it enthusiastically, even if they personally feel less than enthusiastic about the work. In a sales promotion agency, there is (or was then) a different dynamic at work. We are by definition trying to modify consumer behaviour with the introduction of bribes (*surely incentives – Ed.*). Free gifts, special offers, chances to win – anything to get people to buy something they otherwise wouldn't have, or to buy more of something they already buy a bit of. You get the idea. One sales promotion man described the difference thus: advertising takes the horse to the water; sales promotion persuades it to take a drink. That neatly sums it up.

So in a promotions agency, the creative effort is split in two: the suits (us) are involved in devising ever more imaginative bribes (alright, incentives) and defining how we bring said bribes to the notice of our intended targets (that's you, potentially); the creative department designs the communications vehicles specified by the suits: on-pack messages, leaflets, point-of-sale, direct mail, advertising – and these days, increasingly, electronic communications. So the balance of power is very different, and very weighted to the suits, which is just how we like it. We decide whether the execution of our ideas will appeal to the clients or not, and unless there are exceptional circumstances, the creatives are kept at arms' length from the clients. What will they make of a bunch of scruffs armed with Magic Markers (that's felt pens to you)?

Perhaps the fault is ours: the people we recruit are essentially graphic designers, whose core strength is just that: graphic design. Taking on someone who also has creative views about changing consumer behaviour never enters our consciousness: that's our job, isn't it? Maybe, too, it's the effect of the market we're in. Anyone who is genuinely creative in both senses of the word naturally gravitates to the world of advertising, where the money is better, the projects are bigger and more visible, they get more power and influence, and therefore more fun. It's a no-brainer really.

Gaylord runs our creative department, by which I mean we tell him what we want designed – we write the headlines and body copy too, by the way – and he decides which of his staff has the time and skills to execute it best. Naturally he keeps the most interesting and high-profile projects for himself. 'Tis the nature of the beast. He is, however, in one respect, not like his peers – and not just because of his effete manner. Because he's "management", he likes to come to work in a suit and tie. At least I assume he likes to. He's certainly under no pressure from us to do so. Maybe it's his way of allying himself with us – there's no denying that, of the four of us, he's the definite outsider. If it is, it probably also has the effect of keeping his staff at arms' length: by dressing über-smart, he's also making the statement, "I'm not one of you." That can be quite destructive when it comes to fostering team spirit.

In one respect, however, he is an absolutely typical creative type, and that's his inability to spell – it's surely a left-brain, right-brain thing. Hardly any creative types are also good with words, which is why most advertising agencies have teams of two – one to do the words, one to draw the pictures. It's also why you occasionally get right howlers in 36-point headlines, unless you have a rigorous checking procedure. With Gaylord, it gets into his speech too: we laugh like drains when he talks about the Irish Prime Minister, Charles Hawtrey (as I've said before, it doesn't take much), or the blue-chip defence company, Hawker Sidney. Inevitably we've had a few on paper too. One awful drinks client, Coopers of Wessex (part of Allied Breweries at the time) became Coppers of Watford on the rough visual he did. We were so up against the deadline by the time it arrived, that the Cat had to show it to the client too, accompanied by a bit of grovelling, which came particularly hard, because the Cat doesn't do grovelling well anyway, and particularly because, of all the toss-pot clients we've had (and boy, we've had a few – see chapter 4), this is one of the tossiest.

It's one of those things you just have to make allowances for. Forewarned is forearmed etc etc. Actually the people we've recruited, Kev and Judy, are better than most – and certainly better than Gaylord – so the howlers are pretty sporadic. We have, inevitably, a succession of characters in and out of the studio over the years, an interesting mix of personalities, I think you'd put it. From straight family person to social misfit, and most things in between, sometimes all at the same time, it makes for entertaining little cameo dramas every now and then. You do have to keep them busy, as the devil definitely does make work for idle hands. You're lucky if a period of inactivity leads to nothing worse than an impromptu game of cricket, played with bat, ball and stumps fashioned creatively (of course) out of the various art materials at their disposal. Personality clashes are inevitable, given the fragile personalities of some of them, and shouties and sulks are not uncommon. For that very reason, it is the most interesting place in the agency, and of course the only place where a recognisable "product" is created.

Getting the right balance in terms of staff numbers is critical to profitability in any service organisation, and in an agency, nowhere is it more critical than in the studio. If you don't have enough people, you can't get the work done on time; missed deadlines equal late delivery of sales materials; all clients work to strict promotional calendars; no materials equals no campaign; no campaign equals fired promotional agency. QED. Too many creatives, and the salaries come to more than the income, which is not an equation to be recommended for anything other than the very short term, and preferably not at all.

The way you traditionally get round it is to have a nucleus of paid talent on the payroll, and outsource to freelancers what they can't fit in to a reasonable working day. There is always a list of mercenaries who prefer self-employment and who hire them-selves out, at a higher rate than you're paying staffers, to the highest (or nicest) bidder. The upside for them is that they keep control of their own lives and, if they're fully employed, they make more money too; the downside is that they are at the mercy of the market, and if things go quiet and the phone stops ringing, the money stops flowing in too. Few of them build up much of a financial buffer to withstand too many quiet periods, which is why so many of them are pulled in two different directions: the danger/freedom/excitement/higher earnings of working for themselves, versus the security of a regular pay-cheque. There is a qualitative angle too: the more talented a designer, the more demand for their services there is likely to be, even in quieter periods. Gaylord's approach to motivation, where freelancers are concerned, is delightfully simple: he tells every one of them on every single project he briefs out, "This one's important to us."

From the agency's perspective, getting the balance right between full-time and freelance personnel is critical to both profitability and commercial effectiveness. When we first start, Gaylord operates as the sole creative, and everything he can't manage himself, he outsources to freelancers. There is also an issue of supply and demand: when everyone's busy (and by everyone, I mean all the agencies in any given catchment area), finding freelance talent which is available, just when you need it, can be a problem. Anyone who is any good will by definition be in most demand, so the need to put resource on the payroll is also protectionist: you can be sure of getting their full attention at all times (apart from when they're surfing the net for porn or the latest football gossip – we find one of ours is running a football fanzine in his spare time, which includes some of ours). Once you've recruited someone who's any good, and you've got used to their little ways, you want to keep them. Recruitment is difficult enough and fraught with all the usual dangers of taking on someone who turns out to be less than the advertised and anticipated article, so once you get one that has proved him/herself, you don't want to have to let them go, just because you've lost a client or two, unless the figures get really dire – as sometimes, regrettably, they are bound to do.

We try to manage the balancing act by applying a simple equation: when the invoices received from freelance operators come to more than the payroll cost of a full-time employee for two or three months consecutively, we look to take on someone permanently. Then they will be on permanent call, it will cost us a lot less than paying for 40 hours of freelance work, and that's before we take into account the question of working hours. In an agency environment, it is taken as read that meeting deadlines, however unreasonable or unnecessary in the grand scheme of things, is a sine qua non. If we have to work late to get things done, then so be it. We do not as a matter of principle pay overtime. We believe that if we do, all the jobs that would have been finished by 5.30 will magically take until 6.30, 7.30 or 8.00 to complete, with a concomitant additional cost to throw out the profit calculations.

Fostering a team spirit that makes this attitude of mind the accepted norm is vital to the well-being of the agency, and not just financially. If you were to pay overtime to the creatives, why not the account handlers who work equally long hours, when necessary? This would become the thin end of a very large wedge, and each time we confront it, the long-term issues it throws up make us shy away sharply from a change of policy. Our way round it is to treat a couple of hours over as the norm, but if exceptional circumstances find people working till midnight or beyond on a particular project or pitch, we tell them to take their partner out to dinner on us – anywhere of their choosing, no questions asked, money no object, and send us the bill, or put it on expenses. No one ever goes to the Manoir, even though we would pay up without comment or criticism; in fact no one takes the piss at all. The other thing we do is have regular company pub crawls around the bars and bistros of Oxford, all paid for by the state: put it down as staff motivation or whatever, and make it tax deductible, so long as we're profitable... cheers, Chancellor. More on this later, but it all helps team morale. Better than the pirate mantra anyway: "The floggings will continue until morale improves."

About six months after Steve's cops and robbers departure, Jools is manfully (womanfully?) trying to cope with the accounts, with a bit of month-end help from Grant Thornton, to get the regular monthly management accounts into shape. We may be crap at recruiting, but we do run a tight ship financially – if you ignore the little matter of not noticing £35K disappearing from our accounts. Still apart from that ... Every monthly board meeting is accompanied by about 20 pages of accounts information: up-to-date year-on-year figures on profit & loss, balance sheet, cash-flow, forward billings estimates (always a lively discussion piece), expenses (ditto), aged debtors list (who owes us money and how overdue it is), creditor list (who we owe money to and when it's due), year-end profit projections based on current financial information, etc. This last is nearly always a source of pain and irritation: at the start of the year particularly, for the first two quarters even, forward billings rarely go past the next six months, so the back end of the year looks bare and the business consequently unprofitable (pain, gnashing of teeth); there is, however, another six months to put things right. By the last quarter, the figures are more or less fixed and accurate, but if there's a shortfall, there's not enough time to do anything about it, unless we get lucky and a big unforeseen project drops in our corporate lap from an existing or new client. It does happen, but you can't count on it. So it's only in the third quarter that things look reasonably OK, and there's still time to win new business that will make a difference to the bottom line. Why do we do it, then? I guess it's our way of putting pressure on ourselves to keep going out and getting business. Sit back with any sense of complacency and you get an eventual kick in the backside.

Anyway, Jools is struggling to keep everything on track. It's hardly surprising, even though Steve apparently spent half his time studying form and laying bets: she's doing at least a job and a half, if not two jobs, and we have to agree to find another financial person. Not being financially trained, some of the demands of the job have started to get on top of her. Since she's one of the most capable people I've ever met, the fact that she says this to us at all means we don't take long to accede to her suggestion.

In the meantime, we have another little conundrum uncovered, relating to the subject of the chapter (the creative department: keep up). A significant number of invoices are being received from an organisation called Sharp Pencil, for services relating to freelance work and design. There's nothing necessarily odd about this at face value: even with four or five full-timers, the peaks and troughs of the business – especially if we have some big new business pitches on the go – mean freelance resource is still needed to a greater or lesser extent most of the time.

What rings the alarm bells in this case is that nobody seems to know who Sharp Pencil is. Usually freelancers come in to the office to take a brief and, therefore, get seen and recognised by the rest of the business; often treated as part of the team; sometimes they go on to become part of the team. But in this instance, there has been no sight or sound of anyone.

Intrigued, we start digging, surreptitiously. Perhaps, having been bitten by Steve so recently, we are a bit more paranoid than we would have been a few months ago. (Still, you know what they say: just because you're paranoid doesn't mean they're not out to get you.) A few casual questions around the creative staff: anyone know an outfit called Sharp Pencil? No one seems to have heard of them – or no one's admitting to. But if they don't commission work from this lot, who does? There is only one person left, and that is our co-Director, Gaylord. We don't go directly to him and ask him though. We start to play super-sleuth. Finding out who owns Sharp Pencil; where they're based; who the Directors are. It's not that tricky: any of the credit reference companies have the information. A smallish cheque secures all the info we need, and guess what? Gaylord's missus is the proprietor. No wonder we've never seen hide nor hair. He's taking work home and getting Ingrid (for such is her name and she is a designer herself) to do it – or doing it himself. Who knows?

What has prompted him to do it? We speculate that the factors that come into the equation, and the sequence of events, may be:

- The studio's horribly busy. Everyone, including Gaylord, is working late on a regular basis.
- Alternatively, instead of working late at the office, he's taking work home.
- Ingrid wonders idly why he doesn't get it done by freelancers and take the pressure off himself.
- Gaylord doesn't trust freelancers to do it as well as he would (or it's a prestige project and he wants control of it.)
- Ingrid reminds him she's a graphic artist herself. Why not sub-contract to her, still keep control, and make a few bob on the side?
- She'll trade as Sharp Pencil, so it's all kept at arm's length – sort of.
- What could be simpler?

This is the charitable version of events. In this version, you will ask why he didn't just tell us Ingrid was doing freelance work and have it all above board? And his reply would have been that we would have seen the arrangement as a convenient way of doing the work himself, effectively claiming overtime and thereby earning a big whack more than us for the same job. And therefore telling him to fuck right off. He'd be right too: we would have. No doubt he feels he's working harder than us: one creative head dealing with the work of three account directors and their staff. Nevertheless, the fact that it's being done in an under-hand way strongly suggests an admission of guilt.

In our endless musings on the why's and wherefore's of this latest affair, there is also a more sinister reading of the runes. Instead of just making a few bob on the side (actually over ten grand in the last two or three months alone, once we add it all up), what if this is the precursor to something a bit more sinister?

As part of our growth plan, Gaylord was challenged to become a profit centre in his own right, selling pure design, as opposed to sales promotion, and acting as both account handler and creative deliverer. To give him his due, he's done a pretty good job too, developing Volvo and Forte Hotels from occasional minor projects into regular major clients, contributing several hundred thousand pounds a year of highly profitable turnover. And he's become virtually the sole client contact. Now you know why the alarm bells are sounding ever more insistently.

So maybe he just thinks: bollocks, I'm making all this contribution, I'm doing their job and mine, I'm working my knackers off, I should have my due reward; Ingrid, send me another invoice. Or maybe he's actually planning a breakaway. Maybe the fact that we've done the same thing ourselves, in the first place, makes us particularly sensitive to the possibility.

He has the makings of a very nice little business, with those two major clients and a few other bits and pieces. With next to no overheads in a one/two-man band, working from home, most of the gross margin is also nett profit, and on a half million pound turnover, he can see himself banking – what? Three or four hundred thou. I can see the possibility must be tempting. What are we paying ourselves currently (we all earn the same now)? £50/60K with maybe a £10K wedge at the year-end if we've had a good one. The chance to earn 5 or 6 years' salary in one year would tempt a saint. And whatever else he is, Gaylord's no saint.

On the other hand, he is a 25% shareholding Director of our business, which, turning over nearly a couple of million and with nett profits running around 10%, makes his shareholding worth, on paper at least, getting on for half a million. OK, in a small private company, with no market for shares, that figure is theoretical, but it does represent where the bidding between lawyers would start, if we have a giant falling out and resort to litigation to sort out our differences. Needless to say, the business doesn't have half a million sloshing around in it to pay anyone off, and even if it did, we would rather cut off our own genitals and eat them than pay out that fat lying tart. And no, that's not hyperbole. Oh alright, a bit.

By this time, Stid and the Cat, who have always secretly despised him (actually, not so secretly, in all honesty), have decided he's crossed the line and they want him out. They don't like him; they don't trust him; and they're not having him in the business any more. There isn't a great deal to be said in mitigation. I certainly don't feel the same antipathy to him that they do, but with all the facts, there isn't much ground for opposing their implacable intentions.

Getting out a shareholder who doesn't want to go isn't that easy. Especially without any financial compensation. So we consult m'learned friends – again. Re-enter stage left our legal city slickers, Biddle & Co, who specialise in advertising agency work inter alia (since swallowed up by a couple of mega mergers, so you will look for them in vain, but in all honesty Stid's introduction to them is probably the best thing he does for us, in retro-spect). They are what the trade calls 'heavy hitters'. On the odd occasion when we introduce them to provincial solicitors, they scare the shit out of them. Yes, they are expensive, but they do get results. Their advice on our creative dilemma, which they don't put in writing, is that we need some prima facie evidence of what is going on, and if the facts bear out suspicions, the best way to ease him out is to put the frighteners on him – legally of course, we're not talking about hiring a couple of hoods with shooters or baseball bats (not that the thought hasn't crossed our less-than-the-pure-as-driven-snow minds.) Threaten him with the full force of the law (see Steve for details), and get him to resign. They will draw up a resignation letter which signs away his share-holding and all his rights, in return for us not pressing charges.

All we've got to do is get him to sign it, once we have more than the circumstantial evidence currently in our possession. And so begins what might seem like an English version of the Rockford Files (old American private detective series), with me, Stid and the Cat jointly and severally playing Jim Rockford. We find out where Sharp Pencil trades from: it does have an address that isn't their house, we're surprised to find. We stake it out for about half an hour, before getting bored: this private detective lark's not as sexy as it's made out to be on the telly (no…really). Too much hanging around for our tastes. We establish via a neighbouring business that Sharp Practice, as we've come to call it, is run by a woman called Ingrid, who looks remarkably like Gaylord's missus. Via our own bank, we establish where the account is held, in a nearby branch in Banbury, and visit it. We pay a Marketing Principles cheque into it and keep the receipt as evidence. Why? I can't imagine what this would have proved in a court of law. Perhaps we're getting carried away by this private investigation malarkey. Eventually we establish to our own certain satisfaction that Gaylord is effectively defrauding us, and we have enough evidence to convict, even if it might not stand up to a rigorous cross-examination by a canny barrister in a court of law.

He's not going to an English court of law anyway. He's coming, by special RSVP invitation, to our unique version of the Star Chamber, at which there will be one defender and three prose-cuting council, who will also comprise the sole witnesses. The venue for this will be our Board Room, but after hours, when all the staff have gone home. Stid is going to secretly record it, so that when he confesses his misdeeds (as he assuredly will), we will have not only the signed resignation, but a recorded confession, witnessed by the three of us, just in case he has second thoughts and consults his own lawyers about challenging the legality of what we've done.

Before inviting him in for a little chat, Stid's had a dry run, to make sure the tape recorder (a little old hand-held Dictaphone affair – no state-of-the-art bugging devices here) works OK, and you can hear the resulting conversation clearly, if he leaves it, already on, on a shelf adjacent to the board-room table. It it's placed among some other display items, it may be visible, but is unlikely to be noticed: he's not expecting it, and once we've got into things, he'll be too distracted by the heat of the action to be taking in the details of his surroundings. That is our thinking anyway. The experiment works, so, having received a draft letter from Biddles, assembled all the "evidence" (Sharp Pencil invoices, bank statements, Rockford Files testimony), we set up the Board Room for our coup d'état and invite him in for a little chat.

I'm fairly sure he hasn't got wind of any of this, but there's no doubt that he looks a mite nervous when he comes in and finds us all seated along one side of the table, with him being gestured to a seat on the other side. You wouldn't need to be a psychologist to realise you weren't being invited to a game of charades. We haven't told him what we want to talk about, but the last time a meeting like this was convened, albeit without the tape recorder, was when I called them all in to tell them of Jools's and my suspicions about Steve's extra-mural activities, not six months ago. So the scenario is relatively fresh in everyone's mind. Usually with meetings, there's a bit of chit-chat, people fixing themselves a drink, generally settling down, before any business of substance is discussed. On this occasion, though, Stid, who is playing Chief Prosecutor, with me and the Cat in supporting roles (think Stephen Fry in the Blackadder IV episode where he's accusing Rowan Atkinson of murdering the judge's favourite pigeon), goes straight for the jugular.

"Sit down, Michael" (for such is Gaylord's name, and Stid only ever uses it in full when he's about to heap a pile of shit on him – a fact not lost on Gaylord). "We'd like you to tell us who Sharp Pencil is. We seem to be receiving rather a lot of invoices from them." He pushes a sheaf of paid and unpaid invoices across the broad expanse of the board-room table in Gaylord's direction. "But no one seems to know who they are." From initial discomfort, Gaylord progresses swiftly to sweating – profusely. He begins some form of explanation, which rambles around the houses for a bit, before Stid cuts him off. "Actually you can drop the pretence. We've carried out our own investigations and we know what's been going on, so we've invited you here to listen to your take on all this, and to see if you have anything to say that would stop us calling in the Fraud Squad (for the second time this year)". The sweating gets ever more profuse. He's soaked. Gaylord uses sentences that begin with, "I thought…", "I didn't mean…", "I didn't think…", none of which adds much to the sum total of our knowledge, but equally seems to confirm our suspicions. He isn't actually denying anything. The only card he has to play is that Ingrid is a freelance, like any other freelance, and if he chooses to use her for certain jobs, so what? Which would be true if, as we point out, it had all been done above board; indeed, why did it take till year three for this to become such a good idea? Why not start from day one? There is no answer to this of course.

After several minutes of letting him flounder around with some vague sentences of self-justification, Stid cuts to the chase. "The thing is, Michael, so far as the Board is concerned, you have lost its trust through your actions, and your position on it is therefore untenable. We believe you are responsible for criminal acts of fraud and deception, and that it is our legal responsibility to deal with those acts appropriately. Now there are two ways of going about this, in our opinion. Either we call in the police, get the lawyers involved and do all we can to send you to jail; or you can admit what you've been doing, resign from the Board and the company with immediate effect, and walk away a free man."

We all know this is an empty threat. We probably don't have enough to convict him of fraud, false accounting or anything else. It's true he's misled us, and he obviously feels as guilty as hell about the whole affair, or he wouldn't be sweating so much and taking our threat seriously. He crumples and looks resigned, in every sense. Stid strikes while the iron is hot, and pushes two copies of a resignation letter across to him, which he intimates has been drawn up by Biddles – just to leave him in no doubt that we have already begun the due process, if that's the way he wants it. He doesn't, of course. "Alright, I'll sign."

The letters signed, Stid can't resist putting the boot in. "Naturally we won't be paying any of these unpaid invoices." We accompany Gaylord down to the Studio, for him to collect his personal effects. We're not expecting to see him in the building ever again, so we relieve him of his keys. To say he looks crest-fallen is an under-statement, whether because we've caught him cheating or trying to manufacture a breakaway is hard to tell. On his way out, however, he delivers an interesting parting shot – there's only me and him at the door – as he leaves the building: "Watch your back. They'll have you next."

And then there were three. Another major drama. But looking on the bright side, we do all now own 33.3% of the business, instead of 25%.

As it turns out, we probably do Gaylord a favour. Not because we're in imminent danger of demise (yet), but because, set free of the shackles of running a department, which he isn't very good at, he can concentrate full-time on the work. In spite of our best endeavours to stop him, he takes the design business from Volvo and Forte Hotels, builds on it, and within a couple of years, working from home with low overheads, he's allegedly turning over half a million (he never could resist bragging, if there was something to crow about) – an allegation which seems likely to be true, since he's by then driving around in a brand new Ferrari. The next time I see him, bumping into him at some client lunch at The Bluebird in the Kings Road of all places, he's so enormous (presumably from over-indulging at too many client lunches), it's hard to see how he can fit in to the bucket seats of his flash car. We've chopped in our Vauxhall Astra GTI's by now, but are still slumming it in relative terms in BMW's and Mercedes.

Of course working on your own, with or without your husband or wife, you're never going to develop a business that's worth anything as a trade sale, but arguably, if you can make half a million a year for a few years (and not fritter it away on fast cars), you can probably come out ahead of the "build something to sell" alternative which we are following. Depending on how much you sell for (if you get to that stage), and/or how much you can rake in as a one-man band. The sole trader certainly has its attractions in terms of not having employment issues to deal with; and all the money you make is yours, all yours. But you don't have the buzz of an office with lots of things going on – even if you don't know what half of them are – so you don't get that consistent hum of human interaction. As a one-man band, it can be quite lonely. Re-reading this paragraph, what leaps out of the page is the preponderance of ifs, buts and maybes. There is no magic way to make a pile: everyone has to do it the best way they know how.

Do we replace Gaylord with another Creative Director? Of course we do. Is he any better at building morale and creating a happy team doing great work? No, but that's another chapter. In the event, we go through two more Creative Directors, both of whom have shortcomings of one sort or another, until it finally dawns on us that, with a bit of input from us, the people we've got can quite easily manage themselves, as a sort of co-operative. We don't need an expensive figurehead with a big ego to boss people about – which is not good management, but it is how many people act, when given the responsibility of managing staff.

Four

Cowboys (and Indians): Dodgy Clients

As an agency, you only have two real assets (apart from your bank account, if it's in credit): the people who work for you and the people you work for. Finding employees who are talented enough and fit in with the team is fraught enough; finding clients who are competent, honourable, nice to be around and have substantial marketing funds at their disposal – well, that's a whole different set of problems. Looking back, I'd have to say the phrase which immediately springs to mind is, "You have to kiss a lot of frogs…"

Looking at a client billings summary covering six years of trading, from 1990 to 1995 (including a rather nasty recession, but that's another issue), I find 112 company names, to all of which we have sent at least one invoice for some sort of service rendered. It may have been an up-and-down time for a number of reasons, to be covered elsewhere, but it does demonstrate brilliantly the 80/20 rule of business, aka the Pareto law. (In case this basic law has passed you by, it states that 80% of the results of any endeavour – not just business – will be achieved by just 20% of the effort applied. In this case, 80% of income comes from 20% of clients. And vice versa). During those six years, we have turned over a grand total of nearly £16 million, and doing the maths, I find our own ratio is actually 90/10. Of 112 companies that we managed to get a start with, just 12 accounted for nearly £13 million of it.

So what the hell were we doing with the other 100?

Looking down the list, there are inevitably loads of small businesses where we'd done something insignificant for them, maybe as part of a larger project, or small design jobs that were never going to turn into anything worthwhile. Why take on the work? Well, when you start out, you're desperate for work – any work – so you grab at anything that wanders past the door. You don't stop to think, is this the sort of work we should be doing? Is it a good use of our time and resources? Once you become more established (and profitable), a different mind-set comes into play. You know it may not be the sort of work you should ideally be doing, but if it's design work, for example, the studio facility is there, it has capacity (probably), so why not take the extra revenue? It's all grist to the mill. Not all the 90% falls into this category however. Looking down the list, there are just as many big company names with a meagre few thousand against them, so we've got through the door, got a start – some sort of project – but haven't been able to turn it into a big-spending regular client.

There are all sorts of possible reasons for this: maybe we've fucked up on the first job (it does happen, particularly when you don't have the inside track on how the client works); maybe the personal chemistry hasn't quite gelled; or the client contact has moved or been moved very early on in the relationship, and the newcomer wants to use the new broom approach (a common scenario, unless you have your feet very firmly under the table and know more about the client's business than they do – then you're an indispensable asset); maybe they look like a big name (are a big name), but don't spend that much on sales promotion. Whatever the reasons, there are forty big-name companies over a six-year period, which could have helped us double our turnover if we'd handled them differently, or had a bit of luck, or both.

In practice, therefore, we spend a huge amount of time and

energy on opportunities that do not repay the investment. The problem is, it's really difficult to know which ones are going to make you rich, or, as Bob Dylan put it, which are just wasting your precious time. To compare and contrast, we get more than a start with a Coca Cola subsidiary, Refreshment Spectrum, aka Five Alive; we run a commercially successful multi-media promotion using Phillip Schofield to front it (seemed a very nice chap from the photo-shoot, by the by; turns out his manager, ex-DJ Peter Powell, comes from about three streets away from my parents originally); all based on the popular kids' programme "*Going Live*" – *Going Five Alive*: what else? We even do a decent follow-up promotion, milking the theme for all it's worth, on the cheap (ie we don't use Phillip's image or pay him or the BBC a second round of fees for the privilege). Then the client, who has taken us on in spite of the fact that we're not on the company's recognised agency roster (which she's supposed to use – demonstrating her own independence, I guess), fucks off on a career move to Geneva or wherever, having probably established a reputation as a bit of renegade, and we're left high and dry, with no champions left in the house with any influence. Not sure how much of a champion she is anyway, come to think of it. We run the most successful and high-profile promotion ever on the brand, and at the year-end agency review, she gives us the worst crit and the biggest ear-bashing I've ever received. At the end, the team is so shell-shocked, we assume we're being fired. Apparently not, however; perhaps this is her way of motivating us to do even better (she is American after all). If it is, it may explain why she is so spectacularly unpopular with her colleagues, and why, once she gets on her bike, we're left out to dry. Kara Langan, that was her name: tall, fit American with attitude – but then all Coca Cola's staff have attitude in my experience, even if they don't have the talent to back it up. Must be to do with working for the world's biggest and best-known corporation. Or maybe the guys at the top are like that, and they all recruit in their own image…

Holsten Pils, on the other hand, represents the other end of the opportunistic scale. When we get an opportunity to present ourselves, we go with the confidence of having more alcoholic beverage experience under our belts than any other trade sector – beer, spirits, cider, vermouth, you name it – so we travel with optimism and confidence. We get a bit of a half-assed brief, make a complete banquet of it, go back with detailed proposals and visuals and, not for the first time (or last) in our existence, hear nothing for two or three months. The capacity of clients to wind you up and waste your time, on whatever pretext, never fails to piss me off, even now. So another false dawn apparently, till one day, out of the blue, the Cat gets a phone call from the Marketing Manager, asking him to go back and take a brief (another one or the same one? The usual excuse is that "things have changed". Like, it's a completely different month now.) Anyway, off to Dorking he high-tails it, with the Weather Girl, about whom more later, and comes back with a million-pound brief, which we're not competing for, which he has the answer to already, which he writes up in the car on the way back (not driving at the same time, in case you're wondering), faxes it over as soon as it's typed up, and by midday the next day is accepted by the client. Our biggest-ever project, our biggest client, totally out of left-field. And suddenly the agency has another million quid on its forward billings.

The only hurdle we have to get over is the level of our fee, which the Cat has put in the budget at an optimistic £70,000. The Marketing Director at Holsten, whom we've not yet met, has a reputation for being tough and scary (she probably has to be, to deal with all the men in her way). I go down with the Cat to face the music – aka do the negotiations – both of us mentally thinking £50K would be a result. In the event, she turns out to be less intimidating than anticipated (the Cat's legendary charm at work perhaps – he has what can only be described as a long history of success with the ladies), and we walk out with £60K: a jolly good excuse for a serious session on the champagne, which we do not forego. More to the point, Holsten turns in to one of our three biggest clients during the next several years, and is one of the handful of lucrative accounts that eventually make us a worthwhile takeover target (see chapter 10).

The vast majority of our clients are much more frugal, of course, but once you've done your first million-pound project, it gets harder to enthuse about a mere £100K, even if it does represent more money than the client's house is worth. In year one, we were celebrating £10K wins.

Talking of clients, in terms of the individuals we have to deal with on a day-to-day basis, it's interesting the sort of people who are attracted into marketing. To use a gross generalisation, I'd say there are two basic types of marketer: the first type has worked in several other departments of the corporation and is appointed from within as a safe pair of hands, even though they know next to nothing about marketing – then appoint an agency as the acknowledged expert, listen to what they say, and on the whole act upon it; the second type is the career marketeer – much younger, probably a graduate, who has chosen marketing because it seems more creative and exciting than most commercial departments in big business (that's why I chose it, for sure). This lot know it all, or think they do. The agency is there to do their bidding, not give advice. With them, you will always be pitching against other agencies for any substantial piece of work: they like the (relatively small) power they wield, and enjoy the many invitations they receive to lunch, dinner, and a whole heap of other entertainments. The more agencies they have on the go, the more invitations they get. It's all done with the excuse of 'keeping the roster on its toes', but frankly that's bollocks.

Given the number of graduates attracted to the business (I won't pretend it's a profession; it isn't), it's surprising how poor the standards are. If they were all as good as they think they are, they'd all be Einstein. In practice, they're mostly neither creative nor imaginative, but think they are. The acid test is to explain an idea in writing and see if they can imagine what it might look like. Generally they can't. They have to have it shown to them as a full design, in full colour, with all the headlines and text incorporated, or they just don't get it. Another test is, how many of them would you employ yourself? Many clients make overtures over the years – some make whole symphonies – but in 13 years, we only ever take on one person from the ranks of our clients, and that isn't an unqualified success, though he does survive longer than many. The truth is, if you work in the marketing department of a major corporation, you are likely to be more bureaucratic than entre-preneurial, a rational rather than creative thinker; largely conven-tional, they think it's witty (or challenging to the status quo) to have a sign on their wall that says, "You don't have to be mad to work here, but if you are, it helps." Oh split, my sides.

Amongst all this mediocrity, there are a few who are crooked, jokily incompetent, or just plain stupid or unpleasant. Over the years we come into contact with all these attributes.

Let's take crooked first. We always refuse point blank to get involved in outright bribery. A few hearty lunches, a day at the races, OK. Once you start paying for their overseas holiday or buying them a car and putting it through accounts as a competi-tion prize or sales incentive, you're on a very slippery slope – a criminal one. Has anyone ever asked me outright for a bit of graft? No, I don't think they have. It is of course entirely possible that I give off clear vibes of incorruptibility, and this is one of many reasons why some of the starts we get don't turn into lucrative long-term business. I am, however, pretty sure that Stid is feathering the nest of his biggest client's MD (Toshiba Air Conditioning), though I can't prove it for sure. As I write this, I have even more reason to think so, but still nothing that would stand up in court.

We do get involved with one individual at Argos who, it turns out, is on the take. I've been wondering why the relatively small amount of design work we do for them dries up on his arrival, but put it down to the usual: people wanting to work with others they already know. However, their Marketing Director asks if I will help their finance department understand how an agency works, financially, so that if there is any naughtiness going on, they can flush it out. Eventually I discover that he is fired for fraud. All I can say is he must have been spectacularly careless and stupid, because if you do it carefully enough, it is very difficult to uncover, unless you are particularly greedy or suddenly turn up in a brand new Ferrari, when you're only earning £40K a year. In spite of this, we still don't reap the rewards of our honesty there. We do some more work – largely for the Property Department, of all things – and it later emerges that my champion, the Marketing Director, is universally loathed by his staff, who do everything in their power not to work with anyone recommended by him. Typical.

In the early days of the business, in particular, we have nicknames for all the clients, few of whom would be flattered to learn them. This is a hang-over habit from our previous employer, where virtually every client had a nickname: Jingly Jangly (always fiddling with the loose change in his pocket); the Parrot (slight speech defect that reminded us of a popular comedian of the day); the Ace (top man at a drinks company); Beelzebub (surname had 'hell' in it, I think). The list goes on. Sure, it's puerile. Much of sales promotion is pretty puerile. It's hard to take purveyors of plastic daffodils, free offers and self-liquidating premiums too seriously, though there are a few who do. Mainly it's a good way of earning a decent living, and having a few laughs into the bargain. The down-side? It's competitive (sometimes cut-throat); the hours can be long; and every now and then you have a really savage Black Friday, when things go spectacularly wrong. Plus, of course, you have to deal with clients with a whole variety of personality defects, often aided and abetted by an unhealthy dose of incompetence.

EXHIBIT ONE: THE UTTER BASTARD

In the second year of trading, we start doing work for a local business that is a national operator in the field of logistics. Let's call it United Transport (because that is its name). Our contact is a friendly guy who is remarkably sane and easy to deal with. It's never going to be a mega-client, but it's quite possible their marketing spend with us might amount to £100-150K a year. At the stage of development we're at when we win it, it's good business. We get our feet firmly enough under the table to negotiate a monthly retainer, with a simple contract. OK, it's only £1500 a month, but that pays for an Account Executive full time (this is the late 80's, remember), for a job that will never take more than a couple of days a week. The contract has the standard 3-month notice get-out clauses. Then one day, a few months in, a new Managing Director is appointed. Phil Something. An arrogant wanker, who thinks mention of P45s is a good way of incentivising people. You know the sort: a bully with power, a know-it-all with attitude, and an all-round nasty bastard. First up, he announces he's terminating our contract. He has no idea whether we're doing a good job or not, and frankly my dears, he doesn't give a damn. He has someone else he wants to work with.

Incidentally, this may all be true and his motives are as pure as the driven snow, but experience suggests that anyone acting this way is usually on the take. There is no point in arguing: apart from anything else, we'd rather eat our own intestines than work with such a toss-pot. However, if he wants to terminate our agreement, then he'll have to adhere to the three-month notice period. We submit an invoice for three months' fees accordingly. Twat face calmly announces he won't be paying it. We inform him we have a contract. He informs us he doesn't give a fuck. What are we going to do about it? Yes, he is that unpleasant. Wish I could remember his full name, not that he'd be in any sense shamed by the publicity. His type never is. What he doesn't count on is that the 'little mickey mouse agency' (I'm ascribing these words to him because he acts as if that's what he thinks) actually uses a fancy-dan bunch of lawyers in the City, called Biddle & Co. They are experts in media, advertising and agency law, and they do not fuck about. They're horrendously expensive of course, but in my experience, over 13 years of working with them, worth every penny. They send him masterly letters, which lay out precisely the situation and the steps they will take to recover the money we are owed (including, if no satisfactory solution is reached, a winding-up order – about which, more later). Big man Phil thinks it's a bluff and tries to call it, but when he's invited to give evidence in the High Court, he folds and settles in full, including costs. Now, while in the grand scheme of things £4,500 isn't a significant sum – something he probably thought – that is definitely one of the best cheques we ever bank.

EXHIBIT TWO: THE SEX PEST

One of our most loyal clients over the first few years is DRG Stationery, who come with us when we set up, on the back of some good close working relationships. Again, it's never a client that going to break the bank in terms of spend – maybe £50-60,000 a year in a good year – but they are nice people to deal with. Inexperienced marketers, they value your advice and make you feel part of the team. Gerald, Shirley, Andy, Brian – they know who they are, if they're still alive! But people move on, change jobs, retire, and new people take their place.

Step into the spotlight Angus Potts. Product Manager on Challenge duplicate books. Stop sniggering, you there at the back. Mr Potts and Challenge duplicate books are a perfect match at first sight. He describes one £20,000 promotion as "a real shot in the arm for the brand." Now you know I'm not making it up.

When we set up shop, the three of us (I exclude Gaylord from all of this, as his opinion is neither sought nor cared about) make a conscious decision to employ, when the time comes, as many fit women as possible as account handlers, and to be fair, we do a pretty good job over the years. Whenever we interview, the good-looking one always has a head start (oo-er, missus). It might be shallow. It might be illegal (prove it, mind). But it gets results. Good-looking women have male clients eating out of their hands and find it much easier to pour oil on troubled waters, if and when things go wrong.

Right now, the Weather Girl (so named by the studio, because she's like the weather – changeable: you never know what mood she's going to be in today) is handling the day-to-day DRG business, and doing a damn good job of it. She will re-appear at regular intervals, because she's still with us on the last page. Anyway, true to our recruitment principles (there's another business in that name), she's blond, with all the rest of the package, and she knows how to flirt, when necessary, to get things done.

Mr Potts, who is married, middle-aged, and about as interesting as the product he represents, has probably never been up this close and personal to a fit, leggy, flirty blond before and gets all smitten. To start with, we all have a good laugh at his expense. What can he be thinking? Amazingly, however, Mr Jekyll turns into Mr Hide, the sex pest, coming on to her, trying to grope her, phoning her. She's pretty cool, but in the end comes to me to ask what to do. Clearly we can't let things go on, but it's always tricky complaining to or about a client, who may wield the ultimate sanction in retaliation and cut off the business. In the end, I have a quiet word with his boss and the trouble stops. Funnily enough, he's not around much longer. No idea whether he jumps (his cards having been firmly marked) or is pushed. Don't much care either. Maybe he's already got form in that regard. The most surprising thing about his particular personality defect is the unexpected incongruity of it.

EXHIBIT THREE: THE COWBOYS (SORRY, INDIANS)

Five years in and we're doing OK. We'll turn over more than a couple of million, and there are clients who are coming to us (or being referred to us by others) instead of us having to go chasing. One such bit of business is Beaufort Palace Hotels. I know you've never heard of them. Now you're going to find out why.

Donna, another client in the hotel sector and particularly well connected (in an article on the five most influential UK hoteliers of all time, relatives with her surname appeared twice), referred them to us, and to be fair, they did come with a financial health warning: we were told the most difficult thing about them would be getting money out of them. Prophetic words.

Basically the company is a bunch of rich Indians on the make: they've bought a few disparate hotels around the South East and are turning them into a branded group, presumably with the medium-term aim, once they've developed a brand and a reputation, of selling at a large profit. Nothing wrong with that, and they do need an agency to build and develop the brand, no question about that either. God knows where the Beaufort Palace name has come from: we assume it's the sort of faux-posh English that a bunch of Anglo-Indians, with a poorer grasp of the language than they like to think, might come up with.

The leader of the pack is called Mustapha Tossa (I know, you couldn't make it up), whose use of hair oil and general slippery demeanour leads to us christening him Chip Fat very early on. He's supported by a cast of characters who – well, it's hard to put your finger on, but it's not easy to warm to them: they just don't feel right. There's a little weasel of a man with a big chip on his shoulder called Azed, who's particularly objectionable.

In spite of these reservations, we get appointed and start work. They've got the business and the money – allegedly; we've got the skills and are prepared to use them to get some of their money. Quite a lot of their money as it turns out. With corporate identity, stationery and literature for seven or eight hotels plus a few incidentals, the budget is north of £150K. So, we reason, it's worth compromising our gut reactions for. Our gut reactions being that we wouldn't trust the lot of them further than we could throw them.

They are full of front, I'll give them that. The second or third meeting, for some reason, is held at Chip Fat's house, which turns out to be a palatial pile on the Bishop's Avenue in Hampstead (aka Millionaire's Row: there are only palatial piles down there) with a fat new Bentley in the drive. There's obviously money about, and maybe we're supposed to be impressed, but it still doesn't feel right. There's something about them that says they're not to the manor born. Nevertheless we continue. The design process begins. We still don't know where the money comes from – and you usually get a feel for people and their backgrounds as you work with them and get to know them a bit better: is it venture capital or is it their own? They don't look like people who have already made a fortune. I suppose they could have inherited it, but they act like people who have just won the pools, which makes me think they're playing with Other People's Money. (Still nothing wrong with that, by the way). Halfway through the process, we hear a story that their Finance Director has been distressed to discover £30K missing from their accounts. After a couple of days, it emerges that Azed had just fancied a Range Rover one day, so had taken a cheque out of the company book, popped down the dealership and bought one for cash on the spot.

True to form, after two or three months' work and about £50K in invoices submitted, we haven't received a bean. So our normal debt collection process goes to work – and though I say so myself, we (or at least Pierre and Julia) are good at getting the money in. Our new FD, who is more like a bank manager than a bookie, thank god, and his assistant, who started as our Receptionist a couple of years back, have together got our aged debt down to around 35 days, which, considering our clientele is largely big blue-chip companies (Guinness, Rothmans, Volvo, Lyons Tetley, Heinz) is pretty damn good. Julia sweet talks accounts payable into coughing up before they usually would, and Peter keeps the cash-flow positive by paying our creditors when we can afford to, without ever getting ourselves a reputation for bad payers.

So Beaufort Palace is spoiling their average. Luckily at this stage, we still have something they need. We've done the spade-work, but there isn't really much to show for it yet (not unusual with brand development work), as Azed points out at a meeting: "You have invoiced us for £50,000, and all I have to show for it is this!" He brandishes a business card. It is a fair cop, but that's the way the design process works, especially in fairly big projects like this. So the long and short of it is that unless they pay up, we won't be continuing with the work, and they won't have any publicity material to promote their hotels with.

This carrot and stick approach to managing the client and his errant ways does of course have a limited shelf life. Firstly, it is proof positive that we haven't developed any sort of healthy business relationship on which ongoing business is traditionally built. And secondly, we realise that there will come a point, once we have delivered the project in full, when their immediate need for us will become much more peripheral. Getting the last tranche(s) of money out of them, we can already see, is going to be a challenge.

And so it turns out. We do get paid for all the design work, which is all high-margin stuff, but the lower margin print work at the end of the process becomes a real bone of contention. They've by now paid us over £80K, but there's another £50K outstanding at 120+ days (all of this has been specified in detail and agreed in advance by the way), Julia's best efforts have predictably come to nought and we're left with a seemingly impossible to recover bad debt. Well, Stid and the Cat aren't having that. When it actually *is* your money, you do tend to take it more personally. So they decide they're going to go to their offices (somewhere near Banbury, if I remember rightly) and not leave till they get paid. So off they go, and sit in reception while Chip Fat – and everyone else – pretends to be out (his car's in the car park) and refuses to see them. So they sit in reception for hours and tell every visitor who arrives that the business is run by cowboys (not Indians), that if they're a supplier, they won't get paid, etc. Allegedly, they claim to have seen Chip Fat legging it, having climbed out of a window to avoid them. At which point, I suppose it is fair to say, the agency/client relationship can be described as irretrievably broken.

So we're probably not going to get our money, but are we going to let the matter lie? Are we hell. We're nothing if not grudgers. And now that open war is declared, we don't mind spending a bit of money to exact revenge. It's back to m'learned friends at Biddles, who tell us the cheapest and most effective course of action open to us is to take out a winding-up order on them. It concentrates minds wonderfully, they say, because once details are published in the London Gazette, all their other creditors will pile in on the back of it and give them a severe kicking. So what is the potential downside? Well, if they really don't have the money (remember the Hampstead pad, the Bentley, the Range Rover), then the business will actually be wound up and, as unsecured creditors, we will probably get not a bean. Since at the moment we're not expecting to get anything anyway, it's a no-brainer. Well worth spending a couple of thousand, just for the satisfaction and the harassment.

We set the legal beagles off and running (again), and sit back to enjoy the experience. You can see why rich bastards like Robert Maxwell get all litigious at the drop of a hat: it's a great way of exercising power, and it doesn't cost too much, compared to the resources available. And many (perhaps most) people are really intimidated by the law. Not hardened criminals of course. And not this lot either. Perhaps they think we're just a small outfit and are just posturing. United Transport made that mistake. Or perhaps they really don't have the money, because they allow the whole thing to go through, it gets printed in the Gazette, and all the other creditors whom they haven't been paying come shooting out of the woodwork. The brewery's got £50K of unpaid bills for a start. And you can bet they haven't paid any VAT, which has been the ruin of many a business. The upshot of it all is that the business goes to the wall, and as predicted, all we get is the satisfaction of knowing we precipitated the bastards' downfall.

I occasionally wonder what becomes of these people. Do they resurrect themselves in other scams and business ventures, or is their financial reputation so sullied as to make them untouchable? Or do they all go on to become multi-millionaires through other ventures, building a big pile of personal wealth on a mountain of unpaid bills? Whatever their future, I doubt the leopards have changed their spots.

Oh, and despite their large unpaid debt, we probably just about break even on their business, thanks to the massive margins built in to the £84,000 we did screw out of them. So up yours, suckers.

*   *   *   *

Of course most clients are not as colourful as this. They've gone into marketing, assuming they've made a conscious decision rather than just fallen into it by accident, because it sounds more glamorous than accountancy (what doesn't?) or personnel (sorry, human resources – another lot of pretentious wank, like most business jargon). Most of them are as dull as chuff, and we give them nicknames to liven up their lack of personality. Alright, everyone has a personality: it's just that most put you to sleep at ten paces. And nearly everyone has a personality defect – some of us have several – so we make time to emphasise it and give it prominence.

Here are a few that spring to mind from across the years:

The Parrot, aka Jack Trigg, Sales Promotion Manager at Lyons Tetley, aka the oldest man in sales promotion, aka Mr Scary to all junior (and some senior – especially incompetent) account handlers. Employed by Tetley to oversee all the big-money promotions they run and make sure the wet-behind-the-ears 20-something Brand Managers they employ don't make big fuck-ups that cost them their fortune, their reputation, or both. (Overstatement? See Hoover, for more details). He's always had a chair in his office that is prone to collapse, which I christen the "unwelcome supplier" chair. He used to open phone conversations with a peremptory "Trigg" and finish them without pleasantries once the essential business had been conducted by just putting the receiver down. Once he had the Cat taken off the business in pre-Principles days, for making one of his Marketing Managers look stupid (not the trickiest of tasks admittedly): we called him The Rat (he looked like one and acted like one), who, at a summit meeting on some cash-and-carry promotion, answered the Cat's enquiry about why a photography invoice had not been paid, with a terse, "Because we never approved it"; he managed to look smug and arrogant simultaneously, so was considerably taken aback when the Cat trumped him with, "So why have we got an official signed Purchase Order for it then?" and produced the relevant paperwork for all to see. The Rat was always accompanied by some junior bod who deferred to him in all things and who rarely said a word. We called him The Stooge. No idea what his real name was. After this incident, the Parrot closed the meeting abruptly and wrote a letter asking for the Cat's removal from the account, at the Rat's request, I discover later.

A few years later, having won the Lyons Coffee business at Principles, the Cat makes some smart-alec remark in one meeting and the Parrot immediately quips, "You're trying to get fired again, aren't you?" This is the sort of trivia you have to deal with: be nice to me, or I'll take the business off you. To a larger or lesser extent, most clients are like this. In a big corporation, they don't have much power; they're mainly geeks and wankers in their private lives (ask the rest of any business what they think of the marketing department); and the exercise of power over the promotions agency is about the only way of validating their self-importance. I except very few from this generalisation: Gerald, Shirley and Andy at DRG, Robert at the Dutch Meat Board; er, that's about it.

Most blue-chip companies have a sizeable marketing department manned by middle managers, who are not encouraged to use their initiative and certainly not to take risks. Most are stifled by a giant bureaucracy of senior management and accountancy processes, designed to protect the organisation from serious embarrassment.

Exercising authority over the promotions agency is one of the few ways they get to feel that the term Manager actually applies to them. The styles of exercising their authority vary: some pretend to be your friend: but wait till you lose the business (you're bound to eventually – short-termism is the rule), and see whether they still take your calls. Others practise their Senior Management/Board ambitions on you, so everything's very formal. A significant proportion treat the budgets entrusted to them as if it were their own bank account, interrogating the pence column in invoices with utter seriousness. Most are just plain ineffectual, employing agencies to take the rap if anything goes wrong, which by the law of averages and the nature of the work is sure to happen occasionally. Every agency has its black Fridays. Here are a couple of ours. Funny how they both revolve around drink.

1. FREE MOBILE PHONE WITH BAILEYS

Back in the early 90's, it's hard to remember or believe that the mobile phone is still in its infancy. Only a few people have one, but it is patently the coming thing. (If there's one thing that sales promotion is good at, it's latching on to the zeitgeist.) When some outfit contacts us with a deal whereby every single person who applies can get a mobile phone free, it sounds too good to be true. And we all know what that means. If it sounds too good, it almost certainly is too good. Although to be entirely fair here, as everyone now knows, much of the mobile phone industry is based on the provision of free handsets, in return for service contracts of 12/18/24 months, which effectively deliver the revenue to pay for the phones.

At this stage in the industry's development, however, such key dynamics are only just emerging. It's a novel idea: buy a bottle of hooch (OK, Baileys) and get something worth, ostensibly, ten times as much, if you can be bothered to apply. So we present the idea to the brand manager at IDV, which owns the Baileys brand, and he's as enthusiastic about the idea as we are. So off we go, designing collars to go on millions of bottles that will be on sale in the critical pre-Christmas period.

All proceeds as normal, apart from the fact that, just as the bottle collars are going to print (only a million or two, you understand, so no big deal), the Cat gets a call from one Cecil Suarez at BT – he swears he'll never forget that name, even if hell freezes over – telling him that the herberts we are dealing with (he may not have used that actual word to describe them, but that is the clear implication) are neither affiliated to or recognised by BT, and that the use of BT in any literature is therefore likely to be the subject of a court injunction. Here come m'learned friends again: god, they must love us. What to do now? It's all doubly complicated: apart from the immediate difficulties of this promotion – potential product recall, god knows whether our professional indemnity insurance is enough to cover such an eventuality and save us from bankruptcy (probably not) – we've also been officially fired by IDV, the company that owns Baileys and Smirnoff, another brand we've been working on. Reason? Several months earlier, agencies were warned that they would no longer be allowed to add mark-ups to any bought-in products or services, but would have to live off the fees they negotiate. This may just about be acceptable if the client is prepared to pay higher-end fees as compensation, but the company's purchasing department, who are getting their eager fingers into ever more of the company's processes, have also had their marketing managers sent on a negotiating course designed to help them drive down fees during the course of the decision-making process. Something has to give. And anyway, we're not having the piss taken by Marketing Directors who know fuck all about the economics of running an agency: they want premiership service, but only want to pay 3rd division prices. (We'll skate over the old adage that if you pay peanuts, you get monkeys).

Of course getting round this is a piece of piss. Doing deals with suppliers is easy: you send us an invoice for the marked-up amount, plus a credit note for the amount of the mark-up; we append a copy of the former to our invoice to the client. Mostly this works because suppliers need business from agencies as well as direct from clients. They know the game and on the whole they play the game. It's our misfortune to buy some metal pin badges – total amount of the mark-up no more than a couple of hundred quid and certainly not worth risking the business for – from a company who are as thick as thieves with the Marketing Director at IDV, and shop us. (And yes matey, we haven't forgotten you, and one day, grudgers that we are, we'll have you. Feeling paranoid? I do hope so.) Result? Hefty bollocking all round and repayment of the mark-up. Just as we're thinking that's the end of it, and just as the Baileys fiasco is unfolding, new Marketing Director arrives, probably looking for an excuse to fire a few and bring in his mates, and decrees that all agencies who have ever transgressed the unwritten law (or in this case the written one), should have their services summarily dispensed with.

So this Baileys deal is going to be the last promotion we ever do for IDV, however successful it is. Given the shit and derision facing us, the temptation to tell the client that we can't deliver the promotion, and therefore they'll have to let their big retail customers know that there won't be a Christmas promotion, even though they've sold in on the back of it big time, is considerable.

(The Fuck 'Em principle). On the other hand, we stand to make £5 for every "free" phone redeemed, and the temptation to make one last pile from the bastards is also great. In the end, the Cat and Stid throw a Yes/No dice to determine whether to try to continue with it. The dice comes down "Yes."

So, we have a possible BT injunction because the supplier with whom we've negotiated the deal turns out to be a bunch of crooks and cowboys. They may not have much of a leg to stand on, but they also think we're so committed to making it happen that we're effectively up shit creek without a paddle. We, on the other hand, do not like having our collective plonker pulled, or being threatened with injunctions by BT come to that, and start to cast around, even at this horridly late stage, for an alternative supplier. To no one's astonishment, the Cat finds one who is BT-accredited and agrees a deal in principle, then tells the first lot to fuck right off. Which is when the fun really begins.

They may be a bunch of chancers (really there's no maybe about it), but they're also nasty bastards who cut up rough, when they see a fat wad disappearing over the horizon. First up, they send the head bastard down to Oxford (they're based in York, I seem to remember) to try to intimidate us into honouring what he claims is a contract. As you will know from our previous scrapes with clients and the law, we don't do intimidation. So he retreats in his over-specified BMW to continue the dirty fight by other means.

The client of course is shielded from all this. It's not his concern anyway – that's what he pays us our fees to look after. And if we're having a little local difficulty with suppliers, that's our problem. All we have to do is deliver the promotion as shown and agreed. He will only become interested and involved if, say, he gets a call from his biggest customer (let's call them Tesco) warning him that they have been contacted by our supplier (aka the head bastard) to tell them they're running an illegal promotion because … naturally there is a whole back-story constructed as to why it's illegal, but basically it boils down to the fact that they have a contract (they say) and have been shafted. Tesco want assurances etc etc or they will consider pulling the promotion.

The distribution warehouses are chock-full of Christmas promotion stock, just waiting to hit the shelves. The costs of pulling a promotion this late (or worse, when they're already in the shops) are too hideous to contemplate. We may have professional indemnity insurance for two or three million, but any product recall will cost lots more than that. Once you're into big million-plus promotions, the costs of a serious fuck-up are astronomical – quite enough to see us disappear into a financial black hole – so this isn't just a little spat with suppliers, it is life and death (of the business). No wonder the Cat's looking worried. In come the lawyers (again!)

Essentially Tesco has to be reassured that there is no risk of the whole thing going pear-shaped. They like innovation; they don't like risk. We have to prove that the whole thing is perfectly legitimate and that the supplier is just using them out of sour grapes. Since we don't have a direct line into them – they are IDV's customer, not ours – everything has to go through our client first. To put it mildly, we have some sleepless nights and nervous days before finally the whole thing blows over and the promotion runs.

Even then the Cat is getting threatening phone calls from the York hucksters, at least one of whom turns out to have form, along the lines of, "We know where you live, and that nice BMW convertible you drive." Bastards.

And then, guess what? Old Johnny Public sees the offer for what it is: not free at all, when you've got to take out a contract to get it, and ignore it in droves. Millions of bottles on the shelves, point of sale everywhere (so all the trade objectives are met, which is key), and consumer applications barely make three figures. So our six-figure, two-fingered salute to the client turns into a just-about four-figure damp squib. Talk about a large fuss about nothing. Just about sums up sales promotion generally.

I'm going to go off at a tangent now, to explain how these deals work in practice, and to use a famous example to show how they can go horribly wrong, if you don't apply some basic principles and common sense. Our little problem was to do with injudicious selection of an unsuitable supplier, not the core principle of the mechanics of the offer.

Even with common sense and the application of good principles, things can still go wrong: pity the poor agency overseeing the Texaco promotion, when they discovered the printer had printed (and distributed) not just one £100,000 instant-win scratch card but dozens – maybe hundreds. Receiving five £100K claims on the first morning the promotion goes live – that's what I call a Black Friday.

Mostly, budgets are worked out on an anticipated percentage of claims, based on long previous experience. So if you're offering a free tea towel using specially marked packs as proof of purchase, the offer is on a million packs and the free offer requires 4 proofs of purchase, the maximum risk is 250,000 tea towels (which will never happen). In practice, the likely redemption will be somewhere between 5 and 10%, ie 12,500 – 25,000.

Promoters, however, just love having something to offer that is mind-blowingly good value – so good that it almost outweighs the basic purchase cost. And that's what undid Hoover – a promotion that went so spectacularly wrong, it cost the company its independence and very nearly its entire existence. And all because of a stupid marketing manager without proper internal controls (what they wouldn't have done in retrospect for a Jack

Trigg character), who thought he knew it all. Didn't need to pay an agency – waste of money; could do it all himself. What do agencies do anyway for the money? A fair question actually, but just maybe they would have spotted the flawed logic in the deal they set up, and vetoed it. There was a clue: apparently the insurers – you can insure big promotions against serious over-redemption – took a look at it and walked away.

Here is the scenario: the year before, Hoover ran a *Free Flights to Europe* offer for anyone buying a new vacuum cleaner (a Hoover one obviously). Immediately, I can hear you say, but that's worth as much as the cleaner itself. True, but the way it actually worked, via the travel agent who set it up, was that the cost of flights would be offset by the offer of accommodation that accompanied the booking, when it was made, the profit on which would cover the cost of the relatively cheap flight. There were half a dozen destinations, dotted around mainly holiday locations, and the correct assumption was that the majority of claimants would need and accept the accommodation offer to go with the flight. Most people are still using package companies for their travel – the days of Expedia and DIY holiday bookings are some way off. Few people have friends or relatives around the Mediterranean to doss with, so they need a hotel. Plus there's the language issue. As long as the major proportion (say 70 – 80%) of claimants go along with this, the flight costs are covered, and the travel company gets a mailing list for future business too. Hoover sells lots of cleaners. Everyone's a winner.

The following year, let's run the same deal again, only even bigger and better than before (in marketing, everything always has to be bigger and better than before: it's the Law.) This time it's *Free Flights to America*. You can see how they talked themselves into it. However there are some fatal flaws in this logical extension, as follows:

1. Whereas the flights for a European holiday are a minority cost of the overall excursion, the flight across the Atlantic is a substantial – probably majority – cost of any holiday in the USA.
2. It is substantially more than the vacuum cleaner itself.
3. They speak English in America (of a sort).
4. Many people have friends or relatives they can stay with.
5. Even if they don't, there is a plethora of cheap and easy-to-book accommodation over there, from drive-in motels upwards.

No one – hardly anyone – will need or want the accommodation, against which the cost of the flight is offset. So thousands of people buy the cleaner (RRP maybe £120) just to get the flight. The travel agency tries every trick in the book to try to "persuade" claimants and mitigate its mounting losses, to little avail, and the inevitable collapse ensues, leaving Hoover holding a very hungry and irate baby. Tens of thousands of hugely disgruntled consumers are demanding their £200 air ticket, and airing their feelings about the company in the media on a daily basis. A promotion that was probably slated for a budget of between a quarter and half a million now has a likely final cost against it of millions – tens of millions even. Enough to make the share price collapse, and for an American competitor to step in and buy the business on the cheap.

And all because of some feckless middle manager who thinks he's a lot cleverer than he actually is. No wonder big corporations put a giant bureaucracy in place to protect themselves.

So now do you think that maybe, just maybe, we do earn the large fees we charge to avoid such fiascos? No matter how much experience you bring to bear, however, there are some promotions that are just destined for disaster. Here's another.

2. FREE WATCH WITH MARTINI

This should have been the easiest promotion in the universe to deliver. It comes at a particularly difficult time for the agency financially (chapter 7 gives a more detailed exposé): it represents not only a new client, which we desperately need, but also a really good income generator, for relatively minimal effort.

The background to the promotion is that the advertising agency are working on a 'ground-breaking' new campaign, which is going to replace the universally-recognised "Anytime, Any place, Anywhere" line which has run for decades, and give the brand a whole new shot in the arm (sound familiar?) Needless to say, it's taking them an era to research and develop the new work to everyone's satisfaction, including the agency's prima donna Creative Director, no doubt. It's going to revolve round the theme of *"Beautiful People"*. There now. You can't remember it, can you? That's how successful it was. But you can still remember *"Anytime, Any place, Anywhere"*, I bet.

Our brief, while the ad agency creatives are fucking around, is to produce a promotion to keep the brand going during the change-over, which also coincides with the busy Easter period, and act as a bit of a bridge-head between the two themes. This latter objective is a bit fatuous of course: as if a promotion could achieve any such thing, apart from in the minds of the marketing department.

We have to pitch for the business against up to half a dozen other agencies. There's no reason to ask more than three or four to respond really, but it isn't unknown for six or more to be wheeled in. This is especially prevalent among a small minority of unprofessional and unethical marketers, who use the process to cast around for free ideas, that they can later implement themselves, thus saving their companies money, and making themselves seem very clever. You just hope the little tossers fuck up, and end up costing themselves dear (like Hoover): the sense of Schadenfreude in that case was almost tangible in agency circles.

The Cat and the Weather Girl go off to do the presentation, and according to the Weather Girl, it's the best she's ever seen him do. The two of them are undoubtedly shagging in their spare time, but still, this is praise indeed. Just shows what he can do when the shadow of the bailiff is being cast across the agency door, and he decides to stretch his arse and really go for it. When we're doing well, he has a tendency to go into cruise control.

I don't know how many ideas they present. It's usually between four and six. With half a dozen agencies presenting in total, probably a similar number of ideas, the client's got 20 – 30 ideas on the table at the end of the process. Does this sound like a sensible, professional business to be in? No, thought not. It's either a lottery or it's crooked, at least half the time.

This time it's a lottery, and amazingly we win it with a free watch deal (Any time…etc: geddit?) It's a Swatch-type watch with three different designs of detachable strap – just the sort of thing the Beautiful People in the new ad campaign wouldn't be seen dead in, but we can pretend that they might. The people who actually buy the product might, anyway. It's a free mail-in: collect two proofs of purchase and send off for your free watch. Awfully simple. And a nice margin on the watches, so the bank manager will be happy too. What could possibly go wrong?

I wouldn't be writing this unless something goes pear-shaped, and in this case it's all to do with the means of communication, in this case a humble bottle collar. And if we could only bring ourselves to stick with the boring old megaphone-shaped paper collars that are prevalent at the time, all would have been sweetness and light. But we have to get all creative and design a cube-shaped one in cardboard, and one furthermore, that for the litre bottle (there are two different sizes) incorporates one of the three designs of watch-strap – so all the customer has to send for is the watch itself. Even so, I can hear all the printers out there saying, "OK, but it's not that complicated, even if there are a million of them to produce." Which is true. If we'd been using a mainstream printer, none of the following would have happened. But we weren't. So it did.

Since setting up the business, there have been ongoing discussions about the best way to buy print. As principals of the business, we're used to doing it ourselves and know just enough of the technical stuff, not to be fooled by the "cuttin' and creasin'" brigade in the print trade, but we're equally aware that more junior account handlers may not have that knowledge. So do we allow them to gain that knowledge on the job, so to speak, as we did, with all the inherent risk of a fuck-up that may cost you money, a client, or even your existence in extreme circumstances? Or do we employ a Print Buyer to take the risk out of the equation? Allegedly. There are two ways of doing this: employ someone direct and full-time, if you are buying enough print to justify his (or her, but they're nearly always 'hims' – nature of the print trade) salary; or use a freelance print farmer, as they are known. The permanent employee should pay for himself by saving on print costs (but only if you charge the clients the amount you would have charged before you employed him). In practice, you probably put the same percentage mark-up on a lower figure, so the only person to gain financially is the client, who is arguably also getting a better service, though probably doesn't appreciate it. But you can't ignore the fuck-up factor. The freelance option means you only pay out of margin on actual print jobs handled, so the cost to the business is not a fixed one; the print farmer, though, does by definition have other clients, and may find himself stretched if several big jobs are going through simultaneously.

We have tried both options. In about year 4 or 5, we employ a chap whose name absolutely escapes me. An extremely nice person – easy going, gets on with people, seems to know his cuttin' and creasin' stuff. The thing about account handlers in an agency, though, is that they jealously guard their own spheres of influence – and especially those that impinge on their abilities to earn profits – and they can spot weaknesses in others, whether clients or suppliers, all too quickly, and know how to exploit them.

In the case of this chap, one or two of ours soon realise that his nice approachability means he probably isn't driving the hardest deal possible with his chosen suppliers, and furthermore they could do better. Once half the account handlers are trying to by-pass him, the arguments for having someone on the staff wear a bit thin. So with some regret, we let him go.

By the time of the Martini fiasco, we've come full circle again and we're now using a print farmer called Keddy, to 'profession-alise' our print buying. Keddy had been the full-time print buyer at our previous employers, brought in for all of the above reasons, and had made a decent job of it. By this time, 6 or 7 years down the track, he's decided to set himself up in business, possibly noting our own success, and has come knocking on our door. We've taken him on and all our print is being handled through him.

Now this is a big job, and Mr Keddy (first name Robert, but no one ever uses it) sees an opportunity to feather his nest and grow his business at the same time. He elects to invest in a cutting, creasing and gluing machine to do all the finishing of the bottle cubes, and to employ a platoon of local home-workers to physi-cally attach the straps on the bigger 1-litre versions. What could go wrong? Answer: any (or indeed all) of the following: he can't make the machine work properly, so the cow gum keeping the cubes together keeps popping open on the production line – batches keep getting returned from the bottling plant at Southampton as unfit for purpose; a million bottle collars may or may not sound like a lot to you, but made up into cubes for delivery, you're transporting an awful lot of air back and forth – an average cardboard box might hold a couple of hundred maximum – so you're looking at in the region of 5,000 cardboard boxes, enough to fill more than one articulated lorry; anyone who has ever watched their promotion being deployed on a production line will testify to the awesome scale of things, when all you can see for hundreds of yards is your work going round and round and up and down: the consequences of any mistakes in the artwork are brought home to you all too graphically – in this case, supplying them with sufficient units to satisfy the needs of a 24/7 production cycle – or not, as the case may be. Because of the failure of the cubes and their rejection by production staff, bottles are being despatched without a promotion on. Keddy, in desperation, has a small army of housewives putting together the things by hand, and it doesn't take long to realise that their rate of progress means the promotion won't run till next year, never mind next week.

The Cat and the Weather Girl are tearing their hair out, caught as they are between a client (a new and lucrative client, remember) baying for blood, and an incompetent printer who can't deliver to specification or on time. The Cat tells me that when things are at their blackest, he would go and sit in one of the city squares with his head in his hands, waiting for the coup de grâce. They spend hours – days – phoning round logistics places that might take on 20/50/100,000 cubes; we pay whatever it takes to get us out of the shit; Keddy wants paying and the Cat keeps promising him he'll send him a cheque when the next batch of 50,000 are safely delivered. Living on a knife-edge seems to go on for weeks, but in the end, somehow, the whole thing goes out into trade, all the objectives are met, the client seems happy enough.

Now come the recriminations. As the price of 28 sleepless nights, the Cat tells Keddy he can fuck right off – he's not paying him a penny. The costs of the clean-up exercise, never mind the heartache, more than outweigh the original quoted costs, and he refuses to pay him a bean. Talk about the breakdown in a relationship. Keddy threatens all sorts, including m'learned friends. The cat introduces him to Biddle & Co., whose opening gambit silences him for the duration. Subsequently, we learn he's gone tits up and is bad-mouthing our name all round the print industry in an attempt to get even – there's even a letter in the Print Trades Journal, or whatever it's called. It doesn't seem to do us any harm – we're paying all our other bills after all – and frankly the Cat doesn't care. Hell could freeze over before he'd part with so much as a shekel.

What happens next? Well the client, whose name is Jean, and is blessed with humongous tits, is naturally largely unaware of the shit and derision that has gone down, trying to deliver our first promotion for her. Account handlers are paid (and paid handsomely, if they're any good) to look like swans on the water: there may be much thrashing about beneath the surface, but to the naked eye all is calm and beauty.

There is one moment of high comedy, when she enquires whether we can source some branded water jugs for her, which allows the Cat to have a telephone conversation with her, witnessed by the entire office, which opens with the immortal phrase, "Now Jean, about your jugs…" As I've said interminably, it doesn't take much.

And then she's gone. New job. New Marketing Manager arrives. Inherits new advertising. Sees our old-campaign promotion. All very ancien régime. New broom syndrome. And we're frozen out. Still, it's given us a life-line.

I've made little reference to it here, but the importance of the income to us at this particular moment cannot be over-stated, since the whole event occurs at a moment when, as a business, we are very much looking down the barrel. If I were writing all this as a straight-line historical account, it would appear somewhere around the start of chapter eight. It may also explain why the Cat is more emotional than usual in his responses to the promotion's problems, and to Keddy subsequently. I doubt that will make Mr Keddy any happier, if he ever gets to read this, but it might act as some form of explanation.

Five

Motivation Motivation Motivation

PETER COOK ONCE DID a wonderful spoof interview as a typical football manager on some chat show, filled with platitudes such as, "If it's about anything, John, it's about something," and the immortal response to the question about the secret of his success: "It's the three M's, John: motivation, motivation, motivation." (For some reason the cod northern accent he used made it funnier.)

As marketing experts, devising (inter alia) sales incentive schemes, I suppose you'd expect us to take motivation seriously, and in the case of Marketing Principles, there are three distinct facets to our motivational activities, which make Mr Cook's line all the more appropriate: motivating our clients – to keep coming back for more; motivating our staff – or at least the ones we didn't fire for incompetence (see chapter 7) – to stick with us through thick and thin (we have both, over time); and, no less importantly, motivating ourselves to keep going, to put into perspective the inevitable black Fridays, when some bastard of a client or supplier (see last chapter) threatens to overturn the whole bleeding apple cart.

1. CLIENT MOTIVATION

You could argue that, if you're doing good work, exceeding your clients' expectations, and generally achieving their objectives (those are subjectively some quite big 'ifs' by the way), you shouldn't need any additional motivation. Certainly we have one or two clients who require or expect very little in the way of client entertainment, which is what client motivation is taken to mean. At least it's what I take it to mean.

Nevertheless, even for the parsimonious types for whom a pie and a pint in the local pub at lunch time represents the height of excitement and extravagance, the chance to join in some organised jolly at someone else's expense is rarely passed up. For other clients – especially the bigger ones, where a large number of staff from both sides work together and interact as a team – organised events and days out are actively courted as part of the team-building and bonding process.

So in addition to the expected one-on-one and two-on-two lunches or dinners, especially at Christmas, we reason that one of the key things that sets us apart from our competition is our geographical location: top university town, world-renowned seat of learning and excellence – as if our lumpen proletariat of a client base gives a hoot about that really. Once we have a big enough client list to justify it – ten or a dozen different businesses, say – wouldn't it be a good idea to entertain them all together at one exciting venue? It might take a bit of organising, but on the upside we'll kill nearly all our birds with one stone, saving lots of executive time, and money.

We start at the end of our first year of trading with what can only be described in retrospect as a pretty cheap affair, involving a wine tasting. The supplier of said wine has drifted off into the mists of time, but it may have been a contact of one Michel Sadone, restaurateur of this and several other parishes, and who will re-appear in the staff motivation section; he is at the time proprietor of a French (what else) restaurant, in Wheatley of all places, called the Côte de Boeuf. You will look for it in vain: it is now a retirement home. That is where the event takes place.

Michel is a well-known figure in Oxford culinary circles, having run a dozen or more different establishments during the last two or three decades. We frequent all of them at various times. In spite of having lived in England for the duration, he still speaks with an outrageous French accent that makes him sound like René on 'Allo 'Allo. He shares one or two other characteristics with him too – such as an eye for the ladies and liking a drink – though I can't recall ever seeing any members of the Resistance in any of his restaurants. Perhaps they were in disguise. Anyway because this event is effectively a tripartite promotional one (one for the wine, one for the venue, one for the clients) we effectively get a virtually free client entertainment event.

Everything passes off satisfactorily, but of course the wine merchant is trying to sell his wares, and it does seem a bit dull and cheapskate; so when we move into the city centre, we decide to up the stakes a bit. Underneath our offices, and indeed the whole of the Oxford Union to which they adjoin, is an enormous cellar complex, which at this time is being run by Davy's Wine Bars as The Crypt. We use it as a company canteen for several years. Sadly the Union upped the rent and forced them out, so it's now a student bar called the Purple Turtle. Anyway we decide to run another, but this time pukka, wine tasting down there, with a proper master of wine, no pressure to buy and appropriate accompanying food.

We get a decent client turn-out and, there being wine involved, everyone eventually gets a bit pissed. Unfortunately for the Cat, his propensity for a cheap verbal comedy shot, heightened by the onset of alcohol, gets the better of him. Off the main cellars where most people are seated is a separate room, known to us as The Office, where you could host reasonably private business meetings, and where I am holed up with four of my clients, among them the recently appointed new Marketing Director of DRG. DRG has been an extremely loyal client of ours, coming with us when we set up and still giving us work in year three; they could not be described as our biggest prospect or indeed our most important client, by some way. They spend maybe fifty grand a year with us, which is great bread and butter, but is never going to make us rich and famous. Nevertheless it is in our interest to make the new man feel welcome and important.

Enter the Cat, a couple of bottles of red down and feeling a bit lippy and arsey. "So what's going on in here?" he says, rather too loudly, from the door, in his best proprietorial tones, borrowed specially for the purpose from the gaffer of our old employer, who used to use the phrase in his occasional inspections of the troops. Up pipes new DRG supremo, "This is where all your most important clients are." "Oh," says the Cat injudiciously, "So what are you doing here then?"

There followed one of those, "I beg your pardon" moments of unease and discomfort among the assembled throng, and the Cat, even in his cups realising that a line that might get a cheap laugh in *The Young Ones* has gone down like a lead balloon at The Crypt, spends the next hour with his tongue down said client's backside, desperately trying to mend fences, assure him it was all in jest, if not in the best possible taste. I've never seen the Cat so arse-lickey, before or since. The truth is of course that he isn't that big a client, eternally grateful though we are for the business in the early days, and the people at DRG have been the nicest to deal with of all our clients, by far.

In spite of this, we still have a successful do, and start thinking about the next big hurrah.

Our next effort is dinner at an Oxford college, based on the premise that it underpins our dark blue 'heritage' (bit of a joke, using such a word after just three years of trading, but we're not short on hubris), that most of our clients probably haven't been in an Oxford college before, and that the surroundings will be sufficiently grand to reflect well on us as an organisation. We select Worcester College – close to the city centre and with a suitably impressive dining hall, just big enough for our needs, so we won't be rattling around in an enormous venue that could seat hundreds. After all, even with all our own staff there, we shall only be a few dozen. Inviting our own, we decide, will give us two bites of the motivational cherry.

We'll have a couple of after-dinner speeches – I'll say a few words, interspersing a couple of jokes with a vote of arslikhan thanks for their business, and then introduce our guest speaker. We mentally set aside a few hundred quid for same, and then go trawling for someone suitable. Requirements: witty, amusing, nothing too heavy or risqué, no taking the piss out of either the business generally or individual clients specifically, and ideally a household name. Then the reality of how much these guys on the after-dinner circuit actually trouser hits home. Most of the people we express an initial interest in want thousands, not hundreds, for a half-hour speech (and a free dinner, natch). In the end, we settle for Nigel Rees *(who he – Ed?)* OK, not a household name, unless you're a regular listener to Radio 4: he was (still is?) the originator and host/presenter of *"Quote Unquote"* – a panel game in which minor celebrities come on and tell amusing stories, probably made up for them by researchers (yes, I am a cynic), about all the funny things they've seen and heard in the last week. A sort of *"News Quiz"* without any provable veracity, apart from the quote from some god-forsaken local newspaper with all the editorial skills of a dyslexia clinic, which brings gales of laughter from the invited audience (where do they get them from?)

Black tie, of course. Pretentious, who, nous? The invites go out. The RSVP's come back, mostly saying yes. The event goes off without any major hitch. A couple of senior clients couldn't make it (or couldn't be arsed), and we have one no-show from the Marketing Director of a major blue-chip conglomerate – no message of regret, before or after: obviously thinks he's too important to show any manners. Anyway he gets fired a year or so later (they all move on sooner or later), so we get a few moments of schadenfreude at his expense in retrospect.

Nigel Rees gives what I presume is his standard after-dinner speech, consisting mainly of amusing excerpts from his show, which is fair enough, I suppose – that's the only reason anyone would book him – but its preparation (several years before, I imagine) could hardly have taxed him. I didn't watch that closely, but I'd guess he gives it from memory without notes; and he gets enough laughs and applause for us to think the few hundred he'd cost us is money well spent.

At the end of the evening, around 10.30, most of the clients depart for home, or to the hotel rooms they have wisely booked. One or two of the more hardcore come out on the lash with us in the middle of Oxford. We might look incongruous in our penguin suits in Downtown Manhattan – the most adjacent of the city centre's generally crap night spots – but we've necked enough red wine at the refectory table not to care.

While down there (it is/was a cellar bar), we bump into entertainer Keith Allen, who's been wowing them, with his hand up Orville's arse, in the theatre upstairs, and he's with some fit totty about two decades his junior, lucky bastard. Alexei Sayle once remarked about the difficulties of what to say to famous people (he used Paul McCartney as an example) when you meet them: you know everything there is to know about them; they know nothing, and care less, about you. His answer was the immortal line, "Buy us a house, you bastard, you can afford it." Well, while we're in the gents, Keith Allen confides – god knows why, we haven't made any reference to her – that the bird he's with is his third wife, makes some reference to the spiralling costs of his marital arrangements, and then gives the throwaway line, "But I've got the money; what else am I going to do with it?" With the Cat at my elbow, a big Alexei fan, I can't resist using the "Buy us a house" line. He looks utterly perplexed and confused, hardly surprisingly, but I'm far too drunk to care.

Buoyed by the success of our first venture into mass (mass?) client entertainment, we elect to repeat the exercise the following year, but in order to retain some novelty value for those clients who have been to the first one, we decide to go to a different college. There's no shortage of choice, so we could potentially go on doing this till the cows come home. This time we select Trinity, just round the corner from our offices, in Broad Street: a bit bigger and grander, but otherwise a straight repeat (including the after-event city centre lager-fest.)

We shall of course require a different after-dinner speaker. Nigel Rees may be versatile, but I'm pretty sure he's only got one after-dinner speech. If this ever gets published, he'll probably write to remonstrate. Too late of course. Anyway, notwithstanding the proven exhorbitance of known household names, we still haven't increased our budget much, if at all. The key is to find someone quirky and interesting, with stories to tell, whom the audience may have heard of but have probably never encountered before. There are a number of specialists on the circuit doing this very thing – the air traffic controller is one who immediately springs to mind, and immediately springs out again when we discover his fee. If you're good at something like this and build a bit of a reputation, you can make a very good living, schlepping from one dinner to the next. Charge three grand an outing (20 years ago) plus expenses, and do one or two a week – you add it up.

After much research, we end up with Cynthia Payne, whom

you've probably never heard of but who, at the time, is the most famous brothel-keeper in all Streatham (*surely England – Ed.*). She's achieved notoriety a couple of years before, when her establishment is busted in the middle of one of her many 'parties', and it emerges that her clientele includes many of the great and the good from the fine British establishment – politicians, judges, lords of the realm, etc – and the media had several field days. Needless to say, the place has been closed down, and this is presumably one way of keeping the bills paid. There's also the autobiography, the film of the book (she's played by some famous actress).

Apart from her notoriety, she is a totally unremarkable woman – no doubt her middle-aged housewife appearance helped her stay under the radar for a long time. Her inside track on the running of a brothel in 80's London, though – and the concomitant stories of judges and their penchant for bondage, or whatever – keeps our audience interested, and elicits an interesting range of questions at the end, when she takes a question-and-answer session. If anyone ever doubted that sex sells, that session would have silenced them for good.

Downsides? There are still one or two of the most senior clients who haven't come, and while Managing and Marketing Directors may not be involved with you on a day-to-day basis, relationships with them can be vital in cementing long-term business. Obviously the Oxford colleges have been good, but not good enough to ensure absolutely everyone accepts with alacrity (and turns up). We've already discovered the same thing with other forms of client entertainment – VIP sports days, participation events (of which more later) – which all suffer from senior people dipping out at the last minute, substituting juniors whom we've probably already wined and dined, and who probably don't have the power of hire and fire over us anyway. We need to find something that no one will turn down, but still with the Oxford heritage and all that. We find it in the village of Great Milton, perhaps 5 – 10 miles from Oxford, in the form of Raymond Blanc's Manoir aux Quat' Saisons, a 2-Michelin-star restaurant that everyone wants to say they've been to (and still do, to this day).

We, as Directors, have recently been invited there to the opening of the then new conservatory, just before the British Grand Prix at Silverstone as it happens, and we've sat on the table next to Ayrton Senna and his entourage of Brazilian lovelies – McClaren were using the place as a base, and helicoptering the drivers into the circuit over my house over the weekend. It is about the time he is jousting with Nigel Mansell for the F1 championship, and we take puerile delight in trying to keep him awake into the wee small hours by making as much noise as possible in the marquee Raymond has had erected in the grounds for the purpose. No idea whether it has any effect. Probably not. Raymond makes a speech in his best gallic accent about how his father had not wanted him to go into cookery as a profession and that finally he had had to tell his father to 'fuck off'. There is an audible frisson, from a few of the middle-aged middle-class matrons present, at his Anglo-Saxon expletive, which makes us chortle, but we realise that if we reserve the entire conservatory for our guests, we could accommodate around 50 people – 30 clients and 20 staff, say – at around £100 a head (much cheaper than taking them to the Grand Prix itself, where VIP tickets burn a two- or three-hundred pound hole in your pocket, and still don't guarantee your desired client list's attendance.)

It would be double that now, if not more, but still it turns out to be an inspired choice, and without doubt the best five grand we ever spend (on the clients at least) – and you can quote me on that, Raymond. Everyone invited accepts and turns up, including the Managing Director of Rothmans UK, whom we have previously had little real contact with. That is the biggest coup, and proof of the success of the venue in attracting senior decision makers – out of all proportion to its actual cost.

We do lunch, not dinner, and dispense with the after-dinner speaker: I tell a few tasteless jokes instead and give the traditional vote of thanks for their business, loyalty etc. The food is infinitely superior to college grub; the surroundings are elegant, classy and modern; and the outlook, onto the Manoir's manicured gardens and croquet lawn, a bonus. The biggest trouble is getting rid of them at the end: no one wants to go home. The staff shunt us all into the pre-prandial drinks room for coffees and brandies, so the staff can clear up and re-set for dinner – it is already getting on for 4.30 – 5.00pm. If there's one thing most of our clients enjoy, as much as we do, it is having a good drink: they've probably self-selected as clients, as a result. So the brandies and assorted digestifs keep coming, finally giving way to trays of cooling lagers, the noise levels rise (drunks always shout – it's the rule) and the Manoir staff keep the liquor coming with no trace of irritation – or maybe we're too pissed to notice. Seven o'clock approaches and dinner guests for the evening are starting to arrive. An alternative pre-prandial drinks room is improvised, so they don't have to confront the handful of lushes who are still giving it sixty at Marketing Principles' expense.

Raymond himself eventually makes an appearance in full chef's garb, presumably to politely suggest it's time to go, as we are in danger of outstaying our welcome (or just to tell us to fuck off, as he did his dad), but no: perhaps we are getting hungry again? Maybe we would like a little soup? His ruse works. Even through the alcoholic mists, we grasp that, on balance, we probably ought to curtail our bibulous activities and finally call a halt to proceedings. Gradually the party, for that is what it has become, breaks up, and we jointly and severally head home. To our shame, we nearly all drive. We are (were) that middle-aged, middle-class hard-core of drink drivers that the police are always going on about, brought up in the fifties and sixties when drink/driving was a game that everyone played, and bragged about. Old habits die hard. Luckily we never killed or maimed anyone as a result. Only the livers suffered.

So successful is the Manoir that we repeat the exercise for another couple of years – we must have been one of Raymondo's best customers during that time – before the events of chapter 9 intervene, and things are never quite the same again. Each one follows the same basic pattern, though Raymond figures it might be best to have a separate (and more distant) pre-dinner drinks room for the evening arrivers, rather than expect them to mingle with the lunch drunks who are still having it large.

After the traumas of chapter 7, we revert to individual client do's. As the agency grows, we are in any event working with bigger blue-chip names, where our marketing (and sales) contacts can often run into double figures. Sometimes the impetus comes from them for a joint event. Given the profile of most marketing departments – mostly 20-somethings, with a smattering of 30-something middle managers, and maybe a 40-something Marketing Director – all with big egos, energy and any excuse to party hard, it isn't too difficult to entice them out on some pissy event, thinly disguised as team building for the edification of senior management (who probably weren't fooled, having already come this way themselves, on the way up.)

Among the events we organise are:

- A cricket match against Rothmans (for the Ashes, naturally) at Worcester College, one Sunday afternoon, with clients' families invited and entertainment for the kids – all very civilised. And the only water present is in bottles. (See punting, below, for explanation).

- Stock car racing at a track in Essex, again with Rothmans. I get a ricked neck after being speared from behind by one of the opposition and going into the crash barrier at 90º and about 30mph, which doesn't sound much, but these vehicles have no crumple zones – they're reinforced with girders, so assholes like us can't write them off – so when they hit anything they just bounce off, in my case in reverse and in the air, so the body takes a bit of a battering. A jolly exhilarating day nonetheless. Particularly when they coat the track with a mixture of oil and water for the afternoon session, after a definitely non-alcoholic lunch.

- May Balls at the university, many of whose colleges, we discover, are open to outsiders. £100 a pop, at the time, seems pretty good value for all-night entertainment, including dinner, live bands (can't believe we are all bopping to Bjorn Again, the Abba tribute band, with no sense of irony), a funfair and lots of side-shows, disco, and unlimited drinking of course. I'd recommend it, but you do need to go as a decent-size party to make it work.

- One unique aspect of Oxford that we exploit to the full is the ability to give our clients the experience of punting down the river on a lazy afternoon with several bottles of champagne for company. We sometimes take quite large parties, several punts strong, from Cherwell Boathouse to the Victoria Arms in Old Marston, where a stop for liquor reinforcements is de rigueur, before returning for dinner at the Boathouse (a well-regarded restaurant in its own right), or elsewhere. Regrettably, I have never experienced the quiet, leisurely meander along the river, with straw boater and stripey blazer, hands dipping suggestively in the water and the stimulation of witty conversation.

It's always been in the company of young 20-something brand managers on a mission (always successful, given our own approach to life) to get pissed. The return journey from the Vicky Arms, as it is known, is always less "messing about in boats" and more "Mutiny on the Bounty". What starts as a bit of harmless water pistol action ends up as a full-scale water fight, with everyone soaked and half the participants in the river, for a cooling-off period.

Word about the way these events tend to turn clearly leak out in advance (no pun intended) after the first few, because when the Toshiba Air Conditioning lot turn up for a late afternoon's jolly boating, they arrive fully tooled up with giant water soakers, that can project a stream of water more than 20 metres at a rate of about a gallon a minute. And everyone has a change of clothes with them for the barbecue afterwards. And everyone needs it. God knows what the rest of the public make of our antics, but I remember my wife coming on one event with Harp Lager – no idea what possessed her; she rarely succumbed thereafter – and being part horrified at events and the appalling behaviour, and part admiring of me. She had no idea what sort of people we deal with as clients until then, and as a result appreciates considerably more thereafter the little difficulties they can present.

To be fair, she did witness the apotheosis (or perhaps that should be nemesis) of all punting experiences, when a water fight between two crews (not ours, luckily) right in front of the boathouse, escalates to the point where one client (he knows who he is) thinks the best tactic is to continually fill a 20-litre cool-box, long since emptied of its alcoholic contents, with river water, and tip repeatedly into the rival punt alongside, which is trying to board them; said punt eventually disappears beneath the surface, going down with all hands on board, leaving various belongings floating on the surface. All within view of the punt owners, who are miffed if you arrive back with a puddle or two in the bilges. The black flag comes out and we are effectively banned till further notice, or until sufficient time has elapsed for memories to fade.

- We have one mixed client outing to Twickenham, to the Varsity Match (what else?) which traditionally takes place – or did then – on the first Tuesday in December. I can't say I'm a great fan personally, not having been to either university, resenting their elitist pretensions, especially in this case: the rugby's competitive but technically shit, and certainly doesn't justify the crowd size or media hoo-hah, though I'm pleased to see that in recent years its alleged importance is starting to shrink. Anyway, we have an early start by coach to a French place in Richmond that does a hearty breakfast. Kick off's not till 2.00pm but the drinking starts promptly at 9.00. Half the party are pissed when the game starts. A couple of hours' respite? No fear: we've issued everyone with hip flasks. Then at the end of the game (no idea who won and care even less) we all repair to The Sun at Richmond – traditionally the Richmond club's hostelry of choice, just across from The Athletic Ground – for the usual post-match bun-fight. By 10 o'clock, the Cat's rolling around on the floor having a mock fight (I think) with one of our clients (Phil Cross from Burton's Biscuits – later the Dutch Meat Board), and when the coach leaves, we seem to have left Stid behind, because there is an assumption that he's getting off with one of his clients. He says he wasn't in the post-match analysis, but you could have fooled us. Obviously. Not a happy bunny. Altogether one of the most drunken days we ever did, and by god we did a few.

- For the first few years we also do the Middlesex Sevens at Twickenham – a bit of a walk down memory lane for me, having played in them so often (Saracens, since you ask, and no, we never won it; got to the semis one year, where we lost by two points to a star-studded Public School Wanderers team, having been 16 – 0 up at half time. Pah!)

We hire a motor home for our West Car Park base, and persuade Craig, the guy who delivers sandwiches to our offices, to act as caterer for the day, from early-doors bacon sandwiches to post-prandial digestifs. Needless to say, things always descend into drunken farce, things are always said (often by the Cat) which are later regretted at leisure and hopefully forgotten in the alcoholic haze, opportunities taken to flirt outrageously with the fitter female clients (I seem to remember a blond girl from Max Factor with a suitably impressive chest) and bad behaviour generally ensues. Being a rugby do, no one notices.

This pattern of behaviour repeats endlessly and ad nauseam, I'm afraid, so if you're already bored, I should jump to the next chapter now. It doesn't get any better. I blame the parents. We may not want a blame culture, but it's got to be someone's fault, damn it.

On the whole, we do what most businesses do, though perhaps (no, not perhaps, definitely) more than most: we do the things the owner/managers like doing, and we hope and assume that the clients will fall in with us. It would be no surprise to learn that, far from cementing business relationships through these activities, we may have lost one or two clients as a result of clever-dick badinage that comes across as downright drunken rudeness to the recipients.

After the events of chapter 7 (I know, you can't wait) and the advent of a couple of women to the Board, things do become more civilised in this respect, and our client entertainment looks a bit less like a rugby tour on speed. We probably become more professional too, but we also have a lot less fun (well, the men do) and the events are so unmemorable that, frankly, I've forgotten them.

For the record, of all the things we did, the Manoir was the most successful. Take a bow, Raymond. Whoever we invited, however senior, even if they're not a regular day-to-day contact, they all turned up, unless there'd been a death in the family: no late apologies; no no-shows; no substitutions of junior staff, whom we didn't want to spend the money on. 30 invitations = 30 acceptances.

But there's more to motivation than just client entertainment. There's the incentivisation of our own staff.

2. STAFF MOTIVATION

Staff motivation? What's all that about, I hear a goodly number of business owners and senior managers say? They get paid at the end of the month, don't they? What else do they expect? Indian head massages while seated at their computer terminals? (*Yes please – Ed.*)

Having visited plenty of other establishments in my subsequent role as a small business advisor, I can report that the conditions in which very many employees operate are excruciatingly poor (I'm talking office workers here; don't get me started on manufacturing): shabby décor, crappy furniture, clutter everywhere (the paperless office? Don't make me laugh). Well maybe all the drones live in shit when they go home too, but that doesn't mean you have to replicate that in their working environment, where they will spend getting on for a third of their working lives.

Staff motivation is about far more than the year-end bonus too, assuming you've made a big enough profit to divvy some of it out. In fact money is very often secondary in consideration to a lot of other factors, when staff decide (not that they do consciously) whether to show loyalty to you as both a person and a business. But why should you care? Why do you need to motivate staff at all? As long as they carry out the duties prescribed in their job descriptions (you do have job descriptions, don't you?) and collect their pay cheque dues, that's the contract complete isn't it?

Finding good people in the first place is difficult and expensive; moulding them into successful working teams takes time and effort; having got to a point where everything is working satisfactorily, the last thing you want is for the rhythm to be upset by sudden departures. Personnel changes – ins and outs – inevitably create new tensions as people learn to build new relationships and adjust team dynamics to new (or missing) personalities. Minimising that disruption keeps the ship on an even keel. More importantly still, if you have a generally happy ship in the first place, your employees will work harder and better, stay later, achieve more. An efficient and highly motivated team will always be more successful than a disorganised rabble, providing they have a clear idea of their objectives and an agreed methodology for achieving them.

So how do we go about building teams that are both motivated and effective? And by the way, nothing in this should lead you to believe we manage to get it all right: we have plenty of comings and goings – too many – that we would rather have avoided. See chapter 6 for more details. First of all, I think we should divide staff motivation into two: fundamentals, and the icing on the cake.

A. Fundamentals

Even as I write this, it emerges from a report on Radio 4's *Today* programme (where else?) that saying "Thank you" and "Well done" to employees is the equivalent of a 1% pay increase. Let's pass over that fact that this is trotted out blithely, without any questioning about how the figure is arrived at or whether it is actually true; it's a good story and, perhaps more importantly from my perspective, it sounds empirically true in all probability.

It is definitely true that, while a decent competitive salary is important, it isn't the only thing to exercise minds and isn't necessarily the main priority of your staff. Status is at least as important to some, both within the business and without. At the time of all this action, the provision of a company car to important employees is all the rage, mainly because it is so tax-efficient, and there is no doubt that spending an extra £100 a month on supplying a BMW instead of a Ford or Vauxhall is worth two or three times that in salary increase. Not only do colleagues see them driving a marque which is associated with success (admittedly, its rush to volume has dented this a bit), friends and neighbours do too.

There are (or at least were then – I used to work for one of them) organisations in which your internal rise through the ranks to senior management is marked by a tiered system of offices, depending on both its size, naturally, whether it is carpeted or not, and whether it's a full fitted carpet or just a loose affair. I overheard the following exchange in one multi-national where I was working: "How's Stan doing then?" "Oh, he's on the up: he's got his carpet." We don't indulge in all this nonsense, mainly because we all work open plan.

Given the state of many small business offices I have visited over the years, it just reinforces my belief in the importance of providing a pleasant, comfortable working environment: make the office more like home, with some comfy chairs in discussion areas, some art on the walls (not those crass 'motivational' posters which say twatty things like "The customer is king" – of what, you may ask), some potted plants – you get the picture. Make the place a home from home and your people will be happier spending more time there.

Oh, and tell them how they're doing: make sure they have some clear, written objectives – as we grow, we start to set monthly ones for our account handlers – and give them professional appraisals once a year. Not a ten-minute chat down the pub. One that is properly documented, and kept in their personnel file (you do keep personnel files, don't you?)

So a comfortable working environment, clarity of job roles and objectives, and in our case (and something I strongly promote personally), a relaxed management style, without appearing too laissez-faire. I hope we achieve this, though I'm equally sure we come up short from time to time. Those are the fundamentals. What about…

B. The icing on the cake

I've already mentioned year-end bonuses, and we certainly do hand out cash to staff members in good years, that we could easily pocket ourselves.

But team spirit is about more than cash. In fact it's entirely separate from it. You can pay the highest salaries in the land and the biggest bonuses and still not have a happy, fully functioning team (though admittedly, if you can afford to do all that, you're probably doing very nicely anyway, thank you, and don't give a tinker's cuss for my opinion.) To create any kind of team spirit, you have to socialise together. And given our pedigree, it will come as no surprise to discover that socialising nearly always involves drinking at some point in the procedure, if not throughout it.

In the first couple of years or so, our favoured pursuit is the organised pub crawl, discovering the many historic pubs of Oxford and the traditional ales they serve, on a pre-determined route, before eventually closing proceedings at the Duke of Cambridge in Little Clarendon Street, our preferred watering hole throughout the business's existence, because it represents the only bar in Oxford, at the time, with any style (though no draught beer) and, more importantly, attracts the fittest totty in the city. These evenings produce no worse than a bad hangover, which is why we tend to do them on a Friday, when work next day is irrelevant. We may work hard and play hard, but only on very rare occasions do we work or ask any of our staff to work at weekends.

The extension to the pub crawl is the Christmas party – always the last Friday before Christmas, unless Christmas is on a weekend – which follows the following routine, as it develops over the years:

Morning: the pretence of work, or in some cases, perhaps, actual work, but mainly inconsequential chat amid the expectation of the antics to come.

Midday: gather everyone together in the Board Room; announce the projected financial results for the year – our financial year is January to December, so by Christmas the year is not effectively done, it is completely done, and we've already announced bonuses (Christmas presents) to those who deserve them; we open champagne and consume a glass or two (or three), and once, famously, some vodka jelly which a thoughtful staff member has made specially for the occasion.

Then comes the raffle. Throughout the year, promotions agencies accumulate product samples associated with various campaigns – before you decide on a supplier, you might look at options from two or three different companies, only one of which can be selected – so the account teams would put into the mix any

items they haven't personally appropriated; these are supple-
mented by the Christmas gifts from said grateful suppliers –
usually bottles of liquor – not spirited away by the recipients, but
rigorously submitted for general distribution by lot, so that in
practice the best item on display (a magnum of champagne, say)
inevitably goes to the Receptionist. Everyone is given two or three
tickets, depending on the quantity of booty on offer – we try to
ensure everyone receives an equal number of gifts overall – and
then the draw is made to general acclamation.

By the time that is over (50 or 60 gifts might be distributed),
lunch beckons, so, already well launched, we head off to some
local restaurant for a decent 3-courser and a lot more wine,
continuing through the afternoon, as the level of noise grows in
inverse proportion to the standard of behaviour. We watch
other office parties quietly depart around 2.30, to return to
desks adorned no doubt with such messages as, "You don't have
to be mad to work here, but if you are, it helps." We tuck into a
second or third bottle of wine (each) and start to play puerile
drinking games. One favourite is called "Frogger". Someone
finds a rubber frog in their Christmas cracker, and it becomes
the ritual that anyone who finds the frog in their drink has to
down it in one. There are other variations on the theme, but by
late afternoon, and by definition pretty pissed, we head off, if we
haven't actually been asked to leave – we rarely visit the same
place two years running, as a result of our antics, which over a
decade in a place the size of Oxford becomes a bit of a challenge
– and begin a miniature pub crawl. This usually, though not
always, culminates at the Duke, and we drink and drink until, in
my case at least, usually some time between 10.00 and 11.00, I
can no longer speak or hold a conversation (though a glass is
still possible), and I head for the taxi rank, where I can do little
more than blurt out the single-word name of the village I live in

(Brill – sounds great slurred) and collapse in the back.

All very predictable, you may think, and relatively harmless. Well, up to a point, apart from the liver. The trouble is, when oceans of drink are par for the course, bad behaviour linked to fraught business relationships (not everyone on a payroll of 20 or 30 can be bosom pals) leads to embarrassment, regret and remorse. And we certainly have our share.

You know that the laws of sexual attraction mean some members of staff will cop off with one another. We have always made a conscious effort, wherever possible, to employ attractive women for all sorts of reason (see chapter 8), so there is never any shortage of potential in that area, but on the whole nothing much happens to create long-term difficulties in the working day.

Rowdy behaviour, too, can be shrugged off. One year – we're probably 15 or 20 strong at the time – we book lunch at Gee's, a smart little conservatory on the Banbury Road. When we arrive, we discover that sitting along the opposite side is another agency from Abingdon – similar size, on the same mission. In fact, we know the managers of the business personally, as a result of one of our advisors intimating that they have financial difficulties and it may be possible to effect a merger (ie take-over) to bail them out, at very little cost. The egos involved have already ensured this is a non-starter, and we have also decided jointly and severally that their MD is an arrogant wanker (I know: it takes one to know one), so before we start, there is already history.

Fast forward a couple of hours, and bear in mind we are not the only customers here: it's a large-ish conservatory and there are plenty of small private parties of up-market Oxford society out for a classy pre-Christmas luncheon. The wine has flowed, and the noise levels have increased significantly. Banter between the tables has started. Once someone throws the first bread roll, a full-on food fight is all but inevitable. After management intervention – we know the guys who run the place, and employ a bit of social charm to pour oil on troubled water – things calm down a bit, and the two parties actually start to mingle. Unfortunately, those old sexual shenanigans now come into play. There are a lot of fit women from a different organisation to have a pop at – ours, not theirs, as I remember. Their management clearly hasn't had an eye for the ladies at the recruitment stage. They do have an eye for ours though. The git of an MD is paying rather too much (unwanted) attention to one of ours, according to the Creative Director, who may have designs on her himself, and before you can say, "Seconds out," he's twatted the MD and there's a major incident a-brewing. Aka a mass brawl.

In the meantime, it's also got messy with one or two of the less experienced female drinkers: the ladies' toilet looks like projectile vomiting on a roundabout has occurred apparently (I don't go to check), and there is some staggering and falling about in public, which doesn't accord with the establishment's credentials at all. Oh no. We are told in no uncertain terms that it is time to go – and quickly – before PC Plod is invited along for discussions. The rest of the evening is spent comparing notes and discussing rights and wrongs, but the general consensus is that we won 1 – 0.

It isn't the puerile school dinners behaviour, though, nor the sexual peccadilloes that can undermine all the good team building that goes on. It's when petty rivalries or dislikes from the office spill over, that long-term animosity is fuelled and "bad atmospheres" invade the every-day working environment. Often, a formal banging together of heads can sort out the problem, at least on the surface. What simmers beneath the surface is best left to itself. But when it's the principals of the business rowing in public, there is no one to act as referee and chief head banger at a later date.

It is at one of these events that the first signs of trouble ahead emerge. For the full story, turn to chapter 7, but there is no doubt that a potentially serious problem first manifests itself at one of these Christmas do's, six or seven years after we first open the doors for business. We've had all the usual preliminaries at an Italian place just round the corner from Gee's. Presciently, they have put us in a private room upstairs, where their regular clientele can be immunised from nuisance. In fact, nothing much happens. The meal is vaguely disappointing – we insist on a high standard of cuisine, even in our cups – and after a noisy, but far from raucous lunch, we all decide it is time to retire to the pub over the road for a few cooling beers.

It is then noticed that Stid and his Account Manager, Sharon, seem to have gone missing. There have been rumours and innuendo a-plenty for some time that the two have been having discussions of a Ugandan nature, as Private Eye puts it, so this is greeted with a nudge and a wink by most of the staff, including me and the Cat, it must be said. What to do? Well, we're not going to postpone our drinking, just because Stid's gone AWOL, so we leave word of our next destination with the restaurant staff, in the unlikely event of the two of them slinking back, and off we go. An hour or two later (time flies when you're on the piss), we emerge to move on to the next watering hole, and the Cat and I bump into Stid in the road outside, at which ensues an almighty shouty. Why the fuck have we fucked off (there is a lot of effing and blinding) without so much as a by-your-leave? We try to explain the realities of the situation, as we see them: he's the one who's gone missing without any by-your-leave, presumably for talks about Uganda (we are drunk, so don't hold back on the innuendo); we've continued our festivities, while leaving messages with the various establishments about our next port of call. End of. Oh, and I'm thoughtfully still carrying for him the Christmas cake he's won in the raffle (why? I have no idea).

Three drunks arguing in the street is not an edifying spectacle. Stid is in no mood for logical explanations. The phrase "incandescent with rage" could have been coined for this encounter. After a few more claims and counter-claims, and a lot of shouting and swearing, he grabs the cake from me, drop-kicks it down the road and storms off with the words, "That's it. That's bloody it" ringing in our ears, not to be seen again that evening.

So what's all that about, you may ask? As indeed do we, at the time. With the benefit of hindsight, it represents probably not the first, but the most visible sign of a split in the ranks, not to mention an over-weaning ambition on Stid's part. Not satisfied with being a Director of a successful and growing agency, he wants to be top dog, and, put simply, me and the Cat moving events along without his say-so reinforces his (in his mind, and it is a labyrinthine one, it will emerge) essentially subordinate position.

I suppose all this teaches you is that the best intentions and motivation in the world cannot paper over cracks in an organisation's fundamental structure, but they can make a solid business stronger and more competitive. Anyway, he's been busted over his relationship with his Account Manager, whatever form it actually takes, and that adds to his fury. Indeed, re-reading this, I wonder whether maybe they've just had a disagreement about the future direction of any relationship, and that is adding more fuel to his ire.

Anyway, all this just shows that whatever the state of our various relationships, we still try to have as much fun as possible while running the business. The delights of client punting have already been explored, and none of the horrors depicted prevent the staff from voting for a similar excursion, without clients, from a different boat-house, on a balmy (barmy?) summer's evening, with similar soggy results. And another black-flag scenario.

Not everything we do has the desired effect, however. I don't know what possesses us, but at the end of most evenings out, (this is an attempt at an explanation, not an excuse) most blokes' thoughts turn to sex. Pole dancing is yet to be invented, but we've all been to our fair share of stag do's – rugby clubs used to put them on quite frequently, until the game got all serious – where the format of a comedian/MC, to keep some semblance of order with a potentially rowdy crowd, and three strippers, who each do a couple of turns, is pretty well established. Unfortunately Oxford is far too classy to sustain anything as seedy as a good old strip club – or the university which owns most of it refuses to countenance any planning applications for same – so one evening, on an ad hoc night out, the guys get to talking about organising an event ourselves. We organise events for our clients: shouldn't be difficult organising one for ourselves. One call to an entertainments agency secures a package deal. One of the photo studios we use did it for their Christmas party a few years back, and not a stag do either: I think many of the women present were more fascinated by the goings-on than the men, either because of the novelty factor, or because they swing (swung?) both ways.

But where to hold it? Well, why not the office? It's in the city centre; we can push back all the desks, import all the settees and easy chairs from the meeting rooms and create a private little performance area. There are potentially about a dozen of us, plus a few trusted suppliers (the two photographers, for a start, plus our old Creative Director from the last place, Michaelmas). It will be a private and intimate affair. We will go out on one of our unscheduled, blokes-only drinking nights in the city – all very secret squirrel – and will return to the office at 11.00pm for a show. What a wheeze. And what could possibly go wrong?

We manage to conceal plans from the female members of staff, book the 'talent', and set up the office to look more like a night club, after hours on a Friday, when we're more or less certain that everyone will be on their toes. And off we go for an anticipatory night on the tiles. By the time we get back to the office for the show, we've been on the sauce for four or five hours and are not so much flying as stalling into a nose-dive. There's more drink at the office, of course, just in case we're not quite slaughtered enough. It is immediately easy to see, insofar as we can see much at all – sense is probably a better word, even though we're sense-less – that the performers are more than a bit nervous about what they've let themselves in for.

I have to say that memories of the event are a bit blurred, but the words 'unmitigated' and 'disaster' certainly spring to mind, even if total recall doesn't. Flashes of fragmented images include: three nervous-looking women, who are certainly not the fittest we've ever met (I cannot picture a single one of them in hind-sight, so they can't have been all that), but who nevertheless put on a show that titillates us up to a point; in particular, one of them (black, I think) introduces a python into her act and, almost inevitably, picks on the one member of the audience with a total snake phobia (Dave the Viking from the photo studio) to help her with her act, utterly freaking him out; the comedian is not very funny, and we're too drunk to be polite about it; I come close to having a stand-up fight with him about something – probably the options of a final lesbian show and the requirement for us to put our hands in our pockets for same; our previous Art Director, Michaelmas is so slaughtered that he hughies all over the office and the courtyard outside the front door; naked women in baby oil draping themselves all over the office furniture, including some of the female staff's desks, much to their disgust when what has been occurring inevitably gets out on Monday morning, as a result of a fully efficient clean-up not having been effected (the Weather Girl threatens her Account Manager with all kinds of sanctions and penalties until he coughs up – takes her about three minutes to wheedle the facts out of him); oh, and to cap it all, the Cat is off on his holidays somewhere exotic the next morning, and Stid and I come close to fisticuffs about who is coming in the next day to clear up the mess. For reasons that I don't remember, I am adamant that it isn't going to be me, which means he's going to be doing it on his own – as far as the Directors are concerned – and to put it mildly, he is not over the moon about it. Which is no doubt why, when Monday comes around, much of the detritus of the event is still in situ, and all the women smell a rat, not to mention the baby oil.

So, as motivational events go, it hardly ranks as an unqualified success. Still, insofar as the memory banks allow, it has to go down very firmly in the 'memorable' column, and as the man said, "You should try to experience everything in life, except incest and folk dancing." And I've already tried folk dancing.

3. Motivating ourselves

As can already be seen, we are not short of ideas when it comes to amusements. I have often thought that if we had spent half the time we devote to having fun to the business itself, we would have achieved our objectives much more quickly. Unfortunately, as Popeye might have put it, "We yam what we yam." And trying to keep everyone pulling in the same direction, when there are blatantly diverging views on what that direction should be, does become a bigger and bigger challenge. In the early days, when we all have our houses in hock to the bank and two or three bad months in a row might well lead to us losing them, it does concentrate minds wonderfully.

From the beginning, we get used to having a formal Board Meeting for the Directors (in the first few months, that means everyone in the business except one), partly because it sounds grand, and partly to get our minds focused on what is needed to take the business forward. It's what American business guru, Michael Gerber, calls working *on* your business rather *in* it. More than anything though, with rare exceptions when there is something properly serious to discuss, Board Meetings generally resemble breakfast scenes in the American soap, "Dallas", when, as one critic wittily put it, all the cast sit round the table to discuss the plot.

It is true that, as time goes on, the business grows, and the organisation of the business becomes more sophisticated, we do have comprehensive financial reporting, based on an up-to-date trading statement which runs to more than 20 pages and which, as our Non-Executive Chairman (when we eventually appoint one – see chapter 8) remarks, would not have shamed ICI.

So far as self-motivation goes, though, there are three distinct strands to our team-building efforts: one is the monthly meeting itself, which soon gets moved to a late afternoon/early evening slot that allows us to go and have a decent dinner afterwards somewhere nice, all on the business of course. Over the years, there are probably no places of any repute within a half-hour drive – though we prefer the 10-minute city centre walk – that we don't bestow our attentions on. These are generally well behaved and civilised, even if we do consume a bottle each and then drive home, as a matter of course. Astonishingly, no one ever gets stopped, breathalysed and banned, which is why we all continue to run the gauntlet from time to time.

The second motivational activity is the Directors' dinner with wives, which is supposed to develop some sort of team spirit among the extended family; either that, or it's a sop to the one or two whingers and moaners, who complain about never getting taken out as part of the perks of owning a successful business. It's difficult enough keeping all the blokes onside, and we've known each other, mostly, for years; the chances of four or five disparate (that's disparate, not desperate) females getting thrown together and hitting it off are pretty remote, but on the whole everyone's polite (while no doubt bitching like buggery about some of the others' character defects after the event). We have a series of convivial enough evenings around the area's finest restaurants.

The only real drama I can remember is in a smart little bistro in North Parade, where everything has gone swimmingly and we've all consumed a shed-load of pre-prandials, vino and digestifs, with the result that Gaylord is utterly pissed and has to go to the toilet for a quick chunder, some time before we leave. He and Mrs Gaylord leave a bit early and the Cat subsequently returns from the john goggle-eyed. "Just come and have a look at this," he whispers conspiratorially in my ear. I follow him back to the toilets, where a scene of Armageddon greets us. There is vomit sprayed on every wall and surface; it looks as if a giant puke-spraying system has been turned on and allowed to run on full throttle for a couple of minutes. God knows how he's managed to distribute it to some of the nooks and corners where it is lodged. It is, quite simply, the most horrendous vomitarium I've encountered, and the Cat and I deliberate for about five nano-seconds on whether to own up on behalf of one of our own and apologise, or whether to beat a hasty retreat and leave an abnormally large tip in compensation, for when they make the grim discovery. The tip wins.

There are one or two discoveries about character quirks that enliven our post-event reveries: our FD's missus allegedly reveals to the Cat that she can't bear being touched (how or why the subject comes up is a mystery), but it leads to much amused deliberations on how their children may have managed to be conceived. In the main, though, they are relatively harmless dinners for 10 on the Chancellor (aka entertainment).

The third and most interesting means of self-motivation,

THE UNPRINCIPLED

however, is also courtesy of the Chancellor. We discover very early on that the expenses of a company's Annual General Meeting can be offset against the tax on profits, so what better way of spending money that would otherwise be subject to tax than having a bit of a do, and calling it the AGM.

As ever, things threaten to get out of hand, but in the first couple of novice years we are quite restrained, satisfying ourselves with a night out on the town in London, with hotel. The first year we go to School Dinners – all waitresses dressed in gym slips, and a Headmaster who addresses the throng in some cod 'Assembly' – "Whacko" meets St Trinians. There are lots of other parties there, making merry with illegal substances and what have you, and one of them panics at the arrival of a police-woman, and starts to eat his stash, before it emerges to general hilarity that she's here at the express request of a neighbouring party, who have a birthday boy among their ranks, and begins removing her clothing. Free entertainment all round.

At any rate, having got a taste for the high life, we definitely get ambitions above our station, and we start to quarter some of the finest hotels in Europe, as the company's coffers swell, and we become bloated by our own success.

In no particular order, successive AGM's are held at the De L'Europe in Amsterdam, the d'Angleterre in Copenhagen, the Negresco in Nice, not to mention the something or other in Rome, Barcelona and Madrid. In each case, we eat at the finest restaurants, we do a bit of token sightseeing and then go looking for nightlife.

In Amsterdam, where we go for a reprise a few years on, there is the obvious attraction of the red light district, and there are a number of outré establishments close by, including a sex theatre and the Devil Club, as it was then known. At the sex theatre, you sit in rows – it's a proper theatre – watching people come on stage and have … well, you name it, they do it. The stage sticks out into the audience, like an apron, and we are in seats at the side, looking across it at 90º. At one point there is a revolving turntable going round like something at the London Palladium, but instead of the Tiller Girls (actually that would have been quite good, sans costume), there's a naked woman bent over a chair, and an equally naked man giving her one from behind. We are all laughing and joking as they come round, not a couple of yards from where we're sitting, and the geezer looks over at us, for all the world just doing a regular job of work, and as they drift past us, knob a-thrusting, he says very politely, "Good evening." I've never been able to use that phrase since, without thinking of that bizarre scene. The show is a continuous rolling one, so to 'persuade' punters that it's time to leave after one revolution, an enormous black woman wearing nothing but a broad smile threatens to come among us and make our closer acquaintance. When some people don't take this 'fate worse than death' as seriously as they might, she steps off the stage in their general direction. We are near the back of the crowd heading for the exits, having been in the side seats next to the stage, and Gaylord (yes, he's still with us at this point) is at the back of our party. Feeling her hot breath descending on him, he panics, climbs up on the seats and runs across the tops of the backs of them – quite athletic, considering his bulk – until he gets to the screen behind the back row, where he catches his foot on the top and comes crashing down the other side, like a novice at Bechers Brook. In fact, Gaylord is responsible for many a laughable gaff, until his untimely demise.

The Devil Club is/was more interactive. You pay a flat rate for the first hour and then it's so much a minute thereafter, so it's in their interests to keep you interested. Drinks are the usual rip-off, but who cares? Some buxom tart comes among us and removes her attire in the traditional fashion, then lies on the floor and inserts a dildo in her fanny, before expelling it with some force across the room – an amusing little party piece made funnier by the fact that the dildo flies unerringly into Gaylord's glass of gin and tonic. He's not amused, but we are. That'll be another tenner for a replacement, sir, unless you want to risk it … no, thought not. We're not doing the pay-by-the-minute routine, so when our time is nearly up, I invite some of the scantily clad girls to "do something dirty." When they don't, we make our excuses and leave, in best News of the Screws fashion.

Copenhagen has more beautiful girls per square metre than anywhere else I've been, and there's plenty of fun to be had in the many clubs and bars, where everyone including women treat you like a long-lost friend (and contrary to what you're thinking, they're not on the game).

We come out of some club at three in the morning and sit at a deserted taxi rank for about twenty minutes, drunkenly hoping for a lift back to our swanky hotel, when suddenly one of our number pipes up, "Isn't that our hotel over there?" Indeed it is, not 300 yards from where we're currently slumped. Doh!

Madrid, on the other hand, is something else again. If some of you are wondering when (or indeed if) the actual business of the AGM might be conducted, let me reassure you: we have the meeting to decide next year's strategy, budget and pay-rises at one of the airport hotels, before we get on the plane. Usually everything is more or less a done deal, and we're ratifying decisions already made, rather than starting with a blank sheet of paper. Unlike the end of the first year, when I wrote the next year's projections on the back of an envelope at whatever hotel we were staying in.

All this means we can get on with the job of drinking at a very early stage. Before flying to Madrid, around midday, we have a

9.00am meeting at the Post House at Heathrow. I apparently finish chairing the meeting wearing a shower cap (no idea why), and when reception, as we check out, enquires if we've had anything from the mini-bar, we reply that it would be easier to tell them what's left in it: a bottle of water and a fruit juice. We've had the rest.

On arrival, someone decrees we should spend the afternoon at Madrid's equivalent of Alton Towers, where, because it is mid-week and not school holidays, we have the rides virtually to ourselves, which means no queuing and unlimited opportunities to be heaved around at every imaginable angle. Admittedly the bumper cars are a bit disappointing, with only us playing on them, but everything else is top-hole, and despite the vomitability of many of the attractions, especially combined with our morning alcohol intake, amazingly we all keep our stomachs to ourselves.

Come the evening, and once again Gaylord excels himself as the self-styled wine buff. You'd have thought he'd have learned his lesson at Langan's, in London, where we set him up with two glasses of wine to prognosticate on blindfold, which he duly does, professing one to be seriously superior to the other, only to be informed they're both the same wine. I don't think he ever did believe us. Now here we are at some fancy Madrid restaurant, and he's insisting on choosing the wine. We can tell from the somme-lier's raised eyebrows what he thinks of it all, and when it arrives, we discover he's ordered the only non-alcoholic wine on the list. Git.

In Rome, our very first overseas AGM, we toy with the piano bars which are quite obviously fronts for prostitution, but never have the confidence to take things further. In any case, there are far too many other delights to sample, from the cultural to the culinary. Going on my own, for some reason, to the Colosseum in the late afternoon makes a big impression: I don't believe in life after death, being a committed atheist, but there's something about the place that is quite eerie. With few tourists about so late in the day, it's quiet as the grave, and the main feeling I get is one of old ghosts. I've had the same sensation once before, at the top of a cliff in Normandy where the Americans all got mown down in the D-Day landing; and they say that Auschwitz is similar. Doesn't change my religious convictions one jot – they're all loopy in my book – but it's still a strange feeling.

The Vatican is pretty impressive too, though for me the church has much more atmosphere than the Sistine Chapel, which is like market day, over-run by foreign hordes with a deafening cacophony of voices. Before we set out for Rome, I've left my car at the garage to be serviced and have no confidence that, when we arrive back on Sunday afternoon, the keys will have been left at the service station counter for me to collect, as directed. (In the event, my fears are well founded). The fact that I am thinking more about this than the glorious works of art tells you everything you need to know. I have, however, subsequently been subjected to much hilarity on the part of the Cat, to whom I made the mistake of articulating my fears at that very moment.

Oh, and one other place you must head for is Harry's Bar at the top of the Via Venuto, where we encounter the most professional barman in the world. Knows his drinks, mixes and serves them with aplomb, while chatting urbanely with the guests on stools at the bar, and then effortlessly getting them talking between one another, as he goes off to the other end of the bar to repeat the exercise. I guess it would be too much to hope that he's still there, and they always say, "Never go back, you're bound to be disappointed," but next time I'm in Rome, I shall have to go back for a quick peek, just in case.

So Rome gives us a definite taste for high rolling and high

living, which leads us to most of the big cities in Europe. We never do Berlin, to my regret, nor Paris until our 10th birthday (chapter 10), by which time things have changed irrevocably, but nevertheless, each and every one leaves me with ineradicable memories. For two days, we live the life of the über-rich, and then return to our (relatively) grubby little sales promotion business to try to earn the pennies to repeat the exercise the following year.

In Nice we manage to cover off two great hotels in one weekend, staying at the Negresco on the Boulevard des Anglais and having dinner at the Hermitage in Monte Carlo, where we also fritter away a few bob at the casino and then negotiate our way into Jimmy's, the nightclub of choice for the rich and famous (and us tonight), where according to Stid, he spots Princess Caroline bopping away. This may or may not be true: celebrity spots are notoriously tricky in the dim light of most clubs. We once blague our way, courtesy of the Cat's silver tongue, into one of London's major record label's Christmas parties, where I get mistaken for Eric Clapton by some dippy female. OK, when we both had beards, there was some vague similarity, and it was his then record label, but it shows the dangers of asserting you have definitely seen so-and-so, just because he or she is known to frequent the place. Probably wishful thinking – not that I give a toss about celebrity anyway, and especially not royalty.

We also hire a fancy fishing boat for a day and spend several hours out on the ocean, casting lines astern in the vain hope of catching something more substantial than a nasty dose of sunburn. There's a huge spread of food and drink, but we're all so horrendously hung-over from the previous night's fun and games that we barely touch it. The only thing we hook all day is a large plastic sheet – could be a symbol of our times – and while the weather is glorious, in retrospect we would have been better off asking the 'driver' to take us down the coast to Cannes, where the film festival is taking place, parking up somewhere adjacent to the action and posing around for a day. We might even have managed a bite to eat.

Mostly the events take place late in the year – November/ December – to coincide with planning and budgeting for the following year, even though that could take place (does take place in fact) in Oxford. We are often lucky with the weather – glorious blue skies in Madrid and Barcelona, though I remember it snowing like a bastard in Copenhagen – but there comes a point when someone asks, "Why don't we do this in the Spring, when the weather's bound to be better?" As if we need an excuse, there is the publication of the previous year's results to celebrate. Then someone else wonders why it has to be Spring *or* Christmas? A fair question, and so, with money in the bank, we have two jolly outings one year. It's all very well when you have something to celebrate, but what if you're down on your uppers?

When the wheels come off, big time, around year five, and we are looking down the barrel, jetting off to foreign climes and blasting £10-15K on living it up is just not an option, and we all have to draw in our horns. Habit is a wonderful thing though, so in spite of a £200K hole in our accounts (we've effectively lost all the profits we made in the first four years, and some), we still feel we have to do something. Our compromise: a night in London, just like the early days, and dinner at Le Gavroche. God knows what the bill is, but I doubt there's much change out of £200 a head. We haven't exactly stinted ourselves on the fine and extensive wine list, and none of Gaylord's non-alcoholic wine nonsense either: we're all a bit staggery when we emerge.

All good things must come to an end, however. It's the law of the universe. For us, big change arrives (yet more change) in year 8, for reasons more fully explained in chapter 7. (Are you as confused as I am?)

Six

Comings and Goings:
Recruitment and Redundancy

MOTIVATION IS ALL VERY well, but you have to find good people in the first place, and even if you can find them, there are all sorts of reasons why you can't keep them, with or without the sort of motivational activity described in the last chapter.

All those doings may imply that we are wonderful employers and all our staff are happy as Larry (who is Larry and how happy is/was he, and why?) but the truth is we have plenty of failings, and failures, and even for the core of loyal employees that surround us, there are events which dictate that either we show them the door (even if they've seen it many times on the way in), or they show it to themselves.

I have already documented the specific failings of Steve, the dodgy accountant, and Gaylord, the Creative Accountant (*surely Director – Ed.*). Personal failings on this scale are generally pretty rare, apparently, but since lightning has already struck twice, I do start to wonder whether it is incompetence on our part, which attracts and encourages people to defraud us. Or are we just unlucky? Certainly we never succomb to Ricky Gervais's recruitment policy: throwing away half of all job applications unopened, so we don't employ unlucky people. But is the recruitment method we do employ any better? Indeed, do we

146

have such a thing as a recruitment method?

As anyone who has ever run a business will tell you, recruitment is horribly hit and miss. The traditional methods of written application and selected short-list for face-to-face interviews is known to be hopelessly flawed, yet no one has found a better way. You never really know how someone is going to perform on the job until the day they start. In the bigger corporations, Human Resources (aka Personnel) try all sorts of layered filtering to improve things (or is it to make themselves more powerful and self-important?) but there is little or no evidence that they do any better than the rest of us. Psychometric testing is a favourite. Sure it tells you what sort of personality they have, but since all successful teams need a mix of all sorts of personalities, that's only useful up to a point: it doesn't tell you how well they will fit in with existing team members, how hard-working or trust-worthy they are, or how bright and street-wise they are. Educational qualifications don't tell you either. You have to try to elicit things at interview, where, as everyone knows, the general tendency is for the interviewer to make a decision about the suit-ability of the interviewee in the first ten seconds, as he or she walks in, and spend the next hour reinforcing that prejudice.

When there are only five of you (my secretary/PA, Jules, joins my three co-conspirators), the first person you take on seems a massive undertaking. No matter that there are already five on the payroll in practice, your first employee seems like a big leap. And whoever you take on is going to have to work and fit in with a tight-knit team that has spent a year together conspiring to take business away from their employer and then actually doing so. It is, as they say in fatuous sports commentaries, a big ask.

As a result, the first few interviews we do, for a junior account handler to do client liaison work or a graphic artist to help Gaylord (can't remember which came first), are carried out by ...

all of us. We have a meeting room with glass partitions, and outside it a separate area with a Habitat sofa and comfy chairs, for informal meetings and think-tanks, nicknamed Club Class by Stid and the Cat. There it is that we surround each applicant and try to elicit whether we like them or not. When all's said and done, many decisions about employment are made as a result of one key unspoken question: are they enough like us for us all to rub along satisfactorily on a day-to-day basis? A bit like marriage without the sex (generally) or the lifetime commitment. God knows what the interviewees make of what soon becomes known as the Star Chamber. Why do we employ such a ludicrous method of recruitment? Quite simply, we don't know any better.

At this initial stage in the business's life-cycle, we are all in a steep learning curve. We may know how to do the business, but as Jimbo, my ex-boss, so succinctly put it, we know naff all about running one. None of us is into reading business management self-improvement books either, so all our learning is on the job. We are going to have to learn by our mistakes, and boy, do we make a few.

Nevertheless, the first few who come on board are all pretty successful, in the sense that they do the jobs we ask of them diligently and well, and we don't have any serious personality clashes, so the team grows gradually bigger and stronger.

Where do we get them from? Mostly through the traditional methods of running a recruitment ad in the local paper and/or the specialist trade papers – Marketing, Marketing Week, Creative Review. Oxford is full of bright young things, enough of whom are keen to work in a young industry (most in it are still twenty- and thirty-somethings), closely connected to the media. And I suppose it is true that it is slightly more glamorous than most office jobs: Jeremy Beadle (*glamorous? – Ed*) comes in to talk about possibly fronting a promotion for a prospective brewery client, and shoots a video for our presentation (we don't win the business); it's not unusual to use page three models for the occasional photo-shoot too – breweries and alcohol again spring to mind, though I remember working with Linda Lusardi on a fags promotion involving free tights. Anyway, it's a bit more stimulating than working for the gas board, but it is also a lot more demanding. Gas board clients (you and me) get the services they provide, insofar as they get them at all, when they're good and ready to provide them. Our clients work to deadlines – often artificially imposed ones, I grant you – and expect, nay demand, that we work within them. This means excuses for late or non-delivery are unacceptable, and means pressure, both on us and on our own supply chain – printers, promotional merchandise suppliers, etc – to hit them. Or be replaced.

Some people thrive on pressure – we all do, obviously, or we wouldn't have come this far – some find the entire manic business a wholly unnecessary charade. They do have a point. If client/agency relationships were longer term and based on mutual co-operation, and less on continual competition against three or four others (sometimes more) to come up with a better idea than everyone else, to make the client – usually a junior marketing person, at the beginning of what is laughably called a career – look good and take lots of plaudits from his or her employer, then we would have a good deal more planning time and a good deal less burning of the midnight (alright, 8.00 – 9.00pm) oil.

The reason so much of this oil is burned is inherent in the way that promotions are developed. A client asks three or more agencies to produce ideas to sell more of their product. We go into a succession of huddles to dream up jolly wheezes that might fit the bill. Rather than back just one big idea, there is a natural tendency to hedge bets and go in with three or four options. The trouble is that anything creative and innovative (ie no one's done it before) is almost certainly dependent on a third-party supplier delivering the specified product or service on time and on budget. You can do all the pre-presentation checks you like – "if we asked you to do so and so or produce this or that, in connection with a promotion for [insert client's name here], would you be interested, and if so, how much and in what timescales could you deliver?" – but if, holy of holies, you win the business, you then have to deliver. Obvious enough, you might think, but once a firm order is placed, the supplier is no longer fielding a theoretical question; he is being asked to do something finite, with real money involved. Perhaps he sees an opportunity to make a few more bob by upping the hypothetical price originally quoted; perhaps his production line for the next two months is literally overflowing, and it is not necessarily an option to go elsewhere: this is an innovative something – there may not be limitless, or indeed any, alternative suppliers. Why do suppliers renege on their word? Because they can. Why don't they take agency enquiries at the pitch stage more seriously? Because they've done the maths. If every pitch involves three or more agencies, and every agency pitches three or more ideas, the chances of any one of them being selected is a 10 or 15 to 1 shot. Not good enough odds to get serious about. And it's the reason why so many agency/client relationships founder, almost at the first hurdle. If they worked together on the idea generation, all of this wasted effort would be minimised. Just think: 10 or 15 viable and perfectly good promotions have been planned and costed, in order for just one to be implemented. OK, we all recycle ideas from time to time, but many are genuinely brand-specific. For every one selected and run, up to a dozen go in the bin. Well lucky old bin, as Basil Fawlty would say, but what a waste of effort and resource. And then clients have the gall to whine about agency fees.

The point of this rant is to demonstrate why some young people take to the pressure and thrive on it, and some see it for the utter waste of time and energy that it in fact is. Inevitably, therefore, some recruits do not take to sales promotion like a duck to water, and move on to better things. On the whole, though, I think most of the recruits enjoy their time with us, even if they do eventually leave, or even if it all ends in tears.

Why would it end in tears? Well after four years of growth and profits, we have a thing called a recession. There is no particular reason why we can't ride it out and outperform the market, but the bald fact is, we don't. This is not a business founded on client loyalty or long-term relationships, on the whole, so it should hardly come as a surprise if we lose some of the business that we gained in the first eighteen months. This may have nothing to do with a recession at all, but simply reflects the cyclical nature of the business. Few of our clients are in their jobs for more than two or three years, and when they move on, you always hope they will move somewhere where they can continue to give you work, while also hoping that the new arrival in their original position will continue to work with you. The fact is, though, that your current client is probably moving up in the world, may not necessarily be staying in marketing, and even if they are, may be overseeing but not directly controlling the promotions budget, and may not wish to impose on new staff an agency they don't know – particularly if they already have perfectly satisfactory arrangements in place. As for the new incumbent, many arrive with an attitude that they want to start with a new broom, doing things their way, etc. Your best chance of keeping the business is if you've been working on it for so long that you know more about it than they do, so you can genuinely help them look good and benefit their career, which is all most of them care about. To do this, you have to survive the first change-over of staff, which can be a lot sooner than two or three years. It can be two or three months. Even if you survive initially though, it still depends on forging a strong and personal relationship with the newcomer. You can't get on with everyone in life, however much of a chameleon you try to be, and sometimes the odds are stacked against you.

As you can see, when clients change jobs, you are unlikely to come out of the move with the same business you had before (or more). If that situation is repeated in several client companies simultaneously, the results are pretty serious. After four or five years of steadily increasing turnover (and profit), we suddenly encounter a lean year. From one year to the next, revenue slumps from £2.3M to £1.3M. There are no simple reasons for the loss of business. It is the year we fire Gaylord for dipping his fingers in the books, and he takes the Volvo business with him, having assiduously built up his relationship with them in the previous twelve months (mea culpa: I should have kept them closer, but in a growing business, you have to learn to let some parts go, and delegate) – that's £200K. The Lyons coffee business dries up – a combination of new Product Manager at their end and a new Account Manager at ours not seeing eye to eye: that's another quarter million. Rothmans has one of its lean years; Birds Eye dries up; great white hopes like Kraft, Heinz and American Express fail to live up to expectations. It is also the year of our legal run-ins with both the cowboy Indians (Beaufort Palace Hotels) and the nasty wanker at United Transport, so maybe we've not been as fully committed to new business generation as we should have been. Nevertheless, it comes as a nasty shock to the system when, over half-way through the year, our full-year projections show a net loss of nearly £200,000. All I can say is, thank goodness we left most of the profits we made in those first few years in the business, to strengthen the balance sheet, because without it, we would most certainly be going out of business. I was going to add, "And have our houses repossessed too", but in fact that isn't true: given the strong showing in our first five years of trading, we have persuaded the bank to tear up the joint and several agreements, putting all our houses on the line in the event of defaulting.

There is a strong lesson here for small businesses the world over. When you're flying, and the business is growing substantially, there is an enormous temptation to pay yourself huge dividends and live the dream, whatever that dream is: country house, yacht, fast car – all the usual trappings of wealth and success. If *we* had done that, we would not have survived, simple as that. A lot of small business owners say they don't want to pay tax on their profits, but really, that's bollocks. You may pay less corporation tax, but whether you have it as dividends, directors' fees or salary to the wife (on the payroll, but doing fuck all, natch), you still pay. But you weaken the company in the process. By keeping the money in the business, and paying our dues, we've looked better at all the credit rating agencies, but more importantly in this desperately poor year, we've kept afloat. Just.

Needless to say, we now need to use that bank overdraft facility we negotiated at the outset but have never dipped into. Indeed, we need a bigger one than that originally negotiated. Also needless to say, the bank now wants all our houses back on the line, if we want an increased line of credit. Talk about fair weather friends. I think it was Groucho Marx who said, "Banks are institutions which lend money to people who don't need it." Never a truer word spoken, though I'd put it another way: they're keen to lend you an umbrella when the sun is shining. Here's a tip for all business owner/managers: when the business is absolutely flying, the balance sheet as strong as an ox and everything in the garden looks rosy, go and negotiate the biggest overdraft you can at the best terms you can get. They won't understand, and you'll have to make up some cock-and-bull story about rapid expansion creating cash-flow tensions etc, but better to do it then than when those tensions really exist and you need the money now. So after five big years, our arses are back on the line, we've lost everything we've made and we're back to square one. Except for one thing: our overheads are now a lot bigger than they were.

It doesn't matter how long you look at it: if you want to cut costs in the service industry, you have to cut jobs. Look closely at our overheads – and by golly we do – and people make up two-thirds of them; and much of the other third is people related too: the phone bill, for example. There are a few fripperies we can lose, without doubt, but in all honesty, this is like re-arranging the deck-chairs on the Titanic. If we want to get the ship stable, then we are going to have to lose some of our head-count. That means redundancies.

We've never done redundancies before, any of us. It's another steep learning curve to negotiate, but thankfully we have Biddle & Co to make sure we don't get into trouble with the employment laws. In a big organisation, that means consultations and a whole heap of bureaucracy. Individuals affected by the cull have to be given an opportunity to suggest other roles in the organisation which they could contribute to. There is a cooling-off period between the announcement of the planned redundancies and their actual implementation. Frankly this just shows how little government understands about the nature of employment in this country. The laws are framed on the basis of enormous corporations' and the unions' lobbying power, but the reality is that 99% of the businesses in this country have fewer than 10 employees. All this bollocks in the media about maternity (and now paternity) leave is so ridiculous, yet still you get these right-on types, who couldn't run a piss-up in a brewery, pontificating about how important it all is to the nation's development.

What actually happens is similar to the way the Italians (for example) deal with EU legislation: everyone signs up to it all, because basically you have no choice, and then either ignores it altogether, or does no more than pay lip-service to it. We are in the latter camp. So we go down the list of employees and see whom we can do without.

Now the thing is, there is a kind of assumption that redundancy is no shame, that it's not your fault (it isn't of course) and is no reflection on either your ability or your performance. Unfortunately – and particularly in a small company – this latter point is not true. If you have, say, 20 people on the payroll and you're going to have to cut down to 12, the last thing you want is to lose your star performers – the very people who can help you get the business back to profitable growth. Of course the easiest way to make savings is to cut out all the biggest salaries. That is why in big organisations, there are always a lot of senior and middle management getting the chop (usually in their 50's, when they've ceased to be as dynamic as they once were and their pensions liabilities are looming large). With us, the biggest salaries are ours. We're not going to make ourselves redundant. OK, we can reduce our salaries a bit, but it still means we've got to take out around half the rest of the staff. And by definition, the ones who are going to go are the ones who, we perceive, contribute the least, or have the least promise, or are most expendable. So being on the list may be no shame, nor their fault, but it is the clearest possible statement about their standing in and perceived value to the organisation. And although all of this is unsaid, certainly in public, privately it is fully understood.

Needless to say, none of us has ever been involved in a redundancy process before. The way we elect to go about it is to have one-to-ones with the affected staff, explaining the situation and telling them what their rights are. It is of course a myth that being made redundant is a lucrative exercise. The only ones who sometimes do well out of it are those who have worked for 20+ years for a large and (increasingly rarely) generous corporation, where the unions have struck a hard bargain. The rest get a week's pay for every year of service, and most of our lot have only been with us for a couple of years tops. To be fair, they're mostly 20-somethings, for whom it's not the kick in the teeth it would be if you were 40 or 50 with 2.4 kids and a hefty mortgage to support. They're pretty resilient. And generally resigned. We have one bout of tears and the question, "Did I do anything wrong?" And no doubt there's a bit of not quite suppressed anger. Looking back on it, I'm guessing we could have handled it better, but in a small organisation, it's hard to see how. Given the way people talk, I imagine the word gets round quite quickly what the content and format of the meetings are, so that any summons is greeted as a death knell, with the rest thinking it's still not them, and will they get away with it?

I'm not sure how or whether we communicate that the culling process is over. Probably once we emerge and stop summoning anyone else, it is assumed that those still standing (sitting) also still have a job. I do know that the ones left behind are both pleased and motivated. Pleased not to have lost their jobs, obviously, but motivated because it is a vote of confidence in them personally and their abilities. And they realise that without this hugely painful process, their own jobs and the whole company would have been at much greater risk. And it has been a painful process. Telling staff whom you like and respect that their services are no longer required, particularly when you've never had to do it before, is difficult. Nothing trains you for it. It's like your first death. With the first one – of a close friend or relative – you just deal with it as best you can; succeeding ones have the benefit of prior knowledge and experience, and you deal with it more easily and confidently. That's probably why survivors of the two world wars are much better at dealing with death than more recent generations: they've simply experienced more of it.

There is however one fly in the ointment, and his name is Rocky. After Gaylord exited, we did without a Creative Director for a while, and the subject of how important this role is (or isn't) is explored in more detail a bit later. Of all the people we are making redundant, he is the most senior, the most high-profile, the biggest salary (and therefore the biggest saving). He's even been away with us on one of our Directors' away weekends, to Nice, and he does not take the news of his loss of office with equanimity. He thinks the word 'Director' in his job title means he should be immune to such actions (as if), and if not, at the very least he should be offered a decent compensation package, and not the measly couple of weeks' statutory redundancy pay which is on the table. As so often, it comes down to money.

There is also, quite naturally, an element of "Why me?" and "Make all the rest of the department redundant and I'll do all the work – easy." This begs the question of why, if he knows he can do everyone else's work and has known for some months that the business has the skids under it, he hasn't suggested such a move of his own volition. Anyway, in this instance there is an added dimension to the "Why me?" question. A couple of months back, one of the guys working in the studio – an amiable, chunky, balding and slightly older lad from up north, with a penchant for cartoons (they can't touch you for it), hands in his notice. He's only been with us a few months, a year maybe, but it is quite normal for creatives to move around the industry like a Monopoly board, though we are immune from the worst excesses of the London scene, simply because there isn't so much alternative work in the vicinity. Moving jobs often means moving house too, a double whammy which tends to act as some form of disincentive.

By this stage in our development, we are starting to take on more defined roles in the organisation, as opposed to everyone doing everything, as we did in the early stages, and the Cat, in his role as Human Resources supremo (aka Personnel), has taken to doing exit interviews with anyone who leaves, for whatever reason. It's a good way of getting honest insights into what they think of the business – they're off, so there's no reason for them not to give you the truth, the whole truth and nothing but the truth, about what they perceive to be its strengths and weaknesses – and of course the strengths and weaknesses of various members of staff. Of course there is the potential for a bit of score settling and character assassination, where personality clashes are concerned, but on the whole you get a reasonably fair statement of what you could do better. Add all those together, and a pattern tends to emerge which you would be foolish not to act on.

Among Les's revelations is the fact that Rocky is a bully. You may, with some justification, express surprise that we are unaware of this fact, (assuming it to be true: it is, because the Cat has similar sit-downs with the rest of the studio – alright, both of them – and they confirm Les's assertion.) In a company comprising less than 20 people, how can we not know that our Creative Director bullies his staff? It is a question we ask ourselves. We do work in a 3-storey office (even though it's only 3,500 square feet) and the studio operates on the ground floor, so we don't see or hear everything that goes on. And the alleged bullying is not so much about physical intimidation as the style of management – hectoring, shouting, belittling – that old middle management problem of thinking that managing people equates to giving orders and acting superior. Actually, it's not just middle management: you see it at every level of society.

It's not just Les, either. The other two are actively considering their positions too, in the light of his antics, apparently. So apart from saving the most money at one chop, Rocky's demise is also fuelled by a desire to sort out a low morale problem and 'lance the boil' of poor management in one stroke. Needless to say, Rocky's view of the matter is somewhat different, or to put it another way, diametrically opposite. When he realises we are not going to change our decision and fire the other three instead (one of whom is leaving anyway, thus saving us the problem), he changes tack and demands silly levels of compensation, as opposed to the derisory amount he is actually entitled to. As we put it to him, if we could afford to pay out that sort of money to get shot of him, we wouldn't be in the deep do-do that we are in. Parting is not so much sweet sorrow as scarcely veiled threats of what he'll do next.

What he in fact does next is take us to the Industrial Tribunal for unfair dismissal. He obviously has a lawyer who thinks he has a case, or a bulging wallet and an inability to simply move on. We of course have Biddle and Co, who assure us we have done everything by the book and put up a barrister to represent us, when the hearing finally comes around. This is another distraction that we can do without, when what we most need to concentrate on is a new business drive.

The hearing is in some government building in Reading, and the room it is held in is like a cross between a class-room and a court-room, with the head honcho sitting at a desk at the front, flanked by a flunky and a secretary, who writes down everything that is said. We (Stid and I represent Marketing Principles) are all sitting in rows facing the front. Rocky sits with his brief, front right, where we can see his every reaction from our vantage point, half-way back on the left. His brief turns out to be some young legal beagle who we guess is a mate, and who hardly fills us with fear and trembling. Our own brief is a 30-something barrister whom we have never met before today. We have maybe thirty minutes with him before the hearing opens, to familiarise him with the facts. While we are talking and he is listening and asking questions, he is also leafing through a lever-arch file about three inches thick with all the relevant papers in it. It is not a situation which gives us much confidence: how can he grasp the key issues and facts, with such a small amount of time to ingest what appears to be a mountain of information?

He does though, through a combination of top legal training and an acutely sharp mind which is presumably a pre-requisite to turning from everyday solicitor into hawk-eyed barrister (and eventually, no doubt, judge). Given the relative simplicity of the case, notwithstanding the lever-arch file full of papers, you could be forgiven for thinking that this should be a ten-minute job, a couple of hours at most. In fact the Chairman contrives to spread it out over a whole day, with adjournments for a lengthy lunch, just when things are getting interesting (from our perspective obviously; not as interesting as stuffing his face – he's probably been thinking about his capacious stomach half the morning). The end of the day comes at some ludicrously early hour, about 4.30, and while we are in sight of the finishing-line, it isn't quite close enough to justify another hour in court to get it finished. There could be no better illustration of the difference between the worlds of government administration and commerce. We wouldn't dream of knocking off half way through the afternoon – not with a project to finish anyway. The Chairman probably gets another day's fee if he can string it out to a second sitting, so we all have to troop back the next morning for his summing-up and judgement.

Most of the questioning seems to revolve round the contractual terms of Rocky's employment and the legal niceties of the manner in which we handled his redundancy. With Stid and I representing the ruling class, Stid takes the stand to answer questions about our motivations and especially, as I remember, Rocky's status as Creative Director. There are a lot of fancy titles in the advertising business: go to any big west-end agency, and there'll be a list of 'directors' as long as your arm. This list is reduced somewhat when the term 'board' is added before their title, but there are still enough to fill a small village hall. I expect they have 'board meetings' too, at which they all drink coffee and chew the fat about their latest work, but there is no way that any business can run efficiently with that number of decision makers. All the key decisions about strategy and direction will be taken by a small core of major equity holders, most of which will be thrashed out in back offices behind closed doors, before any meeting of public record convenes.

Rocky looks flabbergasted at some of Stid's testimony, especially when he minimises his importance to the business, his 'attendance' at board meetings and the seniority attached to the word 'Director'. In all honesty, he probably over-states the case, but if you are going to create an adversarial arena to sort out such disputes, it is inevitable that the combatants tend to over-play their hand, especially given that both sides have a firm conviction that the other side is wrong. No mention is made of the alleged bullying, which would potentially have muddied the waters.

At the end of it all, we are found guilty of having infringed some minor technicality, Rocky is awarded a derisory sum of money, but not his legal costs which will far outweigh the award, and we all adjourn to the pub to discuss events and claim a moral victory, if not quite a total outright one. Vindicated, I think the word is, that is most commonly used on camera on the steps of the High Court (not that an employment tribunal in Reading quite has that aura.) Rocky retreats to lick his wounds, reflect on his Pyrrhic victory, and his further depleted bank account. We hear he sets up a design company, in which he is the only employee, but neither see him or hear of him again until long after this is all history, by which time he has built a successful company and is surprisingly keen to have a beer. At time of writing, this is a one-off, and I take it to be his way of either burying the hatchet and/or satisfying some psychological need. Whatever, none of it is all that important in the grand scheme of things.

So we are left with two people in the studio, one of whom announces shortly afterwards that he's going freelance. We'll still be able to call on his services, but at his rates and convenience, not ours. So then there is one, and a relatively junior one at that. It's all very well cutting costs, but you can't make money if you don't have the skills and resources readily available to deliver (in our case) a degree of innovation to the look and feel of what we do. In fact the whole services industry is predicated on a balance between income (real and potential) and the human resources required to deliver them. Too many people and you make losses. Not enough and you can't deliver the work. Getting the balance right is the secret of success.

Since we're effectively starting the business afresh, albeit with a decent slug of goodwill and real business already in it, there is a chance to construct the business, going forward, in a different shape from the one that was forming before the cuts, if it seems like a good idea. What, if anything, have we learned from the first five years?

One key debate revolves round the role of Creative Director. Not what he or she is or does, so much as whether we need one at all. In an advertising agency, where creatives rule the roost, the whole reputation of the place depends on the quality of its creative output in terms of awards and industry recognition, and the creative department has total control over the end-product.

They devise and implement the work. They take all the credit for it (or brick-bats when they don't hit the spot.)

In sales promotion, we have to devise campaigns that will make people do things, whereas advertising largely devises campaigns that make people think things (in the hope that thinking positively will lead to action). As I have already summarised elsewhere, "Advertising takes the horse to water; sales promotion persuades it to take a drink." I know this is a dangerous simplification, and now most agencies are covering both angles, but in the 90's, that was about it. So our idea generation involves far more than esoteric thought patterns and imaginative execution; we also have to consider the psychology of the man (or woman) in the street and what will motivate him (or her) to do what we want them to, in sufficient numbers to justify the expenditure in the first place, and generate surplus revenue to boot; and we also have to consider the practicalities of what will motivate people to buy the product or service. In part, this is a numbers game: give away a free car with every ice-cream and you'll sell a lot of ice-cream, and be broke; give away a free ice-cream with every car and you'll be ineffectually giving away ice-creams to people who would have bought the car anyway – it won't play any motivating part in the sale. It is also a practicalities game: the idea may be good, but can we actually deliver it and make it happen?

Campaign ideas and development can come from anyone, including the creative department, but in practical terms, the ideas about what will change people's behaviour within budget nearly always come from the account handlers, and the creatives then design it in an imaginative and eye-catching communications package. Maybe that is a criticism of the quality of the creative people we have attracted and recruited, but personally I think it is more a product of the left brain/right brain differences between design people and the rest: the reason you so often get design visuals emerging from the studio with ludicrous spelling mistakes in the headline ("Coppers of Watford" instead of "Coopers of Wessex" springs immediately to mind: there's nothing like mis-spelling the client's name to cement relations.) I'm not sure even the hot-shot Creative Directors in Soho, whose every twitch is faithfully recorded in the pages of *Campaign*, are any better at it, but if they are, they're probably owning and running their own business.

If all this is true, there is an argument for downgrading the role and simply employing a studio manager, to control quality, accuracy and timing of output. The downside to that is that the role is perceived as largely administrative – little more than a traffic cop – and you certainly won't attract top creative talent, who all crave the magic title, Creative Director, to put on their CV and business cards. One answer would be for one of the three existing Directors to become de facto Creative Director, but my feeling is that the person in that role needs to be a properly trained designer, even though none of the training gives them any people or managerial skills, so nearly every Creative Director is a compromise between talent and management. None of us has that training, nor indeed the confidence, truth be told, to carry it off.

For the moment, this is an academic exercise, because we are in no financial position to be attracting high-rollers with fancy titles and salaries, but if revenues and profits turn the corner and head north again, it is a debate we shall have to revisit. For the moment, the Cat becomes the studio's line-manager (and therefore Creative Director in all but name): he's the one with the most ideas and people skills anyway, and slowly is becoming the business's Human Resources Manager, by default. Because he's the one with the most sympathetic ear, staff tend to gravitate to him when they have a problem.

The funny thing is that the whole process of redundancy seems to have motivated the staff left behind in a positive way. I speculate that it is a mixture of relief that their jobs are safe (for the time being) and gratitude that we've effectively given *them* a vote of confidence; perhaps, too, that we have lanced the boil, so to speak, and weeded out the weak links, caused by, let's be fair, our own incompetent interviewing and recruitment techniques. Perhaps at this size, the growth and development of every small company depends to a large degree on the lottery of who responds to your recruitment messages, whatever form they take, and presents themselves for interview. No matter how crap or sophisticated your interviewing is, the bald truth is, you can't take on clever, gifted people if they don't put their hands up and make themselves available.

Ideally you want to create a reputation for the company within the business community – in our case the marketing services sector specifically and local business generally – so that people of talent come to you, unsolicited, and ask for jobs. This rolls off the tongue easily enough, but isn't so easy to achieve in practice. It assumes you are spending time and money on self-promotion – advertising, PR, etc – and are producing good enough work to win awards. The former is easier to achieve than the latter. As the business's MD, I have to try to raise my personal profile as agency figurehead (there is no point having two people trying to do it and effectively competing for space and attention with the various marketing publication editors), by submitting news and views about the company specifically and the industry generally, commenting on the issues of the day and generally acting as a bit of a rent-a-mouth. Winning awards – even getting nominated for them – is altogether a different kettle of fish. The annual Sales Promotion Awards may sound a bit of a joke – actually they are a lot of a joke from any objective outside perspective – but even getting nominated (ie down to the last three) in any particular category means the agency's name gets publicised in areas where complete strangers are likely to get to hear of us.

Unfortunately we are never going to be a premier league, award-winning agency. We will undoubtedly create some interesting, effective and nicely-designed campaigns, but we don't seem to have that spark of creativity that allows us to produce mould-breaking, quirky or radically different ideas: maybe because we've never found a Creative Director with that talent; maybe because, even if we had, we'd stifle the ideas on the altar of practicality and deliverability. Notwithstanding the horrid black Fridays connected with promotions that go wrong (chapter 4), I'd have to describe us as, on the whole, a safe pair of hands. Our promotions are workmanlike.

Although the judging criteria inevitably include such worthy headings as effectiveness and quality of communication, what catches the eye of the judges (and I should know: I've been on a few judging panels) is the slightly quirky, the out-of-the-ordinary; the idea that makes you think, "I wish I'd thought of that" (to which the inevitable taunt, "You will, you will", follows). When you've got categories like "Best Use Of Money-Off Coupons," it's hard not to stifle a yawn or a snigger anyway. At the Awards ceremony itself – hardly a glittering affair in spite of the black ties and frocks: it's full of badly-behaved 20-somethings getting pissed – the after-dinner speaker and award announcer frequently fails to keep the irony out of his voice, when having to intone some of the category descriptors. Best Use Of Women's Tits In A Value Added Promotion. Alright, I made that one up. They also have tremendous trouble quelling the noise and simply being heard. By the time the actual speeches and awards are made, the assembled throng are drunk and ever so disorderly. The winners celebrate loudly; those who aren't in the running don't even listen, but gossip noisily among themselves. The only celeb with enough presence and charisma to quell the racket (more or less) over the years is Rory Bremner, and even he can't resist a dig or two at the ludicrousness of some of the award headings or the titles of some of the promotions. One year, one of our number, Nick, takes it upon himself to sneak backstage and, pretending to be official, stands on the end of the photographs of all the award winners' teams, with their trophies. They must wonder who the fuck he is when they get their souvenir framed copies. It is the only time we get close to sweeping the board, but we keep going nevertheless. If we get a nomination, it's a good motivational night out for the team responsible; and for the rest of us, it's a chance to ogle all the fit women from the other agencies and get legless.

*   *   *   *

Notwithstanding our trials and tribulations in what can only be described as a difficult year, the round of redundancies marks an upturn in the business. Whether it is because we roll up our sleeves and redouble our efforts, or whether it would have happened anyway, is difficult to tell. The see-saw in turnover reverses, and having halved in a year from £2.27million to £1.3million and caused the redundancy round, we start winning business, and existing clients spend more, with the result that in the next twelve months it more than doubles to £2.75million – our biggest ever result, which is eclipsed the following year, to the tune of £3.8million. The big-name clients which underpin this sudden spurt in growth are in booze and fags – Smirnoff, Baileys, Holsten, Rothmans – and, bizarrely perhaps, Toshiba Air Conditioning, a business-to-business client that effectively turns us into an advertising and 'through-the-line' agency at a stroke. Each of the brands I have mentioned spends over half a million with us, and therefore, to handle it all, we've had to staff up again. We also pick up Five Alive, a Coca Cola brand, and Dutch Bacon. Suddenly we're flying.

Within a year, we've recruited another Creative Director, having reasoned that, while they may be a bunch of prima donnas who you wouldn't trust to run a whelk stall, we need the lateral thinking and all that 'out-of-the-box' bollocks, to give us a bit of an edge. We know we can knock the rough edges off the wackiest ideas and ensure that anything we propose is deliverable – that's our natural inclination – so having someone who can think differently is important to sustaining our re-found growth. Finding that someone, however, is not easy. Creative hot-shots want to be in London, not the quiet backwaters (their perception) of Oxford, regardless of its university status. Apart from anything else, there is much movement from agency to agency among creatives up West, facilitated by the sheer number of potential employers on the overall merry-go-round. Coming out to Oxford signals a degree of commitment, of settling down. You could argue that there is almost a self-fulfilling prophesy about all this: if that is the profile of the kind of person attracted to the opportunities in our agency, then we are fated to be more 'safe pair of hands' than 'edgy creative hot-shop' in perpetuity, and maybe we should just accept that and get on with selling ourselves as we are, rather than as we would like to be. After all, there are plenty of clients out there with big budgets who don't want to risk their reputation on high-profile ideas that can go pear-shaped (reinforced by the Hoover debacle) and cost them both their reputation and large wads of cash.

Enter then, Kelvin, fresh from working on the west coast of America on mega-budget Burger King promotions, but with wife and (as it turns out) planned family, ready to take on a responsible role at the top of a growing agency, and with a desire to forge a reputation for himself in the industry. Whether he's good enough to do that is another matter, but he helps us deliver some pretty damn good work, even if, as we would argue, the basic ideas still come from us. Enter, too, another specimen who until now has been conspicuous by his absence: the professional advisor.

THE OLDEST MAN IN ADVERTISING – AND OTHERS OF HIS ILK

You could be forgiven for thinking that, with a trebling of turnover in two short years, everything in the garden is rosy and we are all on easy street. Well, up to a point: it is certainly true that our finances (business and personal) are in much better shape, and we soon persuade the bank to tear up the Directors' joint and several guarantees on the overdraft facility for a second time, on the wholly reasonable assertion that we no longer need it, which is for them a perfect reason to keep it in place. The reality is, though, that it merely ushers in another chapter in the business's progress, personified by the introduction of two quite different business advisors but driven by a combination of over-arching ambition and, increasingly, personality clashes in the hierarchy.

Thomas (not his real name) first makes an entrance during our travails with the redundancy round. I cannot for the life of me remember where he came from or how he arrived on our doorstep, but all the subsequent events lead me to the conclusion that Stid is instrumental in his introduction. Thomas is an ex-agency head (I suspect not a particularly grand or successful agency, though no doubt he would take issue with that) who now spends his time – and makes his money – in two different ways: one, charging fees for offering help and advice to advertising and marketing agencies in resolving issues and difficulties; and two, earning fat commissions by brokering mergers and acquisitions in the industry. As you would expect from any such personality, he is not short on confidence and eager to help (*surely, send us large invoices – Ed.*). His first efforts involve advice on the restructuring required to maintain the agency as a going concern, when it appears our most likely route is down the plug-hole.

That advice is draconian in the extreme and involves us more or less going back to the bare bones of three Directors and a creative person, as we had been at the start of the business – literally starting again, to all intents and purposes. I think it is fair to say that none of us is comfortable with this analysis. We may have had a bad year, but we still have three times the turnover of our first year, and of course three times the goodwill, plus a pipeline of potential new business. If we make the extreme cuts that he is recommending, we'll barely be able to service the business we have and we certainly won't have any capacity for taking on new projects. For me, it is the solution of an accountant, who can see only the numbers, but not the bigger picture.

We know we have to cut back on staff numbers in the immediate short term, but in the end we decide not to cut right back to the bone, as recommended by Thomas, but to take a middle course, losing about a third of our number – a decision which is subsequently justified by the ensuing upturn in our fortunes. Having ignored him, or at least the substance of his advice, first time out, you may be forgiven for expressing surprise at his continuing involvement in our business, once we get back on our feet and start to motor again. At the start of the business, the objective of a £5million turnover would certainly have featured in the business plan, and in spite of a roller-coaster ride, we are suddenly in sight of achieving it. We are, however, now very much outside our comfort zone, and the received wisdom is that we could do with a bit of outside help to help us get to the next big psychological barrier – £10million. For some reason, Stid (and the Cat, though I think the Cat is just going along with it) is in favour of retaining Thomas to do a full report on where (and how) we go from here.

It is fair to say that I am not full of enthusiasm. This is partly to do with personalities: I cannot pretend Thomas is my kind of guy – he's a bit too smoothly self-confident for my liking, and there's just something about him which doesn't feel right. It's an instinct thing, nothing you can put your finger on, nothing logical or arguable, but over the years I've learned to trust these instincts more and more. They invariably point you in the right direction, and I've certainly made more bad decisions than good by ignoring them. But apart from an instinctive dislike and distrust of the man, there is also the practical consideration of the last advice he gave us, which was certainly flawed, and if heeded, would not have resulted in us being in our current happy position. Why then are we using him? Apart from the fact that Stid and the Cat are supportive, there is the subsidiary question of, if not him, who else? Business advisors come in many guises, shapes and sizes: there is (was) that wonderful government organisation called Business Link, which sucks up zillions in taxpayers' money each year, and which is often the first port of call for harassed business owners; there are various umbrella groups of advisors who operate, jointly and severally, in a freelance capacity; and there are innumerable one-man bands, some of whom are specialists in a particular business subject, others of whom purport to be all things to all men. Even if you know about them all and have access to their services, which do you choose? There are certainly no safe bets. The umbrella groups of advisors are largely peopled by 50-something refugees from corporate Britain, who have been finally found out, but who in any event have rarely run a business of their own. Business Link has brought more disrepute to the business advisory sector than any other (not surprising perhaps, given that it's government sponsored), most of whose people are more 'never was' than 'has been'. Business owners who need help should go elsewhere – anywhere else. And as for the myriad independent operators, there is just no way of separating the wheat from the chaff. There must be some good operators out there – some, even, who understand the specific niceties of the sector we operate in – but identifying them is like looking for a needle in a haystack, which, to mix metaphors, generally leads to buying a pig in a poke. So the short answer to the short question posed at the top of this paragraph, via a rambling diatribe on the state of business advisory services, is he's the devil we know. Not a particularly ringing endorsement, I think you'll agree.

Anyway, I go along with it, with misgivings and without any personal enthusiasm for the process. In the end, it probably serves a purpose, though not necessarily the one that was intended. It certainly helps to flush out the key issue in the business, over time, and is, in my opinion, linked directly to the next big event in the agency's history, fully described in the next chapter (can't wait, can you?) though at this point in time, we cannot see it.

Thomas's report, when it arrives, is possibly the most under-whelming document I've ever had presented to me, considering its alleged importance to the business. It certainly isn't presented with a fanfare of trumpets (though why would it be?); it's presented in a nondescript hotel meeting room. The key recom-mendations are two-fold: the agency hierarchy should be reor-ganised and have more clearly defined roles and responsibilities; and the business as a whole should adopt a process known as Total Quality Management (henceforth shortened to TQM).

Taking the second of these first (and by the way, I am being touted to introduce and champion this process), you won't hear much about TQM these days, though at the time it is all the rage in business consultancy circles. What does it actually mean in practice? I could write a book – actually that's not true: I'm having to stifle a yawn just starting the process. Go look it up in Wikipedia or Google the term: you'll get pages of guff on it. The term itself is self-explanatory: total, involving the whole organisation; quality, yes; management, systems for planning, controlling, organising and leading. It's been evolved, almost certainly, from the American military, to ensure everyone pulls their weight, and in the right direction, and has been taken up by manufacturers in particular, whose need to control consistency of output is fully understood, and has then been extended to major corporations for the better command and control of their operations. I'm sure it has its place (as I write, its current iteration is called Six Sigma – and you can get a black belt in it), but applying it to a small business with barely a dozen people in it is faintly (no, make that grossly) ludicrous.

Every business, no matter what its size, needs to have systems and processes in place, so that it operates efficiently; every business needs the input of all its staff into the continual improvement of those systems; every business needs a clear organisational chart and staff with written job descriptions, roles, responsibilities and objectives within it. And when you've said that, you've said it all. All the rest is a load of jargon and bollocks, fuelling an enormous consultancy sector that feeds on weak management and so-called business leaders who are not up to the job. Most of those who are found to be not up to the job magically re-invent themselves as business advisors/consultants/mentors/gurus/ guides (delete as appropriate) the minute they're found out and let go by their employers. I should know. I'm one of them now.

If you're in business now and you get a visit from any potential advisors, here's a clue to help you spot the bullshit merchants (most of them) from the small band who might actually help you (including me, naturally): look out for them using any of the following words or phrases and immediately avoid like the plague: paradigm; outcomes; change management; kaizen (or any other Japanese phrase); stakeholders.

So much for TQM. What about the reorganisation? Well all of a sudden, the entire motivation behind this process becomes blindingly clear, because the primary recommendation in the document is that Stid becomes CEO, I become Chairman, and the Cat gets the title of MD, and that moves are put in place to achieve a management buy-out, so I can leave within two years. Fancy titles for such a small business, but clearly the intention is to put all the operational power in Stid's hands. To describe it as a kick in the balls would not under-state the way I feel; that and betrayal. Stid's over-arching ambition has certainly become more and more apparent, but with this document he's finally broken cover. There's no doubt in my mind that his inky finger-prints are all over the place and that he and Thomas are working hand in glove to help him achieve his ambitions – which, put baldly, is to be in charge.

Discussing the whole thing later with the Cat, I realise that part of the problem lies in what can best be described as careless talk. Thomas has had interviews with each of us to discover what our business ambitions are, and in a flippant moment I've described making a million and getting out in a couple of years. I thought that's what we all wanted, but the other two have been more circumspect: the Cat used a lot of platitudes, he says (which results in him being put in charge of the creative output), and we presume Stid said he wanted to run the business and grow it into a major corporation, or something similar. He's not exactly short on hubris, is Stid. On that basis, Thomas has evolved – I was going to call it a business plan, but this is nothing of the sort – this paper to create a simplistic answer to all our stated ambitions.

The fact that I don't want to leave the business (which was my idea and which I founded) is a minor inconvenience. I suppose the document does serve one purpose though: it finally shows Stid in his true colours. His machinations are without doubt behind all this, but now they are out in the open. He hasn't so much fired the first shot as the opening salvo, and in practice the camaraderie which characterised the opening years of our little venture has gone – and, as anyone knows who's been through a relationship breakdown, once the essential ingredient of trust has been lost, the whole apparatus becomes a slow, grinding and constant struggle.

What do you do when there is major disagreement in the ranks that cannot be resolved by discussion and negotiation? You paper over the cracks and compromise. You go for a short-term fix that doesn't address the fundamental underlying issues but which allows you to continue as if you had. We agree, after much argument, that Stid and I will be joint Managing Directors, with me acting as external figure-head (advertising, PR, trade associations etc) and him as internal leader (company management and organisation). There's a twisted logic to it that can be presented to the staff (as if they don't know the way the wind's blowing in such a small organisation), but it's a fudge, and we all know it, but it means we can keep trading as if nothing much has happened. Stid gets to run the company effectively, while I look like I'm running it to the outside world and casual observers.

Except for one thing: my role is also to introduce and champion TQM to the business and make the whole thing happen. You may say that that is not consistent with an external/internal job split. I couldn't possibly comment. Oh, alright then, of course it's a nonsense. Apart from anything else, I hate administration in all its forms, and if there's one thing that characterises TQM, it's paper-work. Everything has to be documented. I am tempera-

mentally unsuited to such a role, but then so are Stid and the Cat
– we're all similar personalities in fact, and here's a lesson, if
you're ever in a position to choose business partners, as opposed
to them self-selecting through circumstances, which is what
generally happens.

Try and find people with complementary personalities,
strengths and weaknesses. To use the personality profiling jargon,
you need a Driver to lead the business, an Expressive for creative
thinking, an Amiable for human resources and an Analytical for
the detail (like accounts). Admittedly, we've got the detail covered
pretty well: after the Steve fiasco, we've finally managed to recruit
Pierre as Financial Controller, and he's the traditional, suited,
steady-eddy number cruncher. Stid, the Cat and I are all
Driver/Expressives (though the Cat, as we've seen, is good with
people – especially our female employees), and we have in fact
tended to recruit in our own image, so the business is loaded with
similar personality traits. This is possibly why we have more than
our fair share of Black Fridays, when promotions go horribly
pear-shaped – would a few more detail merchants in the ranks
lessen the pain?

We know all this because we have invested some of our hard-
earned lucre in training. Thomas has introduced us to Avril, as
our human resources consultant (and is no doubt taking a
commission on everything she earns as a result). The world of
small business is full of consultants and advisors, mostly corporate has-beens or never-was's, telling owner/managers how to
run their business. There are generalists, like Thomas, who look
at the whole organisation (the "holistic approach"); and hanging
on to their shirt-tails for dear life, and paying juicy little commissions for every introduction, are the specialists: human
resources; market research (helping you to understand your
market – competitors, opportunities – and yourselves –

strengths, weaknesses, etc); sales; marketing (not that we need that, but most small businesses do: it's the thing they're most crap at, and the hardest to find good people to do it for you at an affordable price. It's no coincidence that we work almost exclusively for blue-chip client companies: they're the ones with the budgets to pay our exorbitant fees); health and safety; change management (aaargh); experts in banking and finance; mergers and acquisitions. You name it, there's an expert in it queuing up to sell you their wares.

Now Stid has got hold of the reins, there are specialist advisors coming out of our ears. Avril makes an individual assessment of each member of staff's strengths and weaknesses, and makes training recommendations to address them. Were we to accede to all of them, we would need the GDP of a small country to pay for them, and when you are just getting back on your feet after a jolt to your finances, all expenditure is viewed with a particularly critical eye. After all, that money could be used in a variety of ways – not least as a year-end dividend for us – a short-term consideration, admittedly, but one that necessarily has its attractions.

Avril is also the reason we get banned from the restaurant at our Christmas bash, described elsewhere, as a result of getting horribly pissed and having the MD of a rival agency take a shine to her; he thinks (probably not incorrectly) that there's a good chance of getting into her oversize knickers, while our next and most recently appointed Creative Director, Kelvin, who also has an eye on the main chance, takes exception to some piece of fondling and/or canoodling that goes on between them, has a shouting match with him (not her, naturally) and twats him. Oh dear. Time for a sharp exit, to quote one of our client's advertising slogans.

Anyway, I digress (again). Avril (or is it Thomas himself?) has introduced us to a couple of sales specialists to help us improve our strike rate in new business generation, and we all undergo a full-day (weekend) course in personality profiling, to help us recognise the particular traits in each new client prospect, the better to present ourselves in a way that that they will respond positively to.

As part of the day, we all do a word association test, which allows us to plot our own personalities against a simple couple of axes, which form the personality chart. Normally I'd be as cynical as the next man about such stuff, but I have to admit that it is convincing, not least because, when I have a refresher course fifteen years later, and again five years after that, I always come out in exactly the same position.

Here are the axes which are used to describe the process:

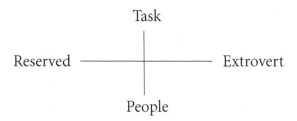

What this mumbo jumbo means (try to keep awake) is that some people are task-oriented and others people-oriented, as one axis; and some are extrovert, while others are reserved on the other. The combination of the two helps provide a description, which summarises the way a person behaves in a work situation. There are two or three variations on this schema being touted by the business advisors who specialise in this field (DISC is another), but they all work on similar principles. Perfectly rounded and well-balanced personalities who appear close to the centre of this chart are as rare as hen's teeth, and being able to spot what makes individuals tick gives you an edge in the sales department. Here is a quick summary of the whole thing (if you're already bored shitless by all this, jump a page), taking into account that few people are far extremes, and most have bits of every trait in them: we're just trying to identify the dominant ones.

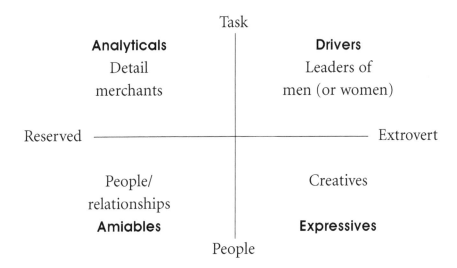

And all bar one of our account handlers fall in the same small segment of the chart: Driver/Expressives on the far Extrovert side of that axis.

What does all this mean in practice?

If you're presenting ideas or campaigns (or any other form of business proposal) to the various character traits, you'll need:

- An executive summary and the clear means of achieving objectives for the **Drivers**.
- Creative ideas and executions for the **Expressives**.
- Profiles of the team who will work on the account for the **Amiables**.
- Fine detail on how everything works, including budget breakdown, for the **Analyticals**.

I have summarised all this rather glibly, but it is by far the most useful training I've ever done, and I still put much of it into practice today. There again, anyone who has ever done any basic psychology is probably laughing themselves stupid. It's not rocket science.

Does it help us win more business though? The cynics would say that the business we win would have been won anyway. Proponents would point to the incontrovertibility of the numbers: from an agency in the doldrums, we're approaching three times the turnover in just two years. At nearly £4million turnover, we're not quite the small business we were, and the need for systems, processes and slickness of operation is all too obvious. Sneer all you like, but anything that seems to give you an edge is worth investigating.

So much for personality profiling. The next subject on the consultants' agenda, and as part of the TQM process (I mentally yawned as I wrote that), is a little thing called BS5750, now superseded by ISO 9000 – a government-sponsored initiative through the British Standards organisation to promote "standards" in British business, through good management, based on standardised (hence the name) practices, systems and processes. You can probably tell I'm not a rabid fan of this: not because the core aims behind it are bad, but more because it comes out of government, so you know it's sure to end up in a bureaucratic mire, like all political initiatives.

Why are we interested in it at all then? I hear you ask. There are two practical considerations. One: it would be a nice badge to put on all our company stationery, and would differentiate us from our competitors (well, most of them). Two: there are signs that some blue-chip businesses are bringing in their own systems, one of which is handing the purchasing of everything, including marketing services, to a department called 'Procurement', and that one of the criteria they may apply to potential suppliers is the BS5750/ISO 9000 badge. It starts (surprise, surprise) with government itself, which spends a fortune on advertising and promotion (aka public information), largely, though not exclusively, through a department known as the Central Office of Information (recently closed, or at least re-badged). There is a growing tendency for it to trickle down into other large corporations, which run a command and control style of management. We probably don't gravitate naturally to this type of business, but that means we are missing out on a decent potential slice of work. And what happens if the types of business that we do get naturally drawn to start taking up the idea?

So we do take it seriously. Naturally there is yet another expert in the field, ready willing and able to take a fee off us for his advice, experience and expertise. For the life of me, I can't remember his name, which tells you all you need to know about his personality and presentation style (I use that last word in its loosest sense). Or maybe it's just the subject matter. At the end of the consultation process, what emerges is that we are already doing most of the things that are necessary to achieve the standard (things like regular personnel appraisals and monthly management accounts). In fact we are probably about 80% of the way there. The only major thing we need to do to achieve the standard is to document all of the actions we are taking, to justify our application. In other words, a load of paper work, that doesn't create anything useful, meaningful or profitable, apart from employment for the geeks who operate the system. Well, it is government sponsored. What do you expect? After careful consideration, we elect to forego the badge and risk the loss of business opportunity, in favour of keeping the agency sharp and business focused. If we do start to lose business as a result, we can always re-visit it later. In fact, we never do.

Notwithstanding that decision, there is no shortage of paper work being generated, as a result of me paying lip-service to TQM and all its doings. For a start, there's the production and publication of the company hand-book, which purports to tell employees (especially new ones) the way we do things round here. It covers everything from invoicing to keeping the papers tidy in reception, and it takes an era to pull together and get a consensus on everything. Is it worth the effort, when it's finally printed and circulated? I guess it fulfils a purpose, in that it forces us to agree lots of things that may have been drifting into grey areas, where different people have different perceptions of what is expected. It just seems like a major distraction from the main business.

This is of course a major problem with most small business owner/managers: trying to get them to spend more time on the business rather than in it – doing the management and long-term vision things that they are less comfortable with and knowledge-able of. (If you want to know more, read The *E-Myth Revisited* by Michael Gerber. It's a business best-seller, and every business owner should read it.) At one all-day sales training, we ask each account handler in turn to stand up and do a 20-30 second 'elevator pitch' (you're in a lift, and someone asks you what you do: you have till they get out to tell them) on what the business they work for does. Every one of them says something different, so it's clear we are not communicating clearly, if at all, any vision about what the company's values are, what it stands for, where it sits in the market place – in short what its core purpose is. Trying to agree a 30-second elevator pitch exercises us longer than it should, and that's only trying to describe the business as it is right now. We haven't even started on where we want to take it.

As part of the process, we also commission some market research into the business – more money lining the pockets of consultant suppliers – to try to get a snap-shot of our strengths and weaknesses. The researchers interview a few of our clients, and then a few potential clients, to find out what they think of us, or indeed in the latter case, if they've ever heard of us. (You'd be a bit worried if your existing clients hadn't). As is often the case with research, the results just tell us what we already know – or "special subject, the bleeding obvious", as Basil Fawlty once put it. Number one: outside of its existing client base, the agency is not as well known as it aspires to be. Number two: within our client base, we are thought of as a safe pair of hands, rather than creative, innovative or strategic thinkers. Number three: as an agency, we tend to appeal to Amiables on the personality profiling chart, rather than creative types or big-shot egos. None of this is news, but again, I suppose it does kick our ass into doing something about it. We carry out annual appraisals with our own staff, but don't think to do the same (or rather ask them to do it to us) with clients. Not doing it means you just don't know what your clients think of you – you're effectively flying blind. Doing it, as we discover, uncovers some uncomfortable truths.

I've already referred to this episode elsewhere, but it warrants more detailed inspection (if you don't agree, skip a page or two). During our bad year, the one ray of light on the client side is that we get in to the giant Coca Cola organisation through the back door. With its zillion-pound promotional budget and iconic brands, Coke runs a roster of top-end agencies, which everyone joins a disorderly queue to try to get on. When widget companies (aka promotional merchandise) come round hawking some new gadget to boost sales, as like as not it'll have the Coca Cola logo on it – not because Coke has necessarily bought any yet, but because it is the prime beacon of a target in terms of unit sales. If Coke runs with it, there'll be hundreds of thousands of sales rather than tens of thousands, and by making it look as if Coke are even considering running with it, they think it gives their widget credibility. Which in fairness, it does partly, even though we know the game they're playing.

Anyway, within the Coca Cola organisation is a separate company (no idea whether it still exists or why it existed then – tax reasons probably) called Refreshment Spectrum, which is responsible for the sales and marketing of its fruit juice brand, Five Alive. Somehow we get an introduction to the woman in charge of its promotional budget, a leggy, strikingly good-looking American woman, called Kara.

We're up against three or four other agencies of course, and while the budget doesn't run into millions, there is half a million to play with, because she's decided to take the media spend and put it into a blockbuster promotion. For whatever reason, we hit it off with Kara from the outset, and not only that, we hit on the obvious promotion very early in proceedings (and check out that we can deliver it OK), so by the time we present our ideas, they're fully formed and developed into a complete programme. The promotion is called, "Going Five Alive" and features Phillip Schofield and Gordon the Gopher (don't tell me you've forgotten Gordon) on all 20 million packs, giving away loads of prizes in a free draw (or sweepstakes, as Kara insists on calling it – she's American, remember). Phillip is currently presenting the popular children's programme, Going Live, and even though it is a BBC production, we are able to negotiate its brand name use with their commercial department. Fifty grand, for the use of the programme title and Phillip's image on all supporting material. Having won the business, I actually meet Phillip for the photo shoot: a nice enough guy, without any airs and graces, and it turns out he's managed by ex-Radio One DJ, Peter Powell, who, it also turns out, was brought up about three streets from me. Never knew him or met him though – he was educated privately, which kept him out of the local hoi palloi.

So we get appeal (mums like Phillip, as well as kids, and the weenies like Gordon), and we have a promotion with genuine media interest and cross-media potential, so it's very PR-able (what a tossy phrase that is). Astonishingly, everything goes like clockwork, the technical problems of printing eight different pack variants in six colours on enormous gravure presses (in Whitby, of all places) are overcome – the skin tones for Phillip's face are a particular challenge – and the sell-in to the trade means all the sales objectives are achieved. Blimey, a (reasonably) creative promotion that works. We should have it stuffed and mounted. Actually, it's not that creative really: a personality-fronted prize draw. But the use of the programme name, in which similar prizes are routinely given away too, and which is so adjacent to the brand name, means this is a promotion which could only work in this form for this brand. It may not be creative, but it does tick all the boxes, and we are like a (corporate) dog with two dicks as a result.

So when we sit down with Kara for our year-end, promotion-end review, we arrive with the confident nonchalance of an agency that has genuinely delivered; and depart two hours later shell-shocked, after being savaged in every single department. There are ten or a dozen categories on the appraisal form, and for each one there is a mark out of ten. We average about three on all of them. There is not a single area in which we excel, or are even just OK, apparently; we are just uniformly crap. I'm not sure whether I ask the question then or later, but does this mean we are being fired? Well, apparently not. What we are being, though, is deflated and demoralised. I can't ever remember being so stunned and non-plussed, partly because of the unexpectedness of it all, partly because of the unjustness, in our eyes. We've done a decent job, damn it. What the fuck is going on here?

There is a rule in all appraisals that when you have criticisms to make of someone's performance, you start and end with positives and give them the bad news in the middle. It's called a shit sandwich. I never find out what Kara's agenda is, but I do know that, by demoralising us entirely, she effectively ruins any working relationship, built on trust and self-esteem, that we thought was between us. My guess, and it is only a guess, is that it's her way of trying to motivate us to even bigger and better things. Of course, it fails miserably. We have a half-assed re-run of the promotion the following year, on half the budget (never a good idea, though not technically our fault), before Kara moves on to bigger and better things somewhere in Europe, and we never see or hear of her again. The suspicion lingers that she is moved because she is not popular with colleagues – her team-building skills being conspicuous by their absence – or else this is just one step on the great ladder of corporate success, and she's made her mark, even if she does leave a trail of destruction in her wake. She certainly behaves like a bit of a maverick, and in a place like Coca Cola, that either marks you out as a loner or as a visionary, who ends up running the business. Given we've never heard of her again, my money's on the former, but either way, once she's gone, we're frozen out gently by the new management, and the great Coke name is no longer on our (current) client list. Oh well, you win some, you lose more.

To be fair to ourselves, the Coke appraisal is not typical. Most of those carried out with other clients merely confirm what the research, and we in our own hearts, already know: we're pretty good at the bread and butter stuff, competent at the creative stuff, but not sparkling. Can you make yourselves more creative? Probably not, without an infusion of talent and a concomitant commitment to giving them their head, neither of which we're massively inclined to.

One thing we can do, though, is to raise our profile in the industry, and we set our brains to thinking how we can achieve this, with some innovative marketing strategy at an affordable price. You may think that, since this is what we do for a living for all our clients, this would be second nature for all agencies, including us. Unfortunately, cobblers' children syndrome prevails: it is generally the last thing agencies (and we) spend money or energy on. When we receive a client brief, unless it is utterly prescriptive, we assemble a team in our Board Room to brain-storm ideas, jotting down thoughts in black felt pen on a giant flip-chart, and then blu-tacking (does such a verb exist? It does now) full sheets of words and phrases round the walls, before reviewing our handiwork and trying to decide whether we've cracked it, and if so, which way to proceed.

For once, we assemble a senior team to consider our own promotion, and eventually come up with a corker of an idea, if only we can deliver it – all the usual caveats applying of course. Amazingly, we discover we can. There are at the time two weekly key trade magazines in the market place: *Marketing Week*, an A4 job that used to be the bible but is looking increasingly tired, as it is overtaken by *Marketing*, a physically bigger magazine published by Haymarket (prop. M Heseltine). There are quite a few sales promotion and direct marketing titles too, but they are without exception yawn-stiflingly awful – the sort of snigger-inducing awfulness that features regularly on *Have I Got News For You*.

We negotiate to put our own cover-wrap on every copy of the magazine, so when it arrives on clients' (and agencies') desks, it will still have Marketing as the banner, but it will be in white out of our corporate dark blue (for Oxford, don't you know), and the rest of the cover (and the other three pages of the wrapper) will be a promotional puff for us, professionally written for a change and slickly produced, before being shipped to the publisher's printing facility, for incorporation into the main paper, to be stapled on as a mock cover. These have become common-place since, but right now, no one has ever done it before, so we are being genuinely creative and innovative about the way we get our message across to our market. It all works like clockwork, and I can tell from the comments of other agency heads – in a tight-knit industry like ours, you're always bumping into them at various do's – they've noticed it (they could scarcely not) and are secretly wishing they'd thought of it. It does, quite simply, make us look bigger than we are. Job done, then.

So after the knock-back and the redundancies, we're doing well again. They say that if you keep doing the right things and doing things right, eventually the business will come right. Out of the blue, apparently, come two or three significant accounts: Holsten Pils and Toshiba Air Conditioning seem to come out of nowhere, and Smirnoff spends over £1 million with us one year. I've already described the way the Holsten account is won – no pitch, promotion proposal submitted and accepted overnight: nought to half a million in the forward billings in 24 hours. Now that's what I call new business generation. Pity it only happens once in a blue moon. Generally we've almost stopped celebrating new account wins, because there are so many false dawns: you're told you've won, and then you find that the budget has been cut back to next to nothing, or something else happens to put everything on hold. It gets to the point where you only feel celebratory when the money is actually in the account at the end of proceedings, by which time it seems a bit pointless going out on a bender on the strength of it (what am I saying?)

Toshiba Air Conditioning is a much more conventional account win: formal pitch against three other agencies. The difference is that it's business-to-business, not consumer marketing, which usually means lower budgets, but greater longevity: once an agency is appointed, generally clients want to develop a relationship with it – become friends, stick with it, ask it to do everything on the marketing front – advertising, direct marketing, brochures, (the internet now, not at this point in time), sometimes PR even, though not here thankfully. We win it through a massive investment in market research, and probably because the opposition are specialist B2B agencies who are demonstrably less creative than we are; and also because the people hit it off – Stid and their MD, Ted, and Marketing Manager, Lorraine, get along on a personal level. Unusually for B2B, air conditioning is big business and the budgets are substantial: for the next three years, they'll spend over half a million a year with us. We've struck pay-dirt, but within the euphoria are the seeds of the next big challenge to confront us.

In the meantime, some mention must also be made of the work we do for Smirnoff, which is high-profile, big budget and, unusually for us, both creative and award-winning – though regrettably not the top gong it deserves, in my opinion, at the annual awards. C'est la vie. As with all great promotions, it's a simple enough idea that represents our best work for the brand. At the time, glow-sticks are just starting to appear at concerts and outdoor events. We take the technology – a flexible plastic tube of two liquids, separated by a membrane, which, when broken and mixed by bending the tube, causes a chemical reaction which glows in the dark in a variety of colours for several hours. We have the plastic tubes inserted into small Smirnoff bottle shapes, branded and converted into pin badges, which are perfect for the clubs and bars where the majority of the product is sold in the on-trade. In participating outlets, anyone ordering a Smirnoff by name (not a generic vodka) gets a glow-in-the-dark badge. If, when activated, it glows red (Smirnoff's core brand colour – there are also blue and black variants, allegedly higher quality), they also win a branded t-shirt. When the promotion goes live, outlets are full of teen and twenty-somethings walking around with highly visible brand messages about their person, pinned to every conceivable part of the body – not just clothing: with body piercing all the rage, they find their way into ears, noses, and heaven knows where else. It's a huge success – popular with the trade, because it works; popular with bar staff, because it's fun and easy to administer (oh, and they get t-shirts too); popular with the client and his sales force, for both the above reasons, but mostly because it actually sells more product. Blimey, a promotion that produces measurable benefits (we have the client's own research on throughputs before, during and after the promotion in participating outlets): we should have it framed and put on display in reception. Actually I think we do.

Amid all this success, the next bit of contentious activity begins. One of Thomas's suggestions is that, to help steer us to the next level (let's say £5 – 10 million turnover), we should consider appointing a non-executive Chairman, who can bring his or her wisdom and experience to bear on our problems and opportunities, introduce us to unthought-of ideas, and, who knows, maybe even some new clients, and generally act as a father figure to us callow youths. Whether it is also part of Stid's grand plan to stop me chairing Board meetings is a moot point (we've already tried rotating the chair, at his suggestion, with limited success, I'd say – but then, I would, wouldn't I?) With Stid acting as advocate, the rest of us are soon running out of objections. The money one doesn't hold much water, because it's only £20K a year. I say 'only': not bad work for half a day's work a month: as I write, my son is working as a full-time press officer for a major political party in Westminster on a similar salary. Soon, we are looking at a list of candidates, thoughtfully provided by Thomas who, you may not be at all surprised to hear, makes part of his living by matching up willing ex-captains of the marketing services industry with young wet-behind-the-ears wannabes like us.

We are eventually presented with half a dozen CV's of the alleged great and good in the industry. There are a couple of advertising agency MD's, a PR agency owner/manager, a research man, a media boss – you get the picture. It is arranged that we will spend an agreeable day at a hotel on the river at Goring, and all the candidates will present themselves in succession – a sort of long drawn-out beauty parade. It is a glorious sunny day, and we indulge ourselves, while all these heavy hitters traipse in and discuss what marvels they can bring to the party. In the end, of course, it's the same old interview process, whereby you decide on the candidate's suitability within two minutes of them entering the room (you only get one chance to make a first impression) and then spend the next hour reinforcing the prejudice. (*You've already done this bit – Ed.*)

The PR man nobody likes: personality clashes all over the place, and he's far too full of himself, when what we really want to be talking about is us! The ad agency man we like; well, the Cat and I do. He's a live-wire, on our wave-length and we hit it off straightaway: here's someone we could work with. The other ad agency head is a woman, who is undeniably bright, interesting, challenging: there is nothing tangible you could posit about why you couldn't work with her. And yet, certainly in my mind, there is a bit of chemistry lacking. Hard to put your finger on, but insistently, there in the background, it just doesn't feel right. I just don't feel naturally at ease in her company. And finally on the short-list, there's the media boss – creator of the first media independent in the industry, so a bit of (a lot of) a ground-breaker and with a reputation for astuteness. Needless to say, we've never heard of him. He turns out to be personable, credible (you'd hope so, with his track record) and utterly ancient. We immediately dub him the oldest man in advertising, and the moniker sticks.

At the end of the day, we all sit round and discuss the pros and cons of each candidate, and as is starting to become increasingly familiar, the Cat and I plump for the agency head, and Stid wants anyone but. When we started with four directors, all on equal shares, there was always the danger that we could have a split decision in board meetings, and nowhere was there any agreement that I would have the casting vote (a mistake I wouldn't make again, even though it never actually cost us). With Gaylord's departure, there are now three of us, so on paper at least, if any two decide on something, it should be a fait accompli. From the beginning, however, I have always tried to have management by consensus, and when we were four, we simply deferred decisions on anything where there was even one dissenter. This could have hog-tied the business, but in practice we disagreed on virtually nothing in the early days. I think the longest debate we had, at which someone had to be won over, was the question of whether a drinks vending machine should replace the mess in what passed for a kitchen. Now we are three, there is a subtle change in the dynamics of the team. The Cat and Stid have always been something of a unit, and indeed Gaylord's parting shot was, "They'll have you next," but in the last year, with Stid's overweening ambitions and muscle flexing, there is a definite cooling in that particular alliance. The Cat doesn't like being told what to do, any more than I do, and is beginning to assert an authority of his own.

So here we have a disagreement of some importance, and we can't just sweep it under the carpet. A decision has to be made one way or the other (of course there is always the option of not having any of them, or indeed anyone, but strangely that is not debated, or if it is, not for long.) Eventually we agree to have dinner with our short-list of three, for a second round of discussions. It puts off the decision and means three nice dinners up in town: it's one way of spending your time. All very pleasant and affable, but it still doesn't change anyone's mind.

The woman, whose special subject now is Third Age Marketing (that's old people to you and me), still gives us reservations about personal chemistry, plus, in our (unstated) misogyny, I suspect none of us can quite bring ourselves to being managed by a woman, however good for us it might be.

The live-wire ad agency man is still favourite for me and the Cat, but he obviously hasn't hit it off with Stid – or maybe Stid can see something in him that might stymie his own ambitions. He just refuses to countenance working with him, and the idea of imposing him via a 2 – 1 vote at a board meeting would just exacerbate the split. We probably should have done it anyway, though it wouldn't have changed anything.

So the compromise candidate (recognise the scenario, all you politicos out there?) is the oldest man in advertising. He's no one's favourite, but equally no one claims they couldn't work with him. On the basis of unanimity between us, he's the least worst option. It's hardly an exciting choice, and certainly not one that fills me or the Cat with any great inspiration, but it is a workmanlike appointment that just might be the glue that holds us together.

I often wonder whether he wasn't Stid's preferred option from the start, and was presented as a compromise candidate as a means of getting his way. Not sure what difference it would have made anyway, because Tomia's (**T**he **O**ldest **M**an **I**n **A**dvertising) arrival coincides with the most turbulent and dangerous period in our whole short history.

Before we leave the world of consultants, advisors and TQM, however, mention must be made of how we present the brave new world encapsulated in Thomas's report to the rest of the staff. Cramming them all in the board-room would have done the job quite adequately, but we never miss the opportunity to squander a bit more cash when there's an excuse for a piss-up. If you have grand designs, you naturally wish to present them in a grand setting. So it is that we find ourselves in the country house splendour of an establishment called Wyck Hill House, down in the Cotswolds, hostelry to the great and good (and us). Thomas must have introduced us to it, because we've had one planning meeting here, and the 3rd Age advertising woman candidate for our role as NEC got the train there from London for her first interview (direct line from Paddington to Moreton-in-the-Marsh, for all you Ian Allen railway buffs).

It is a typically spectacular English country house hotel, set in several acres of magnificent grounds with far-reaching views of the surrounding Gloucestershire countryside. Internally, it's full of wood panelling and chandeliers, and the beds are about ten feet wide – you could easily get five or six in them (and later, we do).

So it is a suitably fine setting to formally present the plans, in one of the many drawing rooms, even if the presentation itself lacks charisma: crappy slides projected on a free-standing screen in one corner, and as I've already demonstrated, the content is all a bit thin – TQM and a bit of a management reshuffle. Still, the venue itself does its best to help us make more of a silk purse out of a sow's ear, and we probably carry it off OK, though none of the staff to whom it is presented are likely to say what they really think about it all, straight off the reel. [If any of you are reading this, god help us, now's the chance to have your say!]

Anyway, business over, it's time to start doing what we do best – eating, drinking and making merry, in best bib and tucker, pretending we might actually fit in to this establishment, instead of sticking out like the obvious sore-thumb parvenus that we are. Pre-prandial drinks, 4-course dinner in a private room (the hotel are very sensible in separating us from their other diners, as the decibel level increases), followed seamlessly by digestifs, more drinks, a disco in the drawing-room where we'd made the presentation (what on earth possessed us? And what possessed the hotel to agree to it? Talk about a grotesque culture clash), and of course more and more drinks. I apparently pass out in the bar (*fall asleep, surely – Ed.*) and am revived by Julia (our erstwhile receptionist and now efficient cash-collecting accounts assistant) giving me the kiss of life. Or something. The staff divide into break-out groups by osmosis, and go off to cavort in various bedrooms, and it all gets horribly messy. Just like the business really.

Seven

The Splitter And Danny La Rue

HAVING ENJOYED OUR BIGGEST ever year, with turnover hitting nearly £4 million, we should be flying. But as ever in business, like the rest of life, just when you think you've got everything cracked, events conspire to send things crazily out of control. And naturally it's not just one thing, but a combination of several that creates the next big drama. Could we have done anything about it with the benefit of hindsight? Overall, not much, though the pain could possibly have been reduced.

Let us start with the positives though. We are planning constructively for how to take the business forward and what its future shape should be. The question of Europe exercises us for quite some time: greater political involvement in the EU and the (still) ongoing debate over the Euro mean Britain is no longer a relatively isolated island off the continental coast. What are we going to do about it? We are currently a strictly UK-based operation, though it is true that we have run a trade promotion for Wiggins Teape across a dozen different countries with half a dozen language variations in the communication piece, though that remains a one-off. (Our client contact departed shortly after, and with him went the business, but thanks, Neil, for the opportunity.) Bigger companies, like Coca Cola and MacDonald's, are already talking about pan-European promotions, driven as usual by economies of scale rather than marketing effectiveness –

communications which work in English don't always translate in other cultures, so there is a tendency to lowest common denominator stuff in what passes for trans-national campaigns, unless you're sponsoring the Olympics or the World Cup, which are by definition universally popular and relevant.

The only practical way of being able to deliver such mega-activity is to be part of a network: generally that means having your agency acquired by an international marketing services group, and wherever the promotion originates (though it is usually the UK or US), there is a local shop to administer and deliver the variants in each participating country. Small to medium-sized agencies like ours just don't have the resources to deliver, so can't hope to get an invitation to the party.

One response by a couple of our competitors is to find like-minded agencies in the various European capitals and form loose alliances that can work together co-operatively as a de facto network to compete for pan-European projects. The problems with this are two-fold: one, finding like minds in various languages is both tricky and time-consuming; and two, there is not the same quantity of agencies operating in our European neighbours – put bluntly, there aren't enough to go round, so once the first five or six have been snapped up, the rest of us are scratching around for poor seconds. It is potentially a viable option, but the sheer time and effort required to make it work mean you inevitably start taking your eye off the main UK business. Someone has to play the role of Manager of European Integration, and spend their time jetting round the capitals of, in order of priority, France, Germany, Italy, Holland, Belgium, Spain and Portugal. The last two would be higher up the list today, but at the time of writing are not yet in the EU.

One other option is to open an office of your own in the important centres and man it with local operatives who speak good English. The lingua franca in all European business is English, thanks largely to America, so the language issue only arises in terms of understanding local customs, phrase and fable. The problem of how much time (and money) needs to be committed to such a project is considerable though: you're bank-rolling a start-up in a foreign land, with different legislation and a whole heap of cultural differences, with personnel that you don't know from Adam. It's your money, so they're quite happy to take a punt on their success with very little downside, but how do you manage them? Proper management is all too time-consuming when you only have 20 or so on the payroll in total; let them have their head, and you could end up picking up some very expensive pieces. One or two of the bigger agencies try this approach, and we watch them nearly go to the wall (I think one actually does) on the back of hugely expensive overseas white elephants.

As the French speaker, this whole issue naturally devolves to me, though everyone has an opinion (surprise), but after twelve months of umming and ahhing, and more than one Board discussion paper, nothing is ever agreed or acted upon – thank God, with the benefit of hindsight – and other events occur which drive the question of Europe off the agenda.

At the same time, we consider other ways of growing the business, other than organically. We've already had a dip at acquiring other small agencies that are struggling financially, or the owners wish to retire, in order to add their billings to ours. Once again, thank goodness, nothing ever comes off: the distractions of merging one business with another, the inevitable personality clashes, the loss of ambition of the leading players who no longer control their own destiny, the probability of business walking away as a result – all conspire to make the whole process very high risk.

Instead we look at building additional services into our 'offer-ing', as the marketing boys put it. At the moment we describe ourselves as a sales promotion agency, pure and simple, but the drive towards 'through-the-line' activities is insistent. (For those of you not of a marketing bent, the 'line' was an invention of the accountants, to differentiate media advertising in all its manifes-tations – above the line – from all the rest of promotional activity, including sales promotion, direct marketing, design, exhibitions, etc – below the line: something to do with tax levies, I believe). While we can blague our way through any design brief, and even, with the help of a media independent partner, an advertising brief (providing it's pretty small scale), there are areas where we could add expertise internally and grow complete new profit streams from within, in semi-independent departments. Add enough of them, and you eventually get a complete marketing services offering in a relatively small microcosm. That's the thinking anyway. The practicalities are a bit more challenging.

Up for discussion as complementary skill-sets are, in no partic-ular order, research, PR, direct marketing, design (of various hues) and of course advertising. If we were having the conversa-tion today, we would have to add digital marketing to that list, and high up it too, but at the time only the biggest brands are toying with web-site development (and are paying tens, some-time hundreds of thousands of pounds for what you can now do at home with Dream Weaver – or so they say). We might also be considering what is called 'Experiential Marketing' – promoting your brands through events – but this too is a west coast of America phenomenon that is still in its infancy, and treated with a degree of caution and suspicion.

Our first dip into new service provision is in fact research. You could say, with hindsight, that it lacks ambition, and it is certainly true that it happens more out of chance meetings than any direct plan, but I suppose it pushes us off in the right direction. It is certainly the next seed sown in the mighty upheaval about to be harvested, though as usual at the time, it all looks innocuous enough.

All that happens is that Stid bumps into someone, probably at a dinner party, who does market reports for a living as a one-man-band, uses him a few times to get background on prospective clients in pitch situations and, after much dancing around the pin-head, eventually convinces him that, rather than operating as an independent from home, his future will be both more lucrative and more secure if he joins us as a paid employee, and brings his operation in-house. His name – well let's call him Danny: he's a dead ringer for Danny la Rue, even the voice (though at parties he prefers doing Gary Glitter impressions), and that's how he's referred to almost from the start. I'm sure his future is more secure and lucrative as a result of his move, even though financial records show that our accounts only benefit from his activities to the tune of £21K. As we shall see.

Let us leave Marketing Eye (for that is what he calls himself) and move on to a much more ambitious and contentious move: the decision whether and how to develop a credible direct marketing service. For our first eight years of operation (yes, nearly a decade has flown by: can you believe how quickly the time goes?) we have presented ourselves to the outside world very firmly as a sales promotion agency. Everyone knows that promotions agencies are jacks of all trades, so we've been able to dabble fairly effectively in many other areas of marketing services – design especially, thanks to our creative studio; advertising, mainly trade, but not exclusively: we've run some national press work for Toshiba and Lease Plan (still with us after all these years); even bits of PR, though we do outsource most of that.

Board meetings, chaired by Tom (you remember: The Oldest

Man…), debate at length the pros and cons of introducing new services into the organisation, to spread its appeal, grow its revenue and generally make us richer. We toy with PR: it's relatively easy to find some presentable totty who will totter round our clients on her expensive heels and promise them the earth in relatively cheap editorial media coverage. The totty bit of the argument is the only attractive one though: none of us really thinks much of PR as a discipline (as you can probably tell, and I know it's a bit rich, coming from a promotions agency, but there you are), so we can't really take it seriously.

We do have a bit of a go at design. Actually 'bit of a go' tells you all you need to know. A middle-aged woman called Jen – still fit and good-looking enough to wear mini-skirts without being accused of looking like mutton dressed as lamb (why oh why did we hire her?) – has been working as someone's PA. Oh yes, mine. And is persuaded, because she has a genuine eye for design, to front up an overt design consultancy arm, presenting us to the more ambitious and profitable local business community as a specialist in that field, to try to maximise profit-earning potential from our design studio facility. You can see how the idea might have developed, but we never really give her the support or investment needed to make it work. Mostly she needs sales training, but she doesn't get it, because we assume everyone either knows how to sell genetically, or can pick it up by watching others (ie us!) Bits of business come in, none of which we're really bothered about, because it's low budget, even though there's some nice work done for one or two local clients (The Old Parsonage Hotel in Oxford is one that springs to mind), but there's just not enough to keep us interested or, more importantly, justify her salary. It's only a question of time before we call time.

Direct marketing, however, is an altogether different kettle of fish. It is a discipline that goes hand in glove with sales promotion, according to Stid; the Cat and I are not so sure. We know however that we can't dabble at it. The only way to make it work is to somehow acquire a team of experts, ideally with a ready-made chunk of business that they can bring along with them, and install them as a fully functioning department that can pay for itself from day one – or at least very quickly. In the last couple of years, we have stabilised the business, and grown it, but there isn't a huge war-chest available to sustain even 6 – 9 months of loss-making from a new department.

Discussions in Board meetings get increasingly fractious, even with the supposed calming influence of Tom. A few months in, and Tom is starting to wonder what he's let himself in for. Having made millions from the sale of his own media independent, he's now a retired blackcurrant farmer on the borders of Herefordshire and Wales. Still, at twenty grand a year for 12 three-hour meetings, it's worth bestirring himself from his currant bushes and trekking up to Oxford to referee a bunch of egos in search of a fortune of their own. We did settle for experience over youth (relatively speaking: all the NEC candidates were elder statesmen – that's the point, but Tom's the far end of the scale.) I'm not even sure how old he is: a small, spare, bald, wizened and bespectacled chap, you would never pick him out at an identikit parade looking for successful business men. Sure, he talks with authority. He's used to running his own show. But to my mind, his business insights are very much limited to his own narrow sphere of business expertise. And media, however hard you try to dress it up, is the least creative discipline of all the marketing services. In fact the only way you can describe it as creative at all is the way you might call accountancy creative. It's about numbers: delivering the biggest audience possible within the available budget, by negotiating fat discounts to increase the amount of money effectively available (while creaming off a bit for themselves), and knowing the channels where promotion messages will best get through. It's a job for mathematicians and salesmen, rather than creative types.

Media companies rarely have to worry about unpaid bills because everything has to be paid up-front. The client may squirm all he likes, but if he doesn't pay, the ad doesn't run. End of. Proof, if ever there was one, that excuses about inflexible end-of-the-month cheque-run systems for late payment are just that. Not that debt collection is a problem with us, in spite of our mostly blue-chip client list. The fragrant Julia, once our receptionist and now promoted to accounts assistant and general company 'mum', is adept at forging relationships with the accounts payable departments and charming the cheques out of them. She may have a machine-gun laugh that can quieten Wembley when unleashed, but she's very good at chatting up clients – and, once chatted, they roll over on their corporate backs to have their tummy tickled.

Tom's knowledge of the creative process is really quite limited. One senses his heart is never quite in it. Strictly a numbers man, and the numbers don't lie, etc. So his insights are not exactly the blinding flashes of the obvious that we may have hoped for, when taking him on. You'd have thought that, of all the other marketing services, direct marketing would have had the greatest appeal – at least half of it is a numbers game (some would say more than half) and creativity has only a limited affect – but he doesn't show any greater knowledge of or enthusiasm for it in our Board shouties (*surely, reasoned debates – Ed.*)

Stid is constantly flexing his muscles and trying to shape the company the way he wants it to be, and the more he tries to railroad me and the Cat into doing his will, the more he isolates himself. When we start, he and the Cat are buddies, hanging out together, smoking dope together; the Cat even lives with him and his missus for a few short weeks when he's house moving (though he did end up having arguments with the other half apparently). Now though, he resents Stid trying to impose his particular vision on us, and the buddy status is definitely one for the past. Loud arguments and long silences alternate; I stand by and watch (what else can I do?) as the ship starts to pull apart through the opposing forces, and Tom … sits and mouths platitudes: "We live in interesting times" is the most common and most irritating.

Two things now happen, more or less concurrently, which makes the whole situation even more unstable. The first is the loss of our biggest client – actually two clients in one: Smirnoff and Baileys. I've already referred to this farrago in chapter four, but still, it's worth examining in a bit more detail the stupidity that can lead to the loss of a million-pound client. It occurs because the parent company, IDV, has a purchasing department that is getting increasingly involved in the procurement of marketing services (as if you can buy creative work by the yard – don't get me started), and decrees that henceforth no mark-ups will be made on bought-in services, and agencies have to survive on the fees they negotiate. Stupidly, none of us has ever had any training in negotiating skills, so those fees are already under pressure. Even more stupidly, we all think we can buck the system anyway.

How can a client know if you're marking up the products and services you buy on their behalf? Sure, they can ask for a covering invoice from the supplier, but that means diddly squat. It's all too easy to negotiate one price, agree they will invoice you for a higher, marked-up price, then invoice them for 'services rendered' later. Even in the unlikely event of them coming to audit your books, which is permitted in some contractual agreements, what are they going to find? Stash any 'commissions' in the nominal account, where they're unlikely to go looking anyway, and as an added cover, ensure they are described as incentive-related bonuses generally, and it's impossible to prove that any particular purchase for any specific client is involved, or to what extent. The supplier has no incentive to snitch on you: they're in a competitive environment (especially printers) and are generally happy to do a bit of administrative sleight of hand to secure the business. What's an extra exchange of paper, when there's a few thousand income at stake? Only one thing could go wrong (you're ahead of me, aren't you?) and that's if the supplier has more direct business with the client than indirect through you: the accounts department receives separate invoices for virtually identical products, one from us, one from the supplier, spots discrepancies and queries them. In this case, the supplier is interested only in covering his own back and protecting his continuing lucrative direct business with the client, and comes clean.

Ridiculously, in our case (but then the whole business is pretty ridiculous), the offending article is a supply of metal pin-badges for some minor Smirnoff trade promotion, total cost a couple of thousand, total unofficial mark-up a couple of hundred. Still, the supplier's testimony – effectively turning state evidence to protect himself – means we're banged to rights. There is an enormous inquest carried out: boy, those procurement people must have enjoyed making a song and dance to justify their positions (and salaries), and strengthen their future positions in buying marketing services – "Just look what we've uncovered; we'll make sure none of this happens again; how much could we be saving the business;" etc etc, ad infinitum. Then we're told we're fired. Never darken their door again. Not just the Smirnoff business, where we've been proven guilty, but by association, the Baileys business too, where there has been no evidence of wrong-doing (though it's likely we've been working the same fiddle, so fair enough, I suppose), where we have a much firmer ongoing client relationship. We sense that it is as big a wrench for the client team as it is for us, when they're told they have to find someone new to work with. More to the point, it puts a big hole in our accounts: in the last twelve months (and indeed for the past two or three years), Baileys has spent a quarter of a million with us, and Smirnoff has spent over a million with us this year and over half a million last year. It is a shattering loss and all for a few hundred quid extra profit.

Allied to that, other clients are spending less: Rothmans might spend half a million with us one year, but only a couple of hundred thousand the next. This is one of the fallow years. Dutch Bacon, which has been spending several hundred thousand a year with us, has its budgets frozen by the Dutch, while they reorganise. The whole business is like trying to control a giant yo-yo, but this year the yo-yoing effect is extreme.

We do acquire new business too – we've recruited a woman called Sue who has contacts with KFC from her previous place of work (beware that particular scenario: what comes in that way can walk out just as easily), and before long we're doing most of their promotional design work. Looking at the accounts in retrospect, it's only a hundred and thirty thousand in a year, but it's all fees – we buy no print or merchandise on their behalf, so no temptation to cheat! – and therefore all gross margin.

However, for the first time in our business lives, the amount of billings under the control of Stid is greater than that handled by me and the Cat. Until this year, he's had Lease Plan as his staple client, but most of the gilt-edged earners have been controlled by us – Guinness, Holsten, Rothmans, Lyons, Smirnoff, Coca Cola, you get the picture. With the advent of Toshiba Air Conditioning and KFC (Sue's reporting to him), he's now controlling a majority of the billings, a fact which is only likely to bolster his ego and reinforce his will to run everything his way.

Things are tense, to say the least. Stid and the Cat go days without speaking, and when they do speak, it is in less than civil terms. It obviously can't go on, and eventually things come to a head at a cricket match, of all things. England v South Africa at the Oval. God knows why the three of us are there – the Cat hates cricket at the best of times – but probably as a day out to try and mend some fences. By the end of the day, most of the fences that remain are flattened, and the landscape looks like a hurricane's gone through it. A day at the test is usually a civilised event: seven hours of sport going on in the background, while the supporters chin-wag, josh, eat and drink – a sort of giant mass picnic. And if the weather's good, work on their tan. Even for non-lovers of cricket, it can be a convivial way to spend a day. Half-way through the afternoon, Stid and the Cat disappear for an hour or more. I assume they're having a heart to heart, so don't go looking for them. I wouldn't know where to start in any event. When they finally turn up, it becomes apparent that the heart to heart has turned into a shout to shout, and far from mending fences, their relationship is in irretrievable melt-down. Needless to say, being British, we see out the remainder of the day in barely contained civility, but the future of the business is very much on the line. Stid wants out, and as the Cat puts it so succinctly, for the first time since we set up, we are in no position to tell him to fuck off then, given the current billings situation.

To no one's surprise, Thomas reappears on the scene, via Stid no doubt, and we are all summoned to a breakfast meeting at some nearby hotel to try to thrash out our differences and find a viable way forward. Thomas presents a proposal for a 'de-merger', which would allow Stid to go off and run his own show, while the two of us continue to run ours – with each having a one-third stake in the other. With the benefit of hindsight (a wonderful thing), or just a cool and unemotional head at the time, it would have been a perfectly sensible and practical way to proceed (and in fact two of us would have ended up a lot richer than we did, but hey ho). Everyone is far too caught up in the emotions of the moment, with feelings of betrayal high on the agenda. There is little we can do to stop him walking out, in any event, but there will have to be negotiation about the shareholding. Neither the Cat nor I can countenance having anything more to do with him if he walks out, so the reciprocal shareholding idea is dead in the water. All we can do is divide the business on current account control lines, and start again (again) with a smaller business and client list. It's déjà vu, with knobs on.

It soon emerges that when Stid goes, he's taking with him Danny la Rue and Sue, together with the Lease Plan, Toshiba and KFC accounts. We can scarcely argue with any of that: Lease Plan was his from the start, and while my input certainly helped win the Toshiba business, he's been running the account and has the client in the palm of his hand; as for Sue, she's never been a Principles person, to my mind – it's been like having a paying (or rather a being paid) guest in our midst, and the Cat tells Stid in no uncertain terms (no uncertain terms is the current lingua franca) that he's welcome to her and will live to regret taking her with him. Prophetic words, since within a year she's left to set up on her own, so fair play to the Cat.

The big contention is over Dutch Bacon, which Stid seems to think he has rights over, as a result of his relationship with the previous client head (not the current incumbent), even though it is an account that I am personally running with my team – none of whom has any desire to go with him. Basically our view is that he can fuck right off, but in the end the decision will be made by the client. As anticipated, the client has no wish to get involved in a tug-of-war and elects to stay with us, subject to the usual reviews etc (which we're effectively subject to anyway). Thank you, Robert: you don't know how much the decision means to us.

It probably is absolutely key to our survival.

Given the loss of Smirnoff and Baileys, the lack of spending by Rothmans, and the failure of one or two other new accounts to develop their big-money potential, the Cat and I are looking down the barrel. Stid proposes to take only Jools, my trusty ex-PA, from the rest of the staff. Everyone else, he's leaving to our tender mercies, the bastard. It doesn't take long with the forward billings, overheads and P&L projections to figure out that the head count is going to have to be reduced by half a dozen. We've had to tell the staff what is happening – this isn't the sort of thing you can keep under the table and then produce like a rabbit out of a hat – and it doesn't take long for them to put two and two together and work out the redundancy equation either. As a result, Stid and his companions are immediately vilified, and the atmosphere in the office becomes even more poisonous.

There now begins an utterly surreal period: we are in the last quarter of the year, and for some weeks we have a situation where there are effectively two businesses operating under the same roof. Stid and his co-conspirators are constantly off in huddles, planning their new venture. No doubt, too, they are trying to defer billings to a date when they rather than we will benefit from them. In the meantime, we have to plan our own future, based, at the moment at least, on less than half the billings but most of the overheads. As I've mentioned previously, in a service industry like ours with personnel representing two-thirds of the total over-head, the only way to reduce costs is to reduce staff. Ancillary costs like phones, postage and expenses come down with the head-count anyway. It is hard to convey the ludicrous nature of the situation, and some of the more emotional members of staff find it difficult to deal with. Our Creative Director, Kelvin, who brings a wealth of experience of big accounts, having worked in America on the Burger King business (and seemingly sourced the big-number free gifts), is particularly exercised by events. He probably suspects – quite rightly as it turns out – that his big salary will be a prime candidate for the chop, come the split. Given that his wife has only recently given birth to their first child (India – how creative is that), the anger brought on by the insecurity is entirely understandable. It all boils over one afternoon when Kelvin is on the top floor, where Stid and his outfit reside, and words are exchanged between him and Danny la Rue. In essence, Kelvin offers (perhaps threatens is a better word) to take him out, and he's not referring to dinner at the Dorchester. In the event, violence is barely averted, and the only damage is that Danny has his desk cleared for him – a simple manoeuvre perfected by Reginald Perrin, whereby one sweep of the arm propels the entire desktop contents on to the floor. It's all jolly dramatic, and sums up the frustrations felt by everyone.

There then follows an even more ludicrous event. For weeks we've been planning a staff night out, with partners, involving a cruise along the Thames from the Head Of The River – food, drink, dancing, you get the picture. Unaccountably, we decide not to cancel due to unforeseen circumstances, but to go ahead regardless – with both factions present. What on earth possessed us, I can't imagine. We must have been mad – literally mad, to quote Enoch Powell. There could easily have been rivers of blood. Astonishingly, miraculously, it all passes off without incident. The conspirators and their partners take up residence at one end of the boat, and we occupy the other. There is barely any communication between the two, and if ever there were an example of good old British sang froid and stiff upper lip coping with a nightmare scenario, here it is in all its understated glory. Conversation is stilted; people try to look as though they're enjoying themselves (a bit), while stealing furtive glances at watches to check out how much more of this purgatory they have to put up with. For the only time in our short history, a company night out ends with nobody drunk and throwing up, or even vaguely tipsy. We all step off the boat, as it moors up, stone cold sober, with alacrity and massive sighs of relief. Thank god that's over, and please god let *all* this soon be over, so we can get on with what's left of our lives (and business).

It is of course very much like a traditional divorce. Technically, I suppose, it is a divorce. It's just that there are three partners splitting instead of two. And the arguments about who takes what with them in this case refer to members of staff and clients. Stid really isn't interested in 'taking his fair share' of the overhead, of course; the selfishness that pervades most of what he does is unlikely to disappear at this particular moment in his personal development, so the fact that he wants to take next to no one with him comes as little surprise. What he's saying effectively is, "I'm starting with three fat clients and a clean sheet; you can go suck." Naturally that would not be his recollection of events: his ego would never allow him to admit that he's fucking us over for personal gain. But he is. And in case you're thinking this is just my ego having its say, perhaps we should leave it to the staff for the final word. The studio, aided and abetted by Nick, one of our Account Directors who came from Rothmans, has taken to producing an occasional spoof company newsletter (after which this book is unashamedly titled) – a scurrilous rag in which the faults and foibles of most members of staff (including me) are mercilessly sent up, Private Eye style. They're probably one of the most creative things to emerge from the engine-room, which may explain a thing or two. The post-split edition, I suppose inevitably, is unlikely to paint a pretty picture of the departing cohorts, and Stid is naturally vilified, but the phrase that sticks with me most is the barbed comment, "He was a legend in his own mind." Says it all really.

With under (well under at the actual moment of the split) half the forward billings and about 80% of the overhead, after you take the departees out of the equation, we soon work out that, even by reducing the head count from 18 to 12 – the minimum we think we need to function and respond to existing and potential new business – there is no guarantee of survival. With these three lucrative accounts walking, so shortly after the debilitating loss of Smirnoff and Baileys, and with Rothmans not spending, we are very much looking down the barrel.

Board meetings are like a war zone, with Tom mouthing fatuous platitudes and contributing nothing practical to events. The 'interesting times' one is his stock in trade, but there are others, most notably in the debate about how we should announce events to our existing clients. "My taste is that we send a hand-delivered letter to all MD's." My taste! Or as the Cat puts it more succinctly, wanker. He's the first on the list of casualties of course – there's no way the Cat and I are going to keep paying him £20K a year for the load of old tosh that he spouts, but it's interesting to note that when he turns up for his final duty, his last act is to produce an invoice and a request that he be paid immediately. Our ship may be going down, but down on the blackcurrant farm the weather's just fine, and he's making sure he gets his pound of flesh before the holed vessel ships any more water (*that's enough mixed metaphors – Ed.*). The ruthless shit. There, that's got that off my chest.

Inevitably there are all sorts of pettinesses going on. Stid has had his golf club membership paid by the company (client entertainment, Mr Revenue) and the Cat insists he personally pay it back. Eventually all things must pass, as George Harrison noted, and there comes a final day when desks are cleared, filing cabinets removed, personal belongings packed up and large swathes of newly vacant office space appear. We've been through the redundancies, with the usual mix of anger, tears and stiff upper lip resignation, and when the dust settles, there are a dozen of us left fighting for survival. We don't tell the survivors that their fate is very much still in the balance, but we don't need to. They know how the business works, and they know what the forward billings are. You don't have to be Einstein to put two and two together and make three. Yes, that's right: one short of what it should be.

As anyone who has ever run a small business will tell you, the idea that you can divorce your private life from your business life is utterly illusory. In big corporate Britain, you know that keeping your job and salary is important to keep paying the mortgage, but if the worst comes to the worst, you can always get another job (unless there's the recession of all recessions going on). In small businesses, not only do you have the livelihoods of all your staff riding on the back of you, but chances are the bank's got your house as security against any overdraft facility – and if they haven't, they soon ask for it, if they get the slightest sniff of trouble in the air. Any business owner who confides in his bank when he's in trouble is barking: they're more likely to withdraw facilities and send you to the wall than be supportive.

Just at this very moment the Cat is moving from his little house-for-one starter home to a converted old school building. It's a big step up the property ladder and one that necessarily began some time before all this blew up. What do you do though? Pulling out is an admission of defeat – an acceptance that we're all doomed, Captain Mainwearing. We have to stay positive and he has to go through with the move, as much as anything for his own motivation. Actually it might be a good thing for him: putting his arse on the line will make him stretch himself and maximise his potential. When he shows me round the new abode though, shortly before moving in, there is a palpable sense of, "Oh my god, what am I doing?" In Monty Python's Holy Grail, there is a moment when the King of Camelot turns to his son and pointing to (through) the window says, "One day son, all this will be yours", to which the wimpy son replies, "What, the curtains?" We're both fans, so I don't need to explain the reference when I casually comment, "Oh well, one day, son, this won't be yours."

While the Cat is still technically single (his Danish girlfriend, Sanne, recruited on a company AGM to Copenhagen, has moved in), many of our staff have families and mortgages of their own to worry about. What goes on in the office is discussed at length at home, and no doubt dissected ad infinitum, particularly after the traumas of the last few weeks. When I share the news with my own family of what Stid's doing, there is a long silence before my 13-year-old son, Luke, sums up all our feelings in two pithy words: "Splitter … Bastard."

Eight

Sheridan Poorly and The Battle of the Blonds

So THERE WE ARE: WE'VE BEEN in business for nearly nine years, and it feels, for the second time, as if we're starting from scratch again. Even with our reduced head-count, the forward billings look decidedly shaky. Unless we win some substantial new business, and soon, we are at real risk of going under, and don't think for a moment that Stid doesn't know that: he's cut and run at the only time in eight or nine years when his departure genuinely threatens our future, which is why he will forever remain in my top three bastards of all time, and why I will never speak to him again. Actually I wouldn't piss in his ear if his brain were on fire. There, another something off my chest.

While the horrors of the split have been going on, though, there has also been another major development, with short- and long-term implications for the business, and which now requires a major decision to be made: a decision which has to weigh up the potential of a long-term opportunity against the short-term financial risk. And given our current precarious situation, it's a decision which could sink us, before the (possible/probable) pay-back has us swimming back to financial security.

Concurrently with Stid and the Cat's deteriorating relation-ship, the Cat has introduced us to Stuart and Liza, who are senior account handlers with a big London direct marketing agency and with whom we share a client – Rothmans. We create the sales promotions – they develop direct marketing campaigns on the back of them, using the client's growing database of smokers. Given the way that legislation is going in cigarette advertising and marketing, a combination of below-the-line disciplines (promotions, direct marketing, sponsorship) represent a real opportunity for big-budget activity, now they can't spend it on media advertising. Over a few beers (and fags), it has become apparent that the two of them are disillusioned with their current agency employers and harbour ambitions to run their own show.

We have been discussing adding direct marketing to our 'offering', but to be credible, you have to have skill-sets and proven experience in the business. It is particularly ironic that this should come up now, because one of the fundamental reasons for the breakdown (on paper at least) between Stid and the Cat and me had been his insistence on taking us down a direct marketing route, and our resistance to it. Just as he splits to form what will become a direct marketing agency, rather than a promotions agency, here we are discussing the establishment of a direct marketing arm in our own operation.

During all the acrimony of the last few weeks, the Cat has continued talks with them about setting up Marketing Principles Direct – a semi-autonomous arm of the agency, with its own discrete client list, which would allow us to cross-sell the new discipline to our (somewhat emaciated) existing client list. Stuart is a skinny guy with a pleasant enough disposition, who seems credible – you'd be a bit disappointed if he weren't. He's the one who's apparently running the show, so it is with him that the initial meetings take place. He's keen to do the deed and set up what he no doubt thinks of as his own show, albeit under our auspices. It is all predicated on his claim that he can bring with him the Financial Times account, which is worth at least a quarter of a million a year in billings. There are other potential gains, too, not least with the Rothmans account, where their work on the Raffles brand could and should put us in a good position to develop the business into a full-service through-the-line agency, based on comprehensive below-the-line expertise. And there's a development client in organic baby food, called Baby Organix, which he says will also come with them.

The risk, then, comes down to this: with the Splitter's departure, our core business is, to put it mildly, depleted. If they come, these guys are due to arrive on January 1st and will want necessarily large salaries – north of £80K between the two of them is on the table for discussion. We don't have enough fat in the business to sustain this kind of expenditure for more than a couple of months, before, quite simply, we run out of cash and disappear down a large financial black hole. So it all boils down to how quickly they can bring the business over and start billing (while remembering that billing alone is all very well, but the money itself doesn't arrive for another 60 days – assuming our sturdy but fragrant debt collector can work her traditional magic.) Yet we can't make too much of this: it looks like a seriously good opportunity, and we don't want to frighten them off with talk of high risk or early closure, if quick results aren't achieved. And of course there is every chance that Stid's departure, in itself, will put the wind up them. Are they pinning their hopes on a business which looks like it's imploding?

In the meantime, Stuart wants us to meet Liza, the Account Manager whom he proposes to bring with him, to help him manage the business – or to put it more succinctly, to do the business. He may be the brains behind it, but it soon emerges that she's the one who makes it all happen. Liza turns out to be a strikingly good-looking blonde, with an assertive but noticeably flirtatious personality, whom the Cat and I take to immediately, no doubt for all the wrong reasons. Notwithstanding the obvious sexual attraction, however, it is immediately apparent that the two of them make a very viable and complementary team, and assuming the anticipated business does come in, we see no problems in working with them and expect no problems in them running the business, once acquired. So the success of the venture hinges on the speed of acquisition of new business. Actually, the success of our whole business: if we go with this, we're effectively betting the house on it.

I think we both know though, that however agonising the decision, given our current predicament, there is only one choice. Stay as we are, and we risk death by a thousand cuts, or worse – one big chop. Go with it, and make it work, and we can replace the business the Splitter's taken – almost at a stroke – and give ourselves a real chance to stabilise everything and get things growing again. The carrot of the opportunity is so much bigger than the stick of the threat. With some trepidation then – that stick still hovers in the background and could get bigger and beatier at any moment – we decide to definitely go ahead. They too have elected to continue with the move, despite our split and the fact that we're now half the size we were when discussions started. Who knows what informs their decision: possibly the fact that, while they could go back to base and start again with a new agency, one, they have to find another partner they can get on with, two, this opportunity is so far advanced that psychologically it's a done deal and three, they've probably already made hints and overtures to their key clients with intimations, if not outright facts, about their plans.

From our point of view, one original problem, the accommodation issue – where do we put them in the office? – has gone away. Post split, the top floor is eerily vacant, apart from our Finance Director, Pierre's lockable corner office, so it is entirely logical to install them on their own floor and create a whole new identity. It really is out with the old and in with the new.

The main question remaining is how we structure it in financial and equity terms. There is no question that we are going to have full control over the new entity – otherwise there's the potential for having a fifth column in the business at some future date – but it is equally important from my perspective, and from theirs, that there is real motivation to build, and keep building, the business in the medium to long term. We start with the notion of a wholly owned subsidiary in which we own 51% and they own 49% between them, in a proportion to be negotiated by Stuart – likely to be 30/19 or 35/14, if I have read the runes correctly. We all begin working together on this premise on January 2ⁿᵈ: there is a piece of paper which outlines the basic terms and structure somewhere, which no doubt would form the basis of a contract if tested legally, but it certainly hasn't been drawn up by Biddle & Co, who would undoubtedly pull it to pieces in court if requested. Because everything happens so quickly, the agreement is always (in our minds at least) subject to ratification on the basis of detailed advice from our lawyers and accountants (Grant Thornton, about whom, more later).

This becomes significant several months later. You may surmise from this that the new venture works out, both financially and in terms of business structure and credibility, which I will explore in more depth in a minute. But it eventually emerges that for reasons of both tax structure and business flexibility, we will not be best served having what is essentially a separate legal entity in our midst. By which time, a couple of other considerations have also come into play, which mean that the Cat and I need to re-think our overall longer term structure, if we are to build a business with real value – i.e. one a potential purchaser might pay serious money for at some future, and at this moment very unspecified, date.

The first is that we have two teams in the promotions division headed up by people whom we recognise we need to keep onside. We do not want to lose vital members of our senior team to the siren calls of some flash (that's a relative term in sales promotion, to be fair) London agency, waving a fat cheque book. And the only way to head off the constant threat of higher pay demands is to build in some long-term motivation, to keep the team together through thick and thin. We've had plenty of thin to chew on over the relatively short space of our existence, and it would be nice to experience a bit of thick sometime soon, but the only way to achieve this with any real effectiveness is through equity in the business. If we share some of the equity, they have a real stake in the value of the business – not just the actual value if we were to sell it, but also any dividends we may declare, in the event (oh happy day) of a profitable year and some spare cash to distribute.

The Cat and I, with first Gaylord's and now Stid's departure, control 100% of the business between us (equally), so it's a good job that we at least get along and don't squabble constantly. We are obviously concerned not to lose control of the decision-making to anyone, however vital to the business. It would be a less than delicious irony, were we to become victims of a palace coup by the very people whom we are trying to incentivise to stick with us. The experience we've had with the Splitter is a real warning of what can happen when personality defects, such as delusions of grandeur and over-weaning ambition, overturn what you think are solid business relationships.

The second consideration is that, once the new operation fully settles in and we have a chance to view the dynamics of it all, it soon becomes apparent that Liza is far more important to the success of the venture than had been represented by Stuart at the outset. She may have the title of Account Manager, but she clearly has the clients eating out of her hand – women as well as men –

and is the one who actually delivers the campaigns devised by Stuart, who is the direct marketing technician. So fair enough, he may be the brains behind the business and the senior person in age and experience, but she brings equal benefits to the equation, in our opinion, in terms of campaign delivery and client retention. It doesn't take long for us to realise that, for the long-term health of our enterprise, there is a nettle here that has to be grasped. We have a vision of what our business will look like 'when it's finished' (read The E-Myth for a full understanding) and it dawns on us that we have to get that essential structure in place sooner rather than later. Or in other words now.

What it means in practice is creating a proper senior management team for the whole business, effectively putting in place a succession management, in the event that the Cat and I are ever made an offer we can't refuse. This is going to present one big difficulty, because it's going to drive a coach and horses through the understanding, if not contractually written agreement, we have with Stuart. The trouble is, unless we do renege on that, we will have an unbalanced team, with Stuart the most senior person overall, after us, and to be honest, neither of us thinks he deserves that ranking. Instead, we want to put in place a team of equals, beneath the pair of us, the majority shareholders.

Between them, the lawyers and accountants come up with a concept that we've never heard of, called shadow or phantom shares, whereby the holders of them enjoy all the financial benefits of them (dividends, sale of company) but none of the executive decision-making – and only as long as they remain in the business. They do not have title to the shares, and while they will sit on the Board and contribute to team discussions and decision making, when push comes to shove in the event of any contentious issues or major disagreements, the Cat and I retain complete executive control of the business. It's a principle that would help a lot of small businesses keep key people onside, though I do find that most small business owner/managers are far too selfish to share the spoils of their success with the very people who have significantly helped them to achieve it. In practice, they probably do not reach their full potential, simply because they do not involve their senior people sufficiently in the running, management and long-term vision of their business.

All we have to do now is decide how much we are prepared to give away. There are five people to take into consideration: Stuart and Liza; the Weather Girl and Nick, on the promotions side; and our extremely efficient and trustworthy Finance Director, Pierre. After much number crunching and agonising, we come up with a figure of 6% shareholding of the entire business for everyone except Nick, who gets 2% (we're not that convinced about Nick's long-term future, but we know that if he isn't part of it, he'll walk now, and right now we need a bit of stability). That's 26% of the business we're giving away, leaving us with 37% each. As always in these matters, the end result is a compromise between greed, self-interest and effectiveness. No point in giving up chunks of the business if it isn't going to have the desired effect.

Marketing Principles Direct will trade as a separate entity – or operating division – and its results may be extrapolated and compared with the other teams in the promotions division, but all the finances will be consolidated into one financial statement. If we had gone ahead with the two separate businesses, we are told, it would make the payment of corporation tax less flexible and probably more expensive, because the allowance would be halved between the two companies, and if one is profitable and one is not, we could not use the losses of one to offset the profits of the other. I think that's it. Taxation isn't my long suit, and important though it is to our pockets, my eyes still start to glaze over when we are getting lengthy explanations of the pros and cons of this or that. Yawn. So one business it is. And the very fact that I am explaining all this pre-supposes that the new division is a success and that, somehow, we work our way out of the hole that we (and Stid) have got ourselves into.

Where does all the new business come from? Looking at the billings for the first year, post split, there are three or four dominant contributors. The first is The Financial Times, which the new team do bring on board, as promised, and in very short order – we're billing by month two – sending letters to prospective readers, offering free and reduced price copies over several weeks, to get them into the habit of buying the paper, and which nets us over £420K of income in the first 12 months of trading. Perhaps just as significantly, their work with Rothmans, initially with the Raffles brand which had led to our initial introduction, brings in even more: with a major promotion also breaking on the King Size brand, they end up spending over a million pounds with us in a single year.

Because all of this takes place over a protracted twelve-month period, it isn't immediately apparent that we are going to survive. At the start of January, we are still looking down the barrel, and it is amazing how galvanised the Cat becomes when his livelihood's at risk. Given our (especially his) expertise in the drinks market, he sets out to win drinks business to replace Smirnoff and Baileys. This is no easy task: there are only a handful of major corporations controlling most of the spirits brands in this country (even fewer now, after more mergers and acquisitions), and we've just had the doors of the largest one slammed in our faces. Nevertheless, he goes at it with vigour, and before too long we find ourselves on the pitch list for a major Martini promotion.

I've already documented this in chapter four, but briefly the circumstances are these: for decades, it seems, Martini has used the advertising slogan, "Any time, Any Place, Anywhere." Now the ad agency has persuaded them that it's time for a change. The new campaign is due to be ready any time now, but to no one's surprise except possibly the client, the agency is pleading it needs more time to get it right. Approaching Easter, when drinks sales are higher than at any time except Christmas, and the client needs some stop-gap marketing to fill the void filled by the unfinished ad campaign. Step into the breach an on-bottle sales promotion designed to act as a bridge-head between the old and the new campaign (entitled "Beautiful People") and shift stock. Oh, and also get consumers to trade up to litre bottles. All for a budget of £300K.

Our solution: "Time For Martini" – a Swatch-style watch, with three different strap designs using graphics that reflect the new campaign, but with a proposition that harks back to the old one, free with two proofs of purchase. And here's the creative bit: the cardboard cube bottle collars which we design to communicate the offer have two variants – a standard one for the standard size bottles, and for the litre bottles, a slightly larger one which will have an actual strap incorporated into it (though not the watch itself: you have to send for that, but the one-litre bottle qualifies for one on its own). It's hardly award winning, but it is a neat solution to the brief, and in a six-way pitch (six – honestly, clients) it wins the business. Much celebration, naturally. It seems like it's saved us from ruin. We have a major new drinks brand – and a high-profile one – on the client list. All we have to do is deliver it, on a million bottles. A free watch promotion? Piece of piss. Nothing difficult about that. Well you've already heard what can go wrong earlier, so if you're desperate for a re-run, turn back to page 102, but the main thing is that it gets us through the first half of the year with a decent profit (you can make a healthy margin on watches, believe me), and probably more importantly, it gives us a psychological lift, after all the traumas of the split:

we're back on track, with a new and fully functioning direct marketing department (fully profitable too, almost from day one), and a sales promotion business that is recovering its equilibrium.

Stuart soon gets burdened with the nickname Sheridan Poorly, after some Viz cartoon character, as a result of him always having a sniffle, a bad back or some other non-life-threatening ailment, so will be referred to as Sheridan hereafter.

In addition to Martini, Rothmans and the FT, we also run a major promotion for Holsten (you can see why we describe ourselves as specialists in the vice accounts – pity pole dancing isn't branded: today we'd be doing work for Stringfellows, I swear), and there's another £300K comes in from computer manufacturer AST, which we've somehow acquired, and now we're their main agency, doing everything from brochures to leveraging their sponsorship of Aston Villa (ASTon – yes, I know it's tenuous, but we didn't propose or organise it: we're just using it to promote the brand to the trade). Never heard of AST? Hardly surprising. The business is full of complete wankers and within a couple of years it's gone down the swannee. Or been acquired by some Far East corporation and integrated into its own operation. Or whatever. But again, it helps to keep us afloat. Better than afloat, because when I look at the figures for the year, sales promotion turns over £1.75 million and the new DM division well over £1.1million. Together, the turnover is only just shy of last year's £2.89million, which included the Splitter's £1M of client business. At the start of January, we were looking at forward billings of about £750K at their most optimistic (so you can see how the 'looking down the barrel' phrase may have seemed appropriate). By the year-end, we're planning our futures with confidence and looking up at a clear blue horizon with expectation, devoid of all nervousness.

As the direct marketing business grows rapidly, we have to recruit again, and the whole business takes on a new dynamic. Recruitment and redundancy are recurring themes in any service business, which suffers pronounced peaks and troughs in its financial performance. If we had hung on, and kept all our people when the Splitter left, couldn't we have redeployed them all onto the new business, as and when it comes in? No. Well, partly perhaps, on the promotions side, but direct marketing requires entirely different skill-sets, and therefore we find ourselves recruiting from another side of the market sector. The top floor is soon home to a bevy of fit women, and this time the Cat and I have nothing to do with the process, though we naturally approve of the end-result. There is definitely a trend towards women as marketing service account handlers – maybe it's because they're better at multi-tasking and have better people skills when it comes to massaging clients' egos (while selling our ideas to them). There's Sophie and Lucy and Rebecca and then another Sophie – nicknamed Lady Di as early as her first interview, because she's a striking blonde with hair cut into the famous bob, but whom the Cat subsequently renames 'Smugglers' after she's been with us about a fortnight, when he discovers she's been smuggling into the building, under our very noses, the most magnificent pair of tits, camouflaged by a careful sense of dress. In fact, apart from Rebecca, who's a particularly striking brunette, (I don't shag the staff, but if I did, she'd be number one), we have somehow acquired a stable of blonds who can all turn heads to various degrees, and who are jointly and severally intent on giving the promotions division, with our own blond Weather Girl to the fore, a run for their money.

All of a sudden, there is competition between departments over who's making the most money, and who's doing the most business. Before too long there are minor squabbles over whether this or that bit of business should belong to one department or another. Where projects cross over, agreements have to be made about the split in income. Mostly this is healthy competition, but there are plenty of examples elsewhere of businesses where the competition becomes so intense that it becomes poisonous and ultimately destructive. Keeping that balance and sense of proportion is part of what informs our decision to divide the equity the way we do. If the real financial benefits accrue, no matter who is putting the billings on their figures, then the competition is only ever that of personal self-justification, which is itself a strong enough motivator and needs careful control.

As the de facto heads of department, the Weather Girl and Liza soon start to develop a bit of rivalry which, one senses, is never going to develop into a pally girls-night-out sort of relationship. There are never any rows, shouting matches or tantrums, but there are a few snide comments and catty remarks about the other's looks, performance and working methods. The Weather Girl, as already documented, is known to be close to the Cat, and while they may not still be having it off (the Cat will no doubt put me right when he proof-reads this), there is without doubt the bond of the sometime sexual partner between them. The Weather Girl and I have a perfectly affable and good professional relationship, based more on enjoying each other's company than sexual attraction, which is the safest sort to have at work. In fact, years later, she's the only one I'm still occasionally seeing and having lunch with.

Liza has this disarming habit of putting her arm through yours when you're walking together, and leaning in to you, as if you're already a couple. I'm sure she does this with the Cat too, so I don't kid myself that I'm being singled out for the treatment, but it's clear she's not afraid to use her physical attractions to play both ends against the centre, if necessary, to advance her career.

Neither the Cat nor I give two hoots about the rights and wrongs of work-place relationships (destructive as they can be, if they get in the way of good team building), and both of us are more than happy to take advantage of the situation, if and when the occasion arises. In my case, it goes no further than a snog outside the pub at one of the regular pub crawls, but I know for a fact that my wife thinks she's the potential source of a marriage break-up, and possibly ours. (It doesn't happen, miraculously, given all my bad behaviour, most of which she only suspects – I think). Just for a nano-second, there is real temptation, but then I find she's relayed details of it all to the Cat (he and I have developed the close kind of relationship where we do literally tell each other everything, and trust each other implicitly, which is why the business really starts to prosper: there are no competing egos to get in the way of decision making), and I realise the cynical and manipulative way of her. And because we tell each other everything – well, most things – if anyone is playing both ends against the centre in what becomes known as the battle of the blonds, it's him. Fair play.

The key difference between the two departments is indeed sexual. On the top floor, direct marketing is all women. On the middle (sales promotion) floor, there is a better balance, with enough blokes who enjoy all the usual blokeish talk – sex, sport, drinking, more sex – so there is a good deal more banter all round. In these days of political correctness, the received wisdom is that sexual innuendo in the office (of the oo-er, missus variety) is distasteful to women, who feel offended and disadvantaged by it. My experience of it is that they not only join in with gusto, but are frequently better at it than their male colleagues.

We have Jonners – a big lump of a guy with a passing resemblance to Robbie Coltrane and a nice line in chat – and Spence, a young Brummie with plenty of personality, sparking off one another, and it's not long before the female cabale on the upper floor are dubbed the Stepford Wives. Around this time, I have a PA from Auckland called Megan (she pronounces it Meegan), who's with us for 18 months or so before she goes back to New Zealand, and Spence takes it on himself to teach her to speak proper, like. His core achievement, by the time of her eventual departure is that she can say in an ultra-thick Brummie accent, "Oi'd loik a curray, ploise." No, it isn't much, but bringing culture to the masses is never going to happen overnight.

Are there any real stresses and strains though? There are definitely no fundamental fault lines, of the type which developed into the Splitter's departure, but what is happening is that the relationship between Sheridan and Liza is 'developing', shall we say. Liza was brought in very much as Sheridan's Account Manager – his junior, reporting to him – but it doesn't take very long for her to start punching above her weight. When we start taking on staff in the department, she is the one who organises and manages them and to whom they effectively report. Within the first twelve months she has become the de facto head of operations, with Sheridan playing the role of elder statesman, strategist, and source of knowledge. She senses an opportunity to advance her career and doesn't waste the chance to stick the knife in, if she thinks it gives her a bit more leverage. A ruthless, smiling assassin? A bit over the top perhaps, but there is that definite quality in her.

It emerges – and this is after the decision to divide the shares equally between them – that Sheridan has a porn habit, and Liza most definitely does not approve. She comes to the Cat – it's always the Cat that the staff go to, never me, with their troubles, hopes and fears – and makes a complaint about the images which are occasionally on his computer screen and which she finds offensive. It's strange how women seem to split down the middle on this subject: half of them have a totally laissez-faire attitude to it, even getting turned on by it themselves; the other half find it shocking and disgusting. Obviously Liza's in the latter camp. Well, it's a formal complaint, so we have to take it seriously. The Cat and I, as you will readily guess from what has gone before, are not averse to a bit of high-quality, hard-core porn, but this is putting a considerable strain on a relationship which we need to be as strong as mine and the Cat's. What do we do about it? First up, we need to establish the facts of the matter. Is this a bit of harmless dabbling or is there a bit of an issue here? So we go take a look at his computer one evening, when everyone's left. Oh dear. Serial pornmeister. All sorts of grotesque images downloaded. Close-ups of female genitalia a speciality. Hundreds and hundreds. Frankly, a bit of an embarrassment, getting caught with all that material in your possession. He's obviously not getting enough at home. So we are going to have to have a word.

Sheridan knows the Cat and I are not averse to naked women, on screen or in the flesh, but he has to admit that causing offence to his entirely female staff (naturally they all know precisely what he's up to) undermines his authority, diminishes him as a person, and therefore lessens his effectiveness in the work place. It also fully justifies our original decision to divide the equity the way we do. But what pisses me off more than all of that is the sheer amount of our time he's been wasting on online porn, instead of building the business. Never mind the tits, make us some cash.

There is another issue that emerges too, regarding Sheridan, as a result, rather ludicrously, of a week's work placement by my teenage son, Luke. The school gets them to do work experience in their GCSE year, presumably to start the familiarisation process of what it's like out there in the big bad world of work. I have mixed feelings about how useful it really is: by definition, they get a sample of one, so they might get lucky and have a really positive time, or they might end up in the direst place on earth. Rather than doing a bit of work to try to find somewhere else, Luke takes the line of least resistance and asks if he can come and work in our office: the school is happy, because they think they have another option for placing their recalcitrant youth in future years. (I soon disabuse them of that. If you're going to do it, you have to find something constructive for them to do, that's useful both to them and you; this is not only difficult, but takes time and effort which you can really ill afford). It is invidious for him to work in my group, so I get Sheridan and Liza to accommodate him, and they set him up with some relatively simple administrative tasks that need doing but which no one has the desire or time to do. It is a perfectly sensible system, but you do feel like you're creating a 5-day lesson plan which gives the teachers a(nother) break.

So there he is on the top floor, beavering away at whatever they've given him to do and keeping his head down, but absorbing everything that's going on around him (which, I grant you, is possibly the main point of the exercise, educationally speaking). You would think, wouldn't you, with the boss's son in attendance, that you might temper any behaviour that might be perceived as less than professional? After two or three days, however, Luke tells me he's surprised how rude Sheridan is to his staff, frequently shouting, hectoring and generally berating them. His management style, from the description I'm given, borders on bullying in the work place. This is news to me and the Cat, since we've never had any inkling or reportage of such from Liza or Pierre, our finance director, whose office is off their work space and would surely see signs. There again, we never saw or heard any of what was going on in the studio a few years back, so we feel we need at least to ask some questions around the house.

It turns out that his management style is exactly as Luke has reported, which is no surprise to me – he isn't given to over-exaggeration or flights of fancy – but does pose a problem. What to do about it? Apparently the girls just accept that that's the way he is, and he might behave like a right tosser, but what do you expect: he's a man. Everyone's just put up with his little peccadilloes, and because she's already made one formal complaint about the porn, Liza probably thinks that if she steps up to the plate on this issue as well, then their future business relationship really is on the rocks. And she'd be quite right, I'd say. The Cat and I aren't going to put up with it though: we have a very definite management style – we're all going to work as hard as we have to, to achieve our objectives, but we're going to have as much fun in the process as is possible in the circumstances. Work hard, play hard. Firm but fair. We have no time for unnecessary shouting – at people, in particular. Anyone who has worked with me will have a wry smile (or worse) at this point, since I have a reputation for shouting when things go wrong, but mainly at things – like the bloody computer freezing again, just as you've finished a lengthy document, but before you've saved the contents. I have come close to throwing the damn thing through the window and down into the courtyard below, more than once. But I do try very hard not to shout *at* people. It achieves little except alienation.

So the Cat, as self-selected human resources expert, takes Sheridan to one side and (instead of leaving him there, as I might have done) introduces him to the uncomfortable facts. His behaviour is inappropriate, ineffective and is doing him no favours – not least with the two of us: the equity decision is still further reinforced. I'm not sure it is positioned as a verbal warning, but I am sure that that is the way it comes across. It will certainly go on his personnel record for future reference, just in case we have to revisit the problem. We're certainly not envisaging having to fire him, but if things were to deteriorate and push comes to shove, we've been to one industrial tribunal, and we know that the more written evidence you have the better, to back up any decision you make.

I think Sheridan is genuinely surprised by the allegations. We have to tell him they come from several sources, so there is no chance of any recriminations, and Luke's name is never mentioned. I suspect he has turned into this ogre without him even realising it, because if it were deliberate and conscious, he would surely have mitigated it in Luke's presence. As so often, people who find themselves in charge of a few employees equate management with giving orders. He's obviously never played a team sport seriously, so doesn't properly understand the team ethic. We should probably send him on a leadership course, but actually let's just see if the bollocking improves matters. It seems to, though without Luke's presence we don't have any objective witness who doesn't have an axe to grind.

Nine

The Cat and Dave Show

NOTWITHSTANDING SHERIDAN'S little peccadilloes, we are now entering a period of calm, emerging on the sunny uplands of relative financial security after a long climb through sweaty and near-impenetrable rain-forest. Finally it is possible to see where we are going, to plan with confidence, and generally to relax and have some fun again. The nature of the fun must necessarily change a bit of course, as the constitution of the Board is no longer exclusively male. We now have two women – the Weather Girl and Liza – alongside Sheridan, Nick, Pierre, the Cat and me, so the old jaunts akin to stag weekends are off the agenda forever.

As we approach the end of the first year with our direct marketing colleagues, we realise it is also the company's 10th birthday. Thanks to Pierre's careful cash-flow management, and Julia's assiduous cash-collection activities, we have money in the bank, and it seems appropriate to spend a bit on a celebration that will bring closer together the two departments and make the business a holistic one in practice – as opposed to the theory of our new business presentation to prospective clients. What should we do though? Take everyone off for a celebration some-where obviously. But where, and at what cost? We could take over the Manoir for a day, but many of them have been there with us several times, so no novelty there. Fancy hotels and restaurants in the UK, weekends in London are all deemed too so-so. But if we're going abroad, there's the cost of flights to consider, plus the Cat and I have quartered most of the fancy capitals of Europe in our stag weekend phase, so we don't want to re-tread old ground there. That rules out Amsterdam (shame, but probably a blessing), Copenhagen, Madrid, Barcelona, Rome and Nice. The one place we've never been is Paris, which may seem odd, given it's my spiritual second home, having lived there for a year as a student, and I know it as an old friend. Given that I still go there every second year for the France-England rugby match, with the local rugby club crowd, I don't feel the need to promote its many charms to my co-Directors, and they have never suggested it independently. Now, however, and still without any prompting from me, it becomes prime candidate. It's close enough to get there relatively quickly, it has all the boxes ticked in terms of status and image, and it quickly gets the vote. The Cat and Julia are delegated to make all the arrangements in secret and to create an itinerary. The rest of the staff are told we're celebrating our 10th anniversary by taking them on a mystery tour – they're to turn up at such and such a time one Friday, and to bring their passport and overnight bag, but no mention is made of destination. How long can we keep it secret? In a business this size, the chances are slim of making it all the way to the airport departure gate (Eurostar has yet to become the option we would undoubtedly have taken today), but in fact, unless they're all very good actors, no one seems to know for sure, until that moment when we lead them to the gate.

We enjoy an extremely convivial and generally civilised couple of days, only slightly marred by having chosen a date when the French transport unions are on strike (again), so the Metro is barely functioning, the city centre is paralysed by traffic and the coach journey from the airport takes two hours instead of twenty minutes. It would have been quicker and more fun if we'd walked the last couple of miles, leaving the bus to deliver our luggage, and popped in to a few bars en route, but eventually we arrive at our hotel in a quiet courtyard, right in the heart of the Latin quarter, just off Boulevard St Germain.

Dinner is planned for a traditional restaurant with panelled dining-room a short walk away, called Le Procope (think the French version of Rules in London), and quite excellent it turns out to be. We eat well, drink well, exchange Secret Santa gifts and unaccountably, perhaps because Paris is such a civilised and sophisticated place, there are none of the usual behaviour or noise problems. Some of the younger staff can't hold their drink and get pissed – one account executive from the direct marketing department returns from the toilets to announce she's just been sick in her knickers. (More tea, vicar?) It is left to our imagination how this feat probably occurred, but the felony is compounded when she is asked if she's therefore thrown them away: no, they're her best pair, so they're in her pocket.

From there, we have a coach to take us to some club/disco at Etoile. I used to walk from Etoile to the school I was assistant at during my year there, but never came across it: hardly surprising – it's on the narrow outer ring that goes all round the Arc de Triomphe, on the opposite side from the Champs Elysees. According to the Cat, who knows (and cares) about these things, it's supposed to be the place to be. It's certainly well appointed and the clientele well heeled, so he's probably right: the sort of place I couldn't have afforded as a student (if it existed then), and now that I can, I'm damned if I want to. It's full of allegedly beautiful people having vacuous conversations about mindless trivia, to the back-drop thump of crappy disco music – this being France, there's nothing cutting edge about the music. Luckily there's a nicely furnished chill-out room, where you can drink and chat, so excursions on the dance floor can be limited. I'm not planning to get off with any of the staff, and the chances of pulling any of the local totty with my rusty French (and age) are somewhere between nul and zéro.

I find loud music, unless it's very good and preferably live, only bearable for shortish periods, so being there for a couple of hours turns into a test of endurance, which, like all things, eventually stops. I have tinnitus in one ear, so even conversation in a lot of background noise is difficult, and it is with a sense of relief that a move is made to depart by our (non-dancing) clique. We leave the young things to strut their stuff – and later to walk up to Montmartre just before dawn in various states of disarray – and I, for one, show my age by retiring early (alright 3.00am). After a morning 'at leisure' as the travel itineraries put it, the return journey the next day is a necessarily restrained affair, but it's all passed off successfully, and there has no doubt been plenty of 'bonding' between the staff. The business must be maturing and/or I must be getting old, because there doesn't seem to be anything for me to be embarrassed about, memories of which generally come flooding back like a bad dream in the next 48 hours.

We now enter a period of stability and sustained growth – probably inextricably linked. We actually have time to relax and enjoy life, even while still having to put in those occasional long hours. Clients are demanding, as they are entitled to be when they spend £2million with you, as Rothmans do in the year following our 10th birthday, but things are generally quiet, settled and extremely pleasant. Our offices may be a touch inaccessible, tucked away, as they are, in a courtyard off a small alleyway off a pedestrian-only thoroughfare, but the centre of Oxford is a pleasant place to work: we are extremely quiet where we are (unlike our company nights out), but a mere 50 metres away is the buzzy heart of a city that consistently tops polls of places people would most like to live and work. God knows why: it's not that brilliant. It is of course the university that gives it its cachet, and its particular town v gown dynamic; without it, it would be little better than Basildon or Luton.

Because our offices are built on university land (surprise, surprise: they say you can travel from Oxford to Cambridge and never leave land owned by one or other of the universities – is this true or just urban myth?) and adjoin the Oxford Union, which is effectively our head landlord, we have a relationship that permits a few liberties. The alleyway runs down to the Union's main entrance, past our courtyard, and walking through the Union and out into the grounds, we can exit into the back entry in St Michael Street, where all the celebrities who speak here are taxied in and out. This cuts all of 50 metres off our normal walk, but it seems we are permitted to do so, and therefore we do, probably just because we can. It gives us a bit of an insight into current student life, in the slightly rarefied atmosphere of Britain's premier establishment (Cambridge? who cares?) and while we don't actually drink in the bar there – it's a pretty seedy affair in reality and we're not that desperate for cheap drinks – we probably could if we wanted. There is no security to speak of (I bet that's changed now). So as long as your face is recognised by the usual uniformed jobsworths, we can pretty much come and go as we please.

The only time security is stepped up is when someone great or good comes to speak at one of the Union debates. We see them all come and go, from American Presidents (both Hopalong and Clinton make appearances) to Diego Maradona, who entertains the assembled throng with a lengthy bout of keep-up, using a golf ball. This makes the (local) evening news: needless to say, no mention is made of the actual debate, whose subject entirely eludes me. You can always tell when someone of particular note is due to make an appearance, because you turn up for work at 8.30 in the morning and there's a queue of students, who you'd normally expect to be sleeping off the effects of last night's binge drinking marathon (oh no, I forgot, this is 90's Oxford, not 60's London), snaking down the alleyway and along Cornmarket. The bigger the name, the longer the queue, and you might expect, with a cerebral establishment like Oxford, that names like Yasser Arafat and Bill Clinton would pull the biggest crowds. Well of course they are popular, but I have to report that the biggest queue I witness in the ten years we are in the city centre is for … wait for it … Jerry Springer. Yup. Longer than for any of the American Presidents or past British Prime Ministers. Speaks volumes about the current state of both society and education, don't you think?

Usually of course, the alleyway at 8.30 in the morning is deserted; there's a cellar bar half way along with a reputation for loud live heavy metal music – you generally need tattoos to be allowed in – and the stale smells of last night's beer can sometime be detected, if the delivery lorry is making an appearance (it's the only time of day you can get reasonably unfettered access). On the left-hand side is a blank wall with two fire-doors set into it, which are the emergency exits for the department store in the adjacent shopping arcade. The alcoves into which these are set are occasionally used as hang-outs for disaffected youths and the homeless. There's a hostel for homeless people right in the city centre, and a drop-in centre round the corner in St Michael Street, and there are days when you feel sure you're in some third-world country, there are so many beggars. You can certainly not walk from our offices to the bus station (400 yards tops) without being accosted at least three times en route. What is clearly happening is that not all the beggars are homeless: for some, it's a lifestyle choice, or simply a way of getting some easy money to buy a few drinks. We have for example the intellectual beggar, usually to be found in St Giles reading something literary (not Harold Robbins) and muttering sotto voce, "Got any spare change?" as you go by. Apparently he's also to be found most evenings in a pub in Jericho supping Stella.

Then there's the sob story: you're literally accosted with some cock and bull tale of woe. One such – a chap in his twenties, pretty smartly dressed, claims he hasn't got the money for his bus ticket to Aylesbury – can I see him right with a couple of quid, so he can get home? I call his bluff: I'm on my way to Aylesbury and will gladly give him a lift, at which he declines, with the admission, "I only wanted a drink." No wonder the genuinely homeless find it tough, with competition like this. There's a little guy on crutches who's obviously a genuine case and seems to have taken up residence in our alleyway – he's there most mornings, as we arrive, in one of the fire-door alcoves. He doesn't help his cause by shouting banter and abuse at the various passers-by, but inevitably as familiarity sets in, you start to respond less dismissively, and he becomes a bit less challenging. I'm not sure we ever quite get on to discussions about the weather or the meaning of life, but the daily exchanges do take on a more cordial tone. He's there for months and months, even though it's clear he's medically unwell, quite apart from the crutches, which soon enough become his nickname. And then he disappears, as suddenly as he arrived, and you start to wonder what became of him: death, hospitalisation, a new home, or just a better life? That's in the order of probability, by the way.

The alleyway may be peopled generally by students, the homeless and the heavy metal brigade, but it also acts as a shield against the thousands of shoppers in the city centre. Two or three times in quick succession, someone pops out for something from the shops (that's the benefit of being so central) and comes back to announce Cornmarket is deserted and roped off again: for a while there are bomb scares about once a month, it seems, but tucked away in our little hidey-hole, no one thinks to come and evacuate us (apart from once, when we spend a fruitless after-noon kicking our heels in some local hostelry, cursing the police for their jobsworth-ness). Given our location, it would take a bomb the size of an articulated lorry to cause any injury, and since there clearly aren't any vehicles at all in the pedestrianised Cornmarket, what is the worst that could happen? No bombs are ever found, and most people assume it's disaffected former employees of some local firm or nutters that are responsible. Then, years later, when Waterstones are having a major re-fit, they apparently find three or four unexploded fire bombs, tucked away behind books on shelves where presumably stock turnover is particularly low. So not all hoaxes, but still hardly a threat to life and limb.

Right next to our courtyard entrance are the steps down to The Crypt, a Davy's wine bar that we use as general canteen and for casual customer entertainment. It's a dimly lit series of arched cellars running under (and owned by) the Oxford Union, with sawdust on the floor and a slightly musty smell. One day we get a visit from someone at the Union to announce that there's water (or something less wholesome) getting into it from above, and they're going to have to dig up our courtyard, from where the presumed leak is reckoned to be emanating, to fix it. It's not a big courtyard, it's paved in brick and is surrounded on all sides by the built environment. We endure months of drilling, piles of earth, exposed pipes and general noise and nuisance – twice. The first time, they fill everything in and re-pave, only to find they haven't cured the problem, and up it all comes again. This time they coat the whole of the roof of the cellar arch, exposed beneath the pipes, with solid black tar, so nothing can get through. It sounds petty, I know, but the noise and disruption gets quite dispiriting, and there is a feeling of utter relief when they finally disappear, not to return.

You will look in vain for the Crypt today, however, for shortly afterwards (and probably the reason for all the work in the first place), the university decides it wants the place back for its own use, and when the lease comes up for renewal, it helpfully trebles the rent, to ensure Davy's don't renew. Well, that's the way it is told to us by the then current management. Whatever, it eventually closes, and if you seek it now, you will find in its place a (strictly) student bar called the Purple Turtle – about as tasteless as you can get, but that's progress.

Being in the centre of town, of course, also makes you potentially exposed to intruders, and during our time there we have two different types. The first is relatively benign, but a nuisance: not long after we install a drinks machine in the lobby outside reception, we discover a group of youths helping themselves to the free drinks we make available to our staff. It turns out they're from the secretarial college that shares offices in the courtyard, they've discovered this free resource and are availing themselves of it. The brass neck of it. We tell them their fortunes and fuck them off out of it, but around this time we also have an incident in which some blackguard walks in off the street during a quiet moment around lunchtime and removes one of our top-of-the-range Apple Macs from the studio. Just like that. What with that and the odd Mr Sweary coming in to berate our receptionist, it is with some regret that we feel the need to have an entry-phone installed on the front door, to deter the wankers. The code is 6610 (1066 back to front) and in case the alarm, linked to the police station, goes off accidentally, the code word when they call before sending someone to investigate in person, to reassure them that they do not need to respond, is "Hastings". We figure everyone will be able to remember that, but it's random enough not to be guessable.

The second intrusion is more serious, though in the event still no more than another nuisance. We arrive one morning to find we've been burgled. Contents of desks have been rifled and keys left all over the place. They've apparently got in through a window on the top floor (who left that open? slapped wrists), across the roofs of the surrounding buildings. The buildings behind – and linked to – us are the shops and offices on Cornmarket and are a complete labyrinth, going all the way down to St Michael Street, so they could have gained entry at a dozen points or more. Once in, they've obviously tried to find an easier means of egress, hence the keys, which have been used to try to unlock the front door (unsuccessfully) and, having opened the studio window onto the courtyard, the heavy-duty metal gates which guard the entrance to it. (Clanging it shut – I'm often the last to leave – at the end of a long day, I always mentally intone, "Norman Stanley Fletcher … ") If they have any chance of removing anything substantial from the premises, they're not going to be hoiking it over the roof-tops, so they have to find a more amenable way out, and this is where they make a big mistake. There is a fire door in the courtyard as a safe means of escape in the event of a major conflagration, and it leads into, and through, the adjoining Oxford Union. We've never tested it, but these boys do. Given its status as prime British establishment, and therefore potential terrorist target (I've seen more than one cabinet minister wandering around, from my desk and through the only window that looks into the place), and once the opened door had set off the alarm, I'm guessing the police took about two minutes to get there, even at 2.00 or 3.00 in the morning.

Our intruders hasten back into our building and scarper

whence they came, taking with them a few hundred pounds of retail vouchers, which someone has carelessly left in their desk drawer from some incentive scheme. I know: you never think it's going to happen to you. Until it does. The vouchers of course should have been in the safe in Pierre's locked office. If only we had one. That's when we get one (sound of horses bolting and stable doors being shut). Still, it could have been a lot worse, and it does show that, in spite of our central location, so long as we use all of the security measures at our disposal (like shutting the bloody windows – that won't happen again), we are pretty difficult to infiltrate. It's probably only the computers that are worth nicking anyway, and getting them through those "Porridge" gates is always going to be a challenge. Probably too big a challenge for most burglars, who are looking for easier pickings.

So much for the petty goings on associated with any city centre location. What about the business? Having stabilised the ship after the Splitter's departure, and having celebrated ten years of survival, we realise we have a real chance to grow to the sort of size we originally envisaged. I seem to remember having £5million turnover as a target after five years, which for various reasons (Gaylord, the Splitter, events, events) is still not achieved after double that time, but we can now see it as an achievable objective in the not too distant future. And the next piece of business we win will be fundamental to its attainment – and to the events which transpire thereafter. But it's not so much the value of the business we win that is so interesting (vital though that is to our long-term aims), but the manner of it.

The Marketing Director of Rothmans has rocked up, via an abortive role at some sports goods manufacturer, at Mirror Group Newspapers (prop. R Maxwell – another Oxford connection; Editor – Piers Morgan, motormouth and not short on hubris). Not long after his arrival, they issue a sales promotion brief, liberally shared around his various agency mates, no doubt. We know it's competitive – well, it would be with half a million big ones at stake – but you never know how many they've scattered it around. They may say three or four (which is the received wisdom), but that doesn't mean they haven't disseminated it to twice that number. I remember some bunch of wankers at a shower company in Rugby running a six-way pitch for a bit of business that was worth about £20K. Naturally we didn't win it: we went through the motions of presenting ideas (all of which would have achieved their objectives) but frankly we just didn't give a damn, and no doubt it showed. It didn't help that the client was some wet-behind-the-ears 22-year-old, fresh out of college with some marketing qualification and trying to act like a bigshot. I hope the business went where it should have done, to some local one- or two-man band outfit, who would actually care about them and their products, but I've no real confidence that it did. The client probably wanted to work with a big agency that would look good on her CV two years later when she moved on, rather than someone who would do good work and care. Big agency + low budget = low priority: put the trainee (or the cleaner) on it.

On the other hand, a half-million-pound brief to create sales promotions that will strengthen the Daily Mirror's sales, stabilise its position as Britain's 2nd most read paper, after The Sun, and head off the increasing challenge from the Mail for that moniker, is more than enough to get our interest and attention. We put our best minds to it. And we conclude that the premise behind the brief is fatally flawed. You cannot use sales promotion to generate trial and repeat purchase – not with newspapers – or at least if you do, you'll have to spend a small fortune on gifts and prizes to people who would have largely bought the paper anyway. Getting people to change the paper they read is a lot like changing the cigarettes they smoke: because it's a habit, you have to have in place a promotional structure that ensures they read (or smoke) your product for at least a fortnight, and preferably a month, until the new habit is ingrained. Given our experience with both cigarettes (Rothmans King Size, Raffles, inter alia) and newspapers (the Financial Times), we are for once in a perfect position to pitch for the business by challenging the brief, something we've never been in the habit of doing: sales promotion might help engender loyalty with existing readers, but to generate trial and repeat purchase from new readers, more sophisticated and targeted direct marketing techniques are called for.

There's nothing creative about the promotional hook we are going to employ: we're going to identify Sun and Mail readers (half the country has filled in lifestyle questionnaires at some point, so there's an awful lot of information available on the man in the street, if you go looking), and mail them an offer, in the form of dated vouchers, of 12 free copies of the paper over a fortnight, followed by 12 more at half price (money-off vouchers) over the next two weeks. They simply redeem them at their local newsagent, who reclaims the value from the Mirror at the end of the week or month, via the standard voucher clearing house process. Nearly all money-off vouchers go through a company called Nielsen in Northampton, and have for donkey's years. They put a small handling charge on every one and, via the many a mickle makes a muckle principle, have developed a prosperous business, thanks to the zillions of vouchers used a day for promotional purposes on every conceivable consumer product. We know it works, because our direct mail experts have been using the technique successfully on the Financial Times for some considerable time. And if money off works with the middle classes who read the FT, it's an open and shut case with the working-class types who make up the Mirror's readership.

All we need is a creative hook to get their attention – that's the client as well as potential readers: we're still in a four- (six-? eight-?) way pitch. What we come up with is a master stroke, even though I say so myself. Data-driven printing is still in the relatively early stages of its development. Readers Digest and their ilk use it to scatter your name and address details liberally through their communications pieces, but the sophistications that are now widely available through digital printing are still in their infancy. We find a way of creating a small facsimile of the Mirror's front page, with an offer in the headline personalised to the recipient in 36-point type. What the fuck does that mean, I hear you say. **"FREE COPIES OF THE MIRROR FOR JOHN SMITH"** (assuming your name is John Smith, naturally) as a front-page headline, that's what it means. Tens of thousands of test mailers, all with different headlines on. You may still not buy the Mirror if you receive it, but I bet it'll get your attention and you'll read it. And really you can't ask for much more of any campaign.

It wins us the business. Much celebrating naturally. Tempered with caution. The Mirror is a basket case. Maxwell is renowned for not paying his bills. He has a reputation for forcing suppliers to take him to court for payment and then settling on the courtroom steps. That's after a late offer of settlement in full and final, etc – if you'll knock another 10% off the bill. Some may call that astute business. I'd call him an obnoxious cunt, and I've yet to meet anyone who worked for him (and I've met a few of his direct line managers over the years) who shed any tears over his demise. We assume we won't be working for them for long, simply because of their reputation for fickleness and unreliability in the industry. If you'd told us then that we'd still be working for them at the dawn of the new millennium, we'd have expressed more than mild surprise and disbelief. I suppose the fact that the relationship prospers is testament to the effectiveness of the campaigns. Under severe pressure from the Mail, our give-away/money off activity keeps the paper in the coveted number two slot for the thick end of 18 months – 20-30,000 copies being the crucial difference.

When our first mailer is placed on (then Editor) Piers Morgan's desk for his comments (scathing comments about wanky marketing anticipated), it is with some pleasure and pride that we hear it is greeted with the simple words, "That's pretty cool."

How big and important a win is it? I think the figures speak for themselves. During the next twelve months, the Mirror will spend as much as the FT with us, and together they will contribute nearly £1.25million of revenue – regular campaign activity that can be put in the forward billings with an above average degree of confidence. Together, they transform us from sales promotion agency doing a bit of direct marketing to a fully-fledged through-the-line outfit, capable of running all aspects of any marketing campaign, including advertising. And that, in turn, gives us the confidence to promote ourselves to a broader audience: in spite of the lip-service paid to 'integrated' campaigns, the truth is that most client businesses still compartmentalise their marketing, treating direct marketing as one specialism, sales promotion as another, and advertising as a (much more important) third. So new business means targeting the Marketing Director who controls it all, rather than the Marketing Managers who implement strategy, who have been our first port of call during the first decade.

New business is a vital component in our operational structure and one which we've never really cracked. We've done lots of marketing of one sort and another, but we've never put together what you might describe as a long-term strategy or campaign. (Physician, heal thyself, I hear you say). Most of our biggest clients have come as a result of either referrals or targeted mailings. We sent IDV an unsolicited idea for a promotion for Smirnoff (a free tin of caviar – which never ran: why not?) That got us through the door and on the pitch list. Rothmans came the same way: the result of a promotion idea sent cold. The FT came with the new DM guys; the Mirror was an ex-client who moved and effectively took us (or at least the opportunity) with him (thanks, Charles, by the way). But all of this activity is occasional: big spurts of stuff (oo-er) every now and again, when we have the time and inclination to do it, or are desperate and looking down the barrel.

New business is one of my responsibilities in the post-Splitter regime, though even before then, it has more or less always devolved to me, with the others chipping in their fourpence-worth. We try appointing someone as New Business Manager, and within a couple of years are on our third or fourth, which tells you all you need to know about their success ratio. Our first effort is a striking, tall, leggy brunette in her 20's (yes, I know, straight off the casting couch: all right, officer, we'll come quietly), with a nice telephone manner but no previous in the industry. Helen. We give her a year, in which the activity reports always make promising reading, but nothing concrete ever happens, before finally suggesting that new business might not actually be her métier. It is with lots of regret that we let her go, and not just because she's fit – she fits in with the team too – but in the end this is a purely results-driven exercise, a numbers game, in which the only number that matters is the one in the bottom right corner of the summary sheet. Maybe I didn't manage her well enough; maybe we should have given her some proper sales training; maybe I should have given her more support. Maybe, but if you're not careful, you end up doing their job for them – having a dog and barking yourself. You have to give people clear objectives and the responsibility for achieving them, otherwise you end up like most small business owner/managers: trying to do everything, because no one does anything quite as well as you'd do it yourself. This is arrant nonsense anyway, but as anyone will tell you, sales is the hardest slot to fill in any organisation, and genuinely good operators can pretty much name their price (and often do.)

After Helen comes Barry – a balding American with the gift of the gab and a convincing line in sales patter at the interview. We buy all his sales talk and think we're on to a winner – like all who sign on the dotted line, we want it all to be true. OK, so he thinks he can sell snow to eskimoes, but can he sell marketing services to big, hard-bitten corporate clients – figuring out, along the way, who are the real decision makers and influencers in any department where he gets through the door? And having got in, does he know enough about our business to convince them to give us a shot?

The answer, many months down the track, is provided on the front page of *The Unprincipled*, a scurrilous piss-take of the business and the people in it, produced occasionally by Nick, the Cat and the creative department. For our Christmas bash, we take the staff for an afternoon's team building, driving quad bikes, Pilot cars and the like, followed by dinner and an overnight stay at Charingworth Manor, a pretty and suitably upmarket Cotswolds hotel for us to embarrass ourselves (and the other guests) at. With our numbers we'll have reserved most of the rooms, but pity the poor saps who've booked in for a romantic weekend, not realising they'll be tagged on to the fringes of Oxfordshire's premier piss-up. And the latest edition of *The Unprincipled* is unveiled and distributed before dinner.

You may change the names a bit to protect the innocent, much as I have done in this diary, but with only a couple of dozen people in the business, everyone knows who is referred to in every situation. Nearly everyone's little ways and foibles are exposed to mirth, and when this goes into formal print as a properly published book, I'm wondering whether I should incorporate a copy as exhibit 'A' for the prosecution (if there isn't one here, the printing was too expensive). For the record, the front-page head-line runs, **"Barry Is The New Bond – The Man With The Golden Dome Is Back."** It uses the photo-shopped poster graphics of a new James Bond film, "*Goldeneye*," to parody the failing new business efforts, featuring Barry as Bond and a new sub-title: "**New Business Never Comes**." It's both funny and cruel at the same time, and while the rest of the staff also get plenty of stick, there's no doubting who the star of this pig-circus is. While having a laugh, the producers of this less than subtle organ are saying effectively what everyone else is thinking: he's on a fat salary, he's a quirky American with no track record, he's producing plenty of paper to cover his tracks, quite ineffectually, but ultimately they (and I) all know: he's failed to produce the goods.

New business in all sales arenas is a numbers game, and in our business the numbers are quite limited. Working primarily with blue-chip brand names, even doing business-to-business work as well as consumer marketing, and having added direct marketing to the specialist offering, there are still only two or three thousand contacts out there. We know who and where most of them are, because we pay for a monthly updated database of marketing personnel in all key companies, called (at the time) Black Box. The job of the Business Development Manager, as he or she is called, is to get messages to as many of these as possible, in order to a) get us through the door for initial talks and credentials presentations, b) on the pitch list when one is eventually formu-lated, or indeed in a perfect world, which rarely exists, c) get auto-matically appointed and start work.

Of course, as with our own client list, many have happy and stable relationships with an existing agency or roster of agencies and aren't really looking around. That doesn't stop junior members of staff setting up credentials meetings for their own training and education of course (not that they'd admit what they're doing), and it's hard to turn down such invitations. They may – almost certainly will – lead to nothing in the immediate future, but the junior client may one day (and it often doesn't take that long – a couple of years, maybe) turn into a senior decision maker. So is it worth having a conversation with someone who may (or may not – they may leave to pursue other careers entirely: not everyone is suited to the world of marketing or finds it exciting and glamorous) at some future point give you work? All sales is about relationship building, and the short answer is that you have to kiss a lot of frogs – starting and continuing to build relationships with as many people as is humanly possible, on the basis of a numbers game for which, over time, you refine the maths. Eg 100 cold calls = 5 meetings = 2 warm prospects = I eventual (note the use of that word) client. It's never that clear-cut of course. As with Holsten, sometimes business comes right out of left-field and it's hard to put your finger on what triggers it, but you know that, whatever else, you won't get any meetings, briefs or business unless they know you exist and what you stand for.

So the job of new business is to co-ordinate sales calls and contacts on the back of an effective programme of marketing, and build a sales pipeline. Over the years we've done some good and some relatively ineffective marketing, to try to raise awareness of our very existence, never mind what we stand for. The wrap-around cover on *Marketing* magazine was a brilliant stunt, and it certainly upped our profile, but we never consolidated that with an ongoing programme of activity. In a business-to-business environment, there are not that many ways to get your voice heard. The various options include:

- Producing a brochure and sending it to as many people as possible. We do this from the very early days and it works, up to a point. Most go in the bin or into a giant filing cabinet labelled, 'Useful Suppliers' that may as well have 'Bin' labelled on it.
- Running trade press advertising. Good for awareness but expensive: you have to do it and keep doing it, to get anything out of it.
- PR: the way this works best is if someone in the business can get a reputation as a guru of the industry and is asked to comment and write on key issues of the day in the various trade press titles. To do this, you have to put yourself about a bit, and generally get yourself known in the industry as one of the movers and shakers. To this end, in recent years, I've been on the committees of both the Institute of Sales Promotion and the Sales Promotion Consultants Association, and ploughed up to London regularly for some yawn-inducing meetings, few of which achieve much.

I've written a few articles, and we've generally handled PR in-house. We do appoint an agency for a year or more, to try to professionalise the process, but the fact that they achieve no more than we do ourselves means we eventually dispense with them. The fact that the name of the outfit escapes me says it all, but surely there must be some good operatives out there who could have done it better than us. We suffer from cobbler's children syndrome (always the worst shod in the village – too busy making shoes for all the rest): our PR goes out when it floats to the top of our in-tray and/or the spirit moves us. We never do it consistently enough. An outside specialist must be the sensible route. The trouble is we're so cynical about PR practitioners – there are so many flaky individuals out there, charging a grand or two a month and achieving no more than we do with our own desultory efforts – that we can't bring ourselves to go out, find the best and pay the money. When the first experiment fails, we never repeat it.

- Awards and league tables: these are an extension of PR in all honesty. Winning awards gets you column inches in the trade press and marks you as successful by industry peers and clients alike. To win them, though, you have to work on big, high-profile accounts where the campaigns achieve credibility through their sheer visibility, or on small accounts where you are allowed to produce quirky, innovative ideas that catch the eyes of the judges by their very unusualness. We get close with the Smirnoff light-up badges promotion, and finally strike gold with some work for Alfred Dunhill that only stands out because of lack of competition in its rather arcane category. I cannot remember for the life of me the campaign that actually wins it, but for those of you not immersed in the world of sales promotion, it would probably generate a bout of sniggering. When they announce the winners at the glittery black-tie ceremony (cue a thousand bright young 20-somethings to get horribly pissed and lairy), the famous name parachuted in to try to make them look important and try to keep order (rarely successfully) can barely suppress their scorn for the laughable titles given to allegedly the best work done by the industry for a whole year. As an agency, we are not very good at awards, but we go through the motions, play our part, have a go; occasionally we get a Highly Commended, and feature as a bit-part player in the Awards catalogue that showcases all the winners. We never find the magic bullet that strikes real pay-dirt.

League tables are another thing altogether. They simply

show how big you are. So in the early days you make a virtue of being small and fleet of foot, and don't bother to participate in the process. Half the agencies lie about their turnover anyway (I know: it should be a matter of public record, but the bigger units have several arms, are part of bigger groups, and journalists are notoriously lazy at checking facts.) As you grow, and start to play the game, it is important that you are seen to be climbing the table – ie getting bigger and more successful – rather than slipping back. Around our 10th or 11th year, we finally make it into the top twenty, though by that time you could argue that we're half sales promotion, half direct marketing. Bugger it: we put the total turnover figure into both categories at the appropriate time, like everyone else. You have to play the game if you want to achieve any sort of stand-out.

- Telemarketing: these days you associate this with call centres in Bangalore and a sense of irritation, but cold calling, and follow-up calls once proper contact has been made, are an essential part of the sales process, in any market sector, not just ours. So new business people have to be good on the phone: confident, relaxed, knowledgeable, friendly but determined to achieve their objective – which is to get appointments with hot prospects. Define a *hot* prospect: one who controls a worthwhile budget (3M taught me to seek out the MAN – the person with the Money, the Authority and the Need, and those words of wisdom still hold good); one who is actively considering appointing a new agency to do the work; er, that's it. Everyone else who is 'looking around' is just a prospect. The rest, whom we haven't got a line into yet, are still suspects. Being good on the phone isn't the only thing, but it is a critical part of the operative's skill-set if they're going to be successful, and it is still the hardest thing to find in prospective employees; few people are good at or enjoy (the two are linked) telephone selling, so if you are, you'll be in demand and able to name your price. You have to be organised too – knowing how to use a CRM system (and actually doing so) – but most of it is about phone manner, attitude and determination. As one Hollywood actor put it, you have to be sincere: once you've got that cracked, the rest is easy.

- Web-site: we don't have one – only major corporates invest the ludicrous sums being touted to build sites in the mid-nineties, but now a decent web-site costs no more than a good brochure, and forms one of the key pillars in your marketing planning: brand, brochure, web-site. It's the first thing prospective clients take a look at, if you manage to get under the radar, past the gatekeeper and into their consciousness. So make sure it's good, quick, easy to navigate and reflects all the principles that your business promotes itself on.
- SS Oriana: what, you may be wondering, is this all about? Marketing and cruise ships? Well yes, actually. Once a year, there's a marketing conference held on board one of the big cruise ships – in the nineties it's the Oriana – in which marketing services suppliers like us pay exorbitant sums to attend, for the chance to meet senior client figures, who go free. Apart from some set-piece presentations, the whole point of the process is a series of short, half-hour meetings with potential clients that you think you'd like to do business with. We nominate forty or more from the attendees list that we'd like to talk to, and the clients nominate which of the marketing services agencies they'd like to meet, and the organisers try to marry the two together with a schedule which amounts to speed dating for marketers. You also have clients as guests at your meal table for breakfast, lunch and dinner. You board the ship at Southampton on a Wednesday afternoon, the ship pulls out and heads for somewhere in the Bay of Biscay where it can

anchor up and where there's no mobile phone signal or web access (that will have changed now), so the clients can't spend the whole time managing their business remotely, and from Wednesday dinner to Friday dinner, there is an unremitting round of client contacts: 6 half-hours in the morning, 6 in the afternoon, 2 at each meal-time – that's a total of around 40 meetings, so when people allude to it as a bit of a jolly, it is difficult not to rise to the bait and tell them to fuck right off. It's one of the most tiring things you can do business-wise, mixed in, as it is, with plenty of drinking at the bar (aka more networking), and three late nights (there's on-board entertainment too). For the last two or three years, we've paid the twelve grand and have just about got back enough business to justify repeating the process. It opens doors that traditional methods do not and is therefore worth including in the mix. And as with all sales activity, some of it bears fruit months, years even, down the track. We eventually win some six-figure business with Twinings that can be traced back to an initial Oriana meeting two years before. Of course not all the clients you meet are bona fide prospects: the odds are at least three to one against, by my reckoning. A third of them are there for serious business purposes; a third are networking to try to advance their careers; the rest are there on the piss. That still means more than a dozen meetings over two days with people of interest, which at a grand a pop is a lot cheaper and more effective than Barry. I wouldn't mind paying him thirty or forty grand a year if he delivered thirty or forty meetings with personnel of this calibre every year (Marketing Directors or Managers only are invited, and junior substitutes are not allowed, so generally you're talking to the organ grinder, not the monkey); but he doesn't, so I do.

Anyway, you disembark on Saturday morning after a final

late-night hurrah, feeling utterly exhausted and ready for a weekend in bed, but armed with a dozen or more prospects to follow up and schedule longer meetings with.

One year we share facilities on board with our almost namesake from Leeds, Advertising Principles, a successful and growing advertising agency, with virtually every other marketing services discipline under its roof, except sales promotion. They express an interest in some form of loose affiliation or tie-up, with the presumed sub-text of some more formal joining at the hip if things work out. From their point of view, they get a southern office and access to proven sales promotion expertise; while we get a northern office and access to their mainly northern client list. (It is certainly true that most northern clients keep their business up North and eschew the delights of Soho's adland.)

I have an office in their impressive Roundhay building and trek up to Leeds one day a week to try to get the business moving. It's one thing their MD – an engaging black guy called Ruel – setting it up, it's another altogether, persuading their account teams of the potential value of the tie-up. They're all ad agency types who don't necessarily care about below-the-line services at all or see any reason why they should promote it to their clients – potentially risking their own reputation (and the advertising business) on some unknowns from Oxford. So my first job is to sell the arrangement internally, and then wait and hope for introductions, when their clients are ready to talk about sales promotion. For months I schlep up the M1 and sit in an office doing work I could just as easily be doing in Oxford or at home, trying to fly the flag, but it's a dispiriting exercise. On one day a week, you're just not one of them – so most of the time you're out of sight and out of mind. Eventually we do get one or two briefs – one for Seven Seas vitamins, which looks particularly hopeful – but nothing ever transpires and slowly it dawns on me that I am wasting my time. We have seriously considered putting someone senior into the building full-time, as the only way of really forcing the issue and demonstrating and demanding commitment to the venture. I even have a potential guy lined up – a Scot called Stuart whom I know through my Institute of Sales Promotion committee activities, who's interested in a move north. But it is really too little too late. The writing is firmly on the wall when I discover that they are in a major pitch for the Morrisons supermarket business – where sales promotion expertise would seem to be a pre-requisite for selection – and we're not involved in the process; not even informed that the pitch is going on – I find out through the trade press. Very soon after, I decide I've had enough of trying to push water uphill, and pull the plug. In any event, I'm sure they've decided to appoint their own full-time sales promotion expert, whom they control and get all the billings from, should any accrue. To no surprise at all from me, they don't even make the short-list for the Morrisons business, as I retreat to Oxford to lick my wounds and reflect on another 50 days or more of wasted effort and one more failed initiative.

Have we learned anything from it? Probably that we went at it half-heartedly, thinking that the business would come through their efforts rather than ours, partly because the original initiative was theirs, and therefore we never developed a proper or concerted plan of action – or thought through in any detail how it would actually work in practice, or where it might eventually take us. And as every business guru in the known universe will tell you, failing to plan is planning to fail.

What Barry has discovered is that it doesn't matter how much sales training you've done, how much theory you can put into practice, how much paper you generate to justify all the actions you put in place, unless you have a detailed grasp of your subject, you will be found out. Hot prospects ask questions to weed out the wheat from the chaff: if you don't have convincing answers to those questions, you end up with the chaff. Put bluntly, Barry doesn't know enough about our business – and hasn't picked it up in the year or so he's been with us – so he probably comes across to prospective clients as more silver-tongued cavalier than seriously knowledgeable sales person. The *Unprincipled* article cruelly exposes him, and short of a miracle, he and we all know that as a result he's a dead man walking. And in the course of the next couple of months, we inevitably make him an offer he can't refuse. Bye.

And so we finish our eleventh year in a beautiful Cotswolds hotel, with all the usual ingredients. Everyone is issued with a personalised 12-page invitation and itinerary, courtesy of the studio (who obviously aren't busy enough): we start at 10.00 in the boardroom for a review of the past 12 months; an hour later, we follow directions to an activity centre in Aston Magna, where a barbecue lunch will be followed by a 4-team competition, involving Honda Pilot cars, archery, Formula Two racing stock cars, and quad bikes. Being December, it's muddy, but the weather's OK, so the barbecue isn't the soggy affair it might have been. We're certainly taking a bit of a chance, running such an event at this time of year, but we get lucky. The conditions do mean, however, that everyone gets coated in the brown stuff, and there are a couple of situations where personal animosities are relieved by rolling the object of their disaffection in the mud – but it's only a bit of fun, they'll claim, with a wry smile on their face.

Then it's back to Charingworth Manor late afternoon for a clean-up, a swim in the indoor pool, and a change into party clothes for dinner in a private room with one long table to take a couple of dozen people, twelve down each side. It's a beautiful old Cotswold stone manor house, but with a modern twist. After a few pre-prandials and the distribution of *The Unprincipled*, the wine keeps flowing over dinner, and soon we're in to Secret Santa: everyone draws the name of someone else for whom they buy a present (maximum value £10), which is generally used by all and sundry to poke fun at perceived character foibles or deficiencies. You rarely get anything worth keeping or even taking home. The Cat, as I recall, gets a porn mag and a box of tissues, which is about as good as it gets. I have no idea what I receive – or indeed bought for whomever it was I drew in the sweep – but in photographs of the event, which I still have, I appear to be holding some sexual aid for men. Nuff said.

The Cat and I have adjacent rooms the size of a small house, to which we eventually repair en masse to continue the revels: more drinks, more flirting, but no actual action (that I can prove). The Cat ends up in bed with three women, I believe, but still draws a blank. There are complaints from some nearby room about the level of noise: what were the management thinking of? Probably assumed their prices deterred loud-mouthed oafs, and that rooms this size attract high-quality members of the establishment (or aspiring members of it). Not the drinky, shouty, sweary nouveaux riches that we represent. An easy mistake to make. And so a (not so) discreet veil is drawn over the close of what turns out to be our penultimate year.

Ten

What A Sell-out

THE CALL, WHEN IT COMES, is unexpectedly out of the blue. Would we be at all interested in being acquired? Since our original objective was to get the business to £5million turnover and then sell to the highest bidder (well, it was mine), and since we are perilously close to achieving that figure, based on the forward billings that are currently being projected, it would be churlish and more than a little foolish to say a curt "No, thank you." Firstly, I'm flattered to be asked, and secondly, as in all things in life, everyone and everything has their price. And it costs nothing to talk.

(When asked if she would go to bed with a man for £50K, the Duchess replied in her posh voice that she supposed she would, but when asked if she'd do it for £50, she demanded haughtily, "What do you think I am?" To which the riposte was, "We've already established that; now we're just haggling over the price.")

The caller is some bloke from a local agency we've never heard of, allegedly representing some big American agency group. His name is Hunt (rhymes with...) but we shall call him Peanut Head, because that is what the Cat christens him and the moniker sticks.

Thinking back, it is all done incredibly unprofessionally, which should have alerted us to the fun and games to come. A call – no meeting at this stage – followed by a short letter confirming their interest and stating their valuation of the business. Based on what? Not stated. The only other contents of the letter are a threat-cum-warning that if we use the offer to hawk the business round the industry and start a dutch auction, all bets will be off.

Of course at this stage, under the veil of complete confidentiality, that is exactly what we should do. Generally, you only ever get one chance to sell your business, and it absolutely behoves you to extract maximum value out of the sale. But we don't. Before we do anything, though, we need to sit down and take a long hard look at the business, where it's headed, what the rest of the management team think, what our options are. In other words, a root and branch review of the business plan and long-term vision: is now the right time to sell? Or would we be better off continuing to try to grow the business, which we've been doing successfully since the Splitter's departure?

The growth in the business in fact means that we have outgrown our city centre offices and need either to augment or move to pastures new. There are two other offices in our courtyard, but neither tenant shows any sign of either moving on or having spare capacity that we could use (which in any case would only be a short-term solution.) So we have been actively seeking new premises, one of which is a brand new barn conversion in farmland four or five miles out of the city. It would treble our existing space, and there is parking all round it, but it would mean a very different atmosphere from our city centre courtyard: no popping out for a quick sandwich from Marks & Spencer, or to buy a forgotten birthday card – everything would be a car ride away. Plus it would mean a considerable long-term commitment, because as first tenants in, we'll be the head lessees (again), effectively responsible for the rent for its duration. We already have a 25-year lease on the courtyard (about which, more later) hanging over our heads, with about 15 years of it still to go, so the thought of adding to that with a second one of any significant length concentrates the mind wonderfully.

The stark choice, then, is either commit to further growth for at least five years, with the expectation that the business will have a much greater value, and take on a new office commitment, or take the money and run. I have seen one or two agencies turn down offers in recent years, because they think they're too big and successful, and want to double or treble in size before considering a hugely inflated deal, only to find that clients and staff suddenly start deserting them (the two are often linked – generally to an arrogant and overbearing management, which I hope we're not), and they end up with a contracting and virtually unsaleable business. We most definitely do not want that scenario, but all it would take is the loss of Rothmans (billings across both divisions last year £1.25M) and the defection of staff who don't like their new office surroundings, for whatever reason, and that could be us.

We have lengthy discussions round the board table, and it is clear that, at the end of the day, the decision is mine and the Cat's to make: we have 74% of the share value between us and 100% of the voting shares, so ultimately what we say goes. I do get the impression though, that the thought of a substantial six-figure cheque in their back pockets isn't that unattractive, even if it arrives much earlier in the business life-cycle than they have been anticipating, as recently as the Christmas party shenanigans in the Cotswolds.

It is a big deal to let go of your baby though. It's yours: you've given it life. You've made it grow up. Now it's a fully-fledged adult, and here's some suitor come to ask for its hand (torso, legs and all the rest). In return for a very large cheque. It's tempting all right, but how are you going to feel when it's no longer yours? When someone else gives the orders, and decides its policy and direction? When you yourself suddenly find yourself with a boss to whom you're answerable? In short, when you are no longer in control of your own creation? Will you be able to deal with the change in status? The omens are not good. Most business owners who sell out do not last two years in their new role, usually because of a fall-out with the new owners – and that's even when they're on a three-year earn-out: they're so pissed off, they forego the third year (sometimes because they've lost heart and know they have no chance of making the figures – and therefore the earn-out – anyway) and just walk away.

On the other hand, this is a serious offer and represents a real opportunity to realise in cash the business value that we have been building, and for many (most) small business owner/ managers, that represents the Holy Grail. The business is their pension, and here are we, in my case not yet 50, and the Cat not even 40, in a position to make ourselves financially secure, if not for life, than at least for the foreseeable lengthy future.

But is the offer a fair figure? Our gut feel is that it isn't, but then every owner/manager has a tendency to think their business is worth more than it actually is, usually because they themselves are fundamental to the business: if they walk away or get knocked down by a bus, the business ceases to function. That is certainly not the case with me and the Cat. We have quite deliberately put in place a board of directors that would act effectively as a succession management team in the event of our departure, to give the business added value and attraction. We are going to pay for that of course, in the form of diluted earnings if and when we sell, but we figure it is worth that for the stability and added value it puts into the business.

After a good deal of soul searching, we reply to the letter that their valuation does not match ours, which would be £1M more. With hindsight, we should probably have gone higher – probably double. How do you put a value on any business? You can talk about earnings ratios all you like (a multiple of your average annual profit over the last three years, say), but ultimately it comes down to two other important factors: sentiment and liquidity in the market sector you work in (at present the marketing services sector is buoyant and a bit of a darling in the City, with lots of deals being done and several major international corporations – usually advertising based – hoovering up smaller marketing services agencies like ours all over the globe); and inextricably linked to that, the earnings multiple that can be expected in the event of a trade sale. Because advertising agencies are cash rich, they are often paying 10 times earnings – or more – while someone running a factory making building products might expect only 2/3 times. This may be ridiculously unfair, but it is the way it is. In other words, your business is no different from your house or any other valuable asset you own: it is worth precisely what someone else is prepared to pay for it. No more, no less.

How do we arrive at our figure? Well, last year we made a profit before tax and dividends of not far short of half a million, which at ten times earnings would not make a figure of £5-10M completely out of order. And while we haven't been making that sort of figure for the last three years – it's only three years since the Splitter walked out, and year one was definitely a recovery year – we've still managed to accumulate a very healthy pile of cash: we have nearly three-quarters of a million sitting in the bank – or more precisely on the money markets – earning handsomely, courtesy of Pierre's good offices, for doing sweet Fanny Adams. So our figure is fully justifiable, based on ten/fifteen times three years' solid earnings.

On the other hand, that figure might be ambitious but … a) what is anyone prepared to pay for us? and b) once you state a figure, you can come down from it, but you can't go up. It's the rule of haggling – sorry, negotiation. So our number represents a compromise between what we'd like and what we think they might be prepared to pay. It's a mistake. Almost by return of post comes a letter accepting our revised valuation. Our assessment is definitely a figure below what they are prepared to pay. But it's too late. Indeed, by stating a figure at all, we have psychologically accepted that we are going to sell, subject to…blah, blah, etc. The whole negotiating process has been short-circuited: usually the first to name a number effectively loses, but we've started with a number (however reasonably arrived at) that gives us no further room for manoeuvre.

The money's one thing (though let's not underplay it: in the grand scheme of things, it may not be everything, but it still ranks right up there, alongside oxygen), but what actually happens to the business physically, if and when we conclude a deal? The short answer is that it will disappear without trace. Amazed? You should be. We have spent over a decade establishing client awareness of and credentials for our business. In fact, just this year, we have been investing £20,000 in regular trade press advertising in *Marketing* magazine, to further improve the business's standing. But here's the thing: the buyer is working in cahoots with a large – very large – agency group; one of the world's top three advertising and marketing behemoths. They have a direct marketing agency in the group called Draft Worldwide, which is the biggest of its kind in North America; try as they might, however – and they have tried, unsuccessfully, at least twice before – they have been unable to build a major presence in the UK or Europe, far less the market-leading role they aspire to; Peanut Head runs a small direct marketing business outside Oxford, whose name I shall not bother you with, because you'll never have heard of it, and neither have we, in all honesty; he has, however, sold his agency to the Americans and persuaded them that he's the man to achieve their ambitions; he will buy (using their money of course) as many UK agencies as it takes to create a UK Draft that is at the very least in the top five direct marketing agencies.

Essentially Peanut Head has sold them the dream, and they've bought it hook, line and sinker, mainly because (I'm guessing here, but it does rather characterise the American race when it comes to business) they want to believe it. He's sold them this big picture of a successful group of companies bestriding the UK, and by extension, eventually, Europe. And they've gone for it, believing the hype.

So who is Peanut Head? Well, first of all, the name: he is a corpulent individual in his early forties, I'd guess, whose head seems too small for his fleshy body. The Cat coins the name at an early meeting and he becomes that henceforth. Perhaps more to the point, he is a silver-tongued cavalier who has got lucky – falling across a large American conglomerate with deep pockets and large ambitions, and persuading them he's the man to achieve them. He comes across as affable but arrogant, full of himself and what he's achieved (not very much in reality), and what he's going to achieve. Neither the Cat nor I buy the bullshit: after an early meeting, the Cat characterises him as being just like the Splitter in his general attitudes, and he has a point. He does, however, have the Americans' money to play with and he appears to want to use some of it to acquire little old Marketing Principles. Well, yee haa.

Having acquired us, however, the idea is that the two businesses are merged into one immediately – there is room for such expansion in their offices (about which more anon), and there obviously isn't at ours (from an office perspective, we're about to move anyway) – and renamed Draft. You can see the logic of it long term, but. You just knew there was a 'but' coming there, didn't you? But, as things stand right now in the world (alright, in the UK) of marketing services companies, Marketing Principles is better known than either Draft (frankly, hardly anyone has ever heard of them on this side of the pond) or Peanut Head's previous business, put together. A lot better known. But (that word again) in the interests of the big ambition, we have to become Draft. Straightaway. Not Marketing Principles, part of the Draft Corporation; not Marketing Principles, a wholly owned subsidiary of Draft; not even Draft, formerly known as Marketing Principles. This is what any sensible brand owner would do to protect their brand's goodwill in any name change (remember Marathon to Snickers?) But Peanut Head's got so close to the big picture, with him in the middle of it, he can't see the wood for his big corpulent ego.

This does have an impact on the financial negotiations though. Normally a deal like this is done as an earn-out: a tranche of money up front (or better still from the buyer's perspective, if you can get away with it, a tranche of shares in the buyer's business), and the rest comes at the end of years one, two, and three, upon achievement of some contractually pre-agreed financial performance – normally profit. For this to work in practice, however, the seller has to remain in control of his or her business. Usually this is in the best interests of the buyer anyway: it gives them time to get to grips with the business, so that if it is eventually merged with another part of the organisation, it is done from a position of strength, having already assimilated it into the new regime's systems and processes gradually over time. No unnecessary shocks to the system. And yet, isn't it amazing how often businesses are acquired because they have been successful, yet the acquirer immediately changes everything about the business that has made them successful in the first place. The people with the money always know best. I read somewhere that two thirds of all mergers and acquisitions are financially unsuccessful in the long run, yet still the gravy train chugs on.

From our perspective, if you are going to put us in with another business and we don't control it lock, stock and barrel, then an earn-out isn't going to work. Peanut Head does his best to persuade us that we can have separate accounts, but as he knows only too well, it isn't about some administrative sleight of hand (good as he turns out to be at such). Fundamentally, you can't have responsibility without control. And without control, we're just not going to buy any 'join now, pay later' scenario. End of. It's cash up front or nothing (which is probably what we'll end up with if we do the earn-out thing in any event). There really isn't going to be any negotiation on this front. Put simply, it's a deal breaker, and he knows it.

We're his first big acquisition in his quest for UK domination and he needs it to go through for his own credibility with the Americans, about whom we've heard little until now, but when the purse strings start to get loosened, the man with the money is bound to come knocking, to see what his pile of cash is going to get him. Enter stage left, the CEO of DraftWorldwide and the man who, it appears, is driving the business's global expansion by acquisition plans: Jaydon Blumenthal. No, that's not the name of some motor racing team or hair-care product. It's the money man at Draft. Why do so many Americans have utterly silly names? Not that we care: we'll deal with Engelbert Humperdink if he signs the cheques. Jaydon is a short, bespectacled dapper little man, in his late 40's or early 50's at a guess. He comes across as a pretty straight guy: authoritative certainly, but since he's in control of the business's squillions of dollars acquisition fund, that's hardly surprising. He doesn't have Peanut Head's arrogance though. I imagine he's risen without trace from the boring old world of accountancy – he's one of life's number crunchers, who's made it all the way to the top of some corporate structure by keeping his nose clean, the balance sheet balanced, and giving every impression of a safe pair of hands. If you're a venture capitalist or any other form of money man, who do you want running your businesses? A marketing visionary, a sales guru, a technical wizard, or someone who knows how to look after the pennies? Yup, it's most often going to be the money man. Even if he has no vision, ideas or passion.

So Jaydon is here to look us in the eye, give us the once-over, check whether we look like we might know what we're talking about, and generally to establish in his own mind whether giving us his money in return for our business is a good investment. It's part of what is called due diligence, and as becomes apparent (to me at least), it is fatally flawed. What the Americans are interested in are our figures: do the numbers stack up? In short, can the accounts be believed, or is there some horrid little black hole in there somewhere, the equivalent of the Dorian Gray portrait in the attic, that could bring the whole lot crashing down around our ears? Since, as our departed and unlamented Non Exec Chairman remarked, we have monthly accounts that would put ICI to shame, and since we demonstrably have three-quarters of a million in the bank, we don't have much to fear on this count.

What's interesting though, is that the due diligence is just about the numbers: it's classic accountancy. All they want reassurance on is that the figures all add up to the right total. No mention is ever made about due diligence on the people and their personalities (otherwise Peanut Head's silver spurs would have been noticed). Will these two teams of people be able to work together? Will there be a good fit in terms of management styles, systems and processes? In short, is there compatibility? Given the egos that are in place at the top of any organisation, you'd think this might be an important part of the buyer's consideration, but it doesn't appear to have crossed their minds once: if we take the money, we'll learn to work together – that's the apparent assumption.

In fact the three-quarters of a million cash is the subject of a different conversation: obviously (it is obvious, isn't it?) they aren't getting the business with all the cash sloshing around in it – otherwise they're effectively paying three-quarters of a mill less for it. We're going to take it out and divvy it up. They on the other hand want the cash-flow luxury that being cash-rich brings. Well, in the immortal words of Mandy Rice-Davies, they would, wouldn't they? In the end, we agree to "donate" £50K to the cause, and they will pay us £700,000 more as part of the sale contract, so they get our bank account with all the cash neatly stashed. It doesn't say much for the organisation that either they want or need it in the first place, or that it becomes any sort of issue, but it's resolved, so we forget about it.

One thing we can't forget about, though, is the existing office lease, which we negotiated 12 years ago and which still has 13 years to run, at a current rent of £42,000 per year. So, in a worst-case scenario, that adds up to a liability of over half a million, which exercises me and the Cat more than the rest, because our names are on the lease (together with Gaylord and Stid, almost certainly, and it would be interesting to know where they actually stand legally, if push came to shove). The thing is, Peanut Head says he won't take the business with this (potential) liability attached. He doesn't want the dead weight of a useless lease hanging round his shoulders – or more likely his American masters don't – and neither do I or the Cat. As head-lease signatories, we are effectively jointly and severally responsible for the rent for the full 25-year term. Don't start on about why we took on such a long lease: I know it wouldn't happen now, but at the time, it's very much the norm – especially with new-build offices, which ours are: the developers wanted certainty that their own investment would pay back, and there was absolutely no negotiation possible on that front. I know, because I sat and watched Biddle give it their very best shot, when we were negotiating the lease, and they came up short, which is about the only time they ever did. What this means in practice is that it will be our responsibility to sub-let to viable tenants, and if we fail to do so, it automatically reverts to us. Whammy.

This is a big sticking point and is eventually resolved with a compromise that no one is particularly pleased with, I imagine. After the sale has gone through, they will give us back the shell company with a bank account containing £100,000, which will cover nearly two years of void, and the existing office lease. The responsibility continues to be ours therefore (and to some extent our other directors/shareholders, whose names are on the contract of sale, but we all know that it is the Cat's and my arses which are effectively on the line.) Biddle and Co insert a clause in the contract which states this all has to be executed within six months of the sale being completed, and we set about finding an estate agent to market our offices.

The sale contract itself is the usual legal jargon the size of a very large door-stop, containing every conceivable material fact about what is being acquired and how, plus the dreaded warranties – statements from us about any known weaknesses in the company's trading position which could affect its value going forward. So, for example, if we knew that our biggest client were about to call a review of its biggest suppliers and we didn't include the fact in the document, and we subsequently were to lose the business, and with it around a quarter of our turnover and profit, they would be entitled to take us to court to recover some of the purchase price. Warranties force you to think every negative thought in your head about all the worst things that could happen and then commit it to paper, where the lawyers compile a dossier of "bad news shit about to hit the fan." As it happens, we run a pretty tight ship, and the accounts are transparent and free of any tax-avoidance initiatives (mainly because our accountants, Grant Thornton, never come up with any – they may as well have been an off-shoot of the Inland Revenue). If you're ever tempted to set up your own business, shop around for accountants – ask for referrals and don't rush into the arms of the first one to speak politely to you (they can all manage that) – until you find one that really understands the entrepreneurial mindset: knowing and applying the principles of *The E-Myth* is a good indicator. At that time, they are rare as hen's teeth; now there are a few around if you go looking hard enough.

Nevertheless we spend hours with the lawyers imagining what could go wrong, based on our current knowledge. Given the track record of the business in little over a decade, and all the shit that has already gone down, you can imagine that, once the creative juices get flowing, we can make the business look like a geriatric basket case in no time at all. Martin Lane at Biddles (who incidentally I recommend unhesitatingly as the best lawyer I've ever met – if you're in commercial trouble, go seek him out, wherever he's now plying his trade) tempers our enthusiasm for a disaster movie script and plants the cool hand of reality and experience on our heaving shoulders, to help us mould what actually goes in the document, which is comprehensive enough, but doesn't add up to a hill of beans in the grand scheme of things.

Having fancy-dan city-slicker lawyers may be costing us a fair old whack and may look like a giant ego ride, but as I've stated elsewhere, they always get you a result. Peanut Head is using some local (for local, read parochial) little practice in Oxfordshire, whose representative can best be described as unprepossessing. What his actual track record is in putting together merger and acquisition deals, I have no idea, but my guess is that this represents the biggest (if not the first) one he's ever done. God knows why Peanut Head has chosen him, but on the basis of his normal modus operandi, which we discover as we get to know him, he's probably either an old family friend and retainer, or he's bumped into him at some dinner party or other (which we discover over time is one of Peanut Head's common methods of recruiting). Biddle and Co run rings round him at every stage of the process, and as we shall see, his incompetence eventually costs them dear.

The final session at Biddle's palatial City offices comes after the Cat and I have had a night out in London of biblical proportions, ending in the early hours at Stringfellows (where else?) – and consumption of their ultra-trendy Tynant bottled water (blue designer glass bottles: I thought blue glass equals poison) apparently hits a new record, as, hung over, we try to concentrate on the fine detail of the sale document. I really do not recommend the combination.

While the legal beagles have been doing their thing, of course, life has been continuing apace. The business doesn't stop, just because we're trying to sell it, but there is a real risk in this situation that you start to take your eye off the ball. I suppose we're lucky, in that we have the business in the kind of shape where it can more or less run itself. Well, not lucky. We put a succession management team in place specifically for this purpose and eventuality, so when Rothmans puts us on a pitch list for a new cigarette that they're planning to launch in the UK, it's pretty much business as usual. It's a brand called Winfield, which is big in Australia. The fact that in the UK it's also Woolworth's own label brand doesn't seem to trouble them, so either they're unaware of it, or they've thought through the implications and don't think it matters. Personally I think it gives the brand an initial additional hurdle of appearing cheap and down-market, but since I'm not a smoker, what do I know? Perhaps they're aiming it at

Woolworth's customers, though knowing the marketing people there, I somehow doubt it.

Either way, it represents an opportunity for another half million or more on the billings, and while they've got a roster of agencies competing for it, we're confident we can produce the goods. Just the thing to bolster your finances and make you look even better, as the sale document is starting to take shape. We elect to present a campaign using Aussie road signs as the core graphic that links all the various communications, and it seems to work well at every level – from advertising to branded merchandise, like ash-trays. We make the presentation and wait with bated breath.

Meanwhile, we're invited to go and take a look at the new offices, where we'll be working, once the sale goes through – it is scheduled for December, with us moving over between Christmas and the New Year. It's a farm building complex in a village to the west of Oxford, with two or three separate units. Draft has two sides of a horse-shoe shaped building round a large central courtyard, containing a swimming-pool. Across the car park at the rear is another rectangular building with three or four smaller units in it, behind which are a couple of tennis courts. It's all very bucolic and a far remove from our city centre eyrie. It all looks very beautiful and Country Life, but I remember the last time I personally made this kind of move, coming out of an office in Covent Garden opposite the entrance to Drury Lane theatre to an office on the edge of Thame with views of a field with pigs in, that you do feel a real sense of loss. There's a vibrancy and an energy to city centre life which, for a business, seems to transfer to the people and attitudes within it. Of course there are the practicalities of being able to pop out for a skinny latte or a sandwich at a moment's notice, but there's also a strange dislocation between the pace of countryside life and the often frenetic client needs, associated with running a marketing services agency. It feels a bit like having a split personality. (There's a meeting of the Schizophrenic Society tonight: I've half a mind to go.)

The offices themselves are essentially a large barn conversion job. At the moment, the Draft lot are rattling around in half-empty accommodation, which has clearly been chosen for its ability to house another organisation of at least the same size. This is quite a gamble in a place like Oxfordshire, where there aren't that many agencies of our ilk, full stop, never mind ones of a sufficient size to be of interest. Still, it looks like they've got away with it. There are two floors on each side of the building, and the upper floor is almost completely empty at present. That's where the bulk of our people will go, in the long side of the horse-shoe. Downstairs on that side is a large board-room and three or four private offices, one of which is slated for me, next to the much larger one that Peanut Head shares with his financial person, a woman in her sixties with glasses and a shock of white hair, who is almost immediately dubbed Fanny Craddock, and who will be described as such hereafter. She does all the number crunching, and she speaks in a tone of voice that brooks no dissent – Joyce Grenfell with a harder edge. She seems a strange choice of running mate and we wonder what particular personal chemistry has brought (and kept) them together.

The other player in the drama is Peanut Head's creative director, Pete, who was obviously a partner in the original three-man management team that sold out to Draft (his name was in the agency's name – the third one has mysteriously disappeared, with only a sketchy explanation). He's an amiable enough char-acter, but quite clearly defers to Peanut Head on just about every-thing, so he isn't likely to feature much in our discussions and negotiations. Since we have given up trying to find a Creative Director, our studio personnel will simply join theirs – the creatives have their own space in the office across the car park, in the rectangular building next to the tennis courts – and he will become their de facto boss. To be honest, we don't think about it too much, because it doesn't strike us as being an issue. Bung together two lots of complete strangers. They're all doing the same sort of thing. They're sure to get on, aren't they?

In fact the whole question of who does what, post acquisition, has barely been asked. It may only cover a few pages of text here and has probably taken you ten minutes to read it, but the process has been going on for the best part of six months, and yet we've never asked what the structure of the new organisation will look like – what we are all expected to do, what staff to manage, etc. This is our failure of due diligence par excellence and is evidence, if any were needed, that all we're really interested in is the money.

Nevertheless it doesn't prevent it being a bolt from the blue when, at a getting-to-know-you lunch at the Old Parsonage (fancy boutique hotel just off the city centre), Peanut Head introduces us to the business's new Managing Director, Pauline. Who the fuck is Pauline? We're barely a month to six weeks away from the sale and merger going through, and she's never been mentioned – nor the role that she's going to play, ill defined as it is. Pauline's background is in mail-order; she's had some senior position at a well-known national name company based in Oxfordshire, but she's been persuaded to forego whatever success she's been enjoying there to come and play referee (my analogy) between two similar but fundamentally diverse organisations in terms of management style. What her precise role is, her core objectives, her job description, are not explained; I doubt she has any piece of paper with anything written down. She's what? Forty-something, shoulder-length brown hair, presentable enough, affable enough, bright enough; but here she is, being dropped into the conversation as effectively my and the Cat's *boss* in the new regime. We've never seen or heard of her before, yet all of a sudden she's being presented as a key player.

Of course, as we shall see, job titles can be (and often are) spurious, but the point is, this is no way to run a whelk stall, never mind a multi-million pound organisational merger. It is, though, in retrospect, typical of Peanut Head's management style, insofar as the word 'style' can in any way be associated with the man. He equates the word 'manage' with giving orders, making decisions and bossing people about, and his idea of taking people with him is to let them know what he's decided after it's a fait accompli and telling them to get used to it. If you don't like it, you know what you can do. He is, as we've already established, an arrogant (and ignorant – not a pleasant combination) piece of shit, and here is our first experience of his utter uselessness at first hand.

Why has she been brought in? My analysis is that the two companies are hopelessly unbalanced. We have a strong management team of six, who play an active part in decision making; he has himself been making all the decisions, with Fanny Craddock to whisper in his ear about the finances, and Pete to go along with everything he says and does – the ultimately not-very-bright yes man, carrying his spine around in a bucket. We have the bigger billings, stronger balance sheet, the better client list, the more developed organisational structure, the greater industry profile and reputation, and by far the best management team. If there were any logic or justice, we should be taking over them and acting as the lead Draft agency. But he's the one with the ear (and money) of the Americans, and he's feeling, notwithstanding his naturally arrogant chutzpah, just a teeny bit vulnerable and exposed – out-numbered actually. He's trying to even up the numbers a bit.

I don't know whether he realises it or not (I'm not sure he's that bright: of course he thinks he is, but that's what makes him such an arsehole), but this is potentially a deal breaker, not least because of the manner in which it is presented. I doubt he even thinks of it as such, so up his own orifice is he, but the Cat and I are utterly shocked by the whole pantomime. Unprofessional. A chilling illustration of things to come, if we continue with the process. Can we really work with this guy as our superior? As the Cat says, knowingly but much later, he'd always had him down as a dead ringer for the Splitter in terms of ambition and ego, so we can't really argue that we haven't been warned.

Given that our business has a defined and logical structure, with a 6-person management team at the top, and theirs has Peanut Head shouting the odds and everyone else doing what he says, who actually is going to do what, post merger? Obviously all our junior board members are going to lose that status and go back to being plain Account Directors. The Cat will be given the title Client Services Director and have all their account handlers as well report in to him (in other words, all the billings are his responsibility). I'm to be given the ceremonial title of Chief Executive, with no clearly defined roles and responsibilities, which may sound all fine and dandy in principle, but in practice is quite unnerving. So what *do* you do all day? Swan around, asking, "What's going on here?" (as our ex-boss in Thame was wont to do), and generally making encouraging noises? Pierre's role as Financial Controller, or whatever title they're proposing, looks like a demotion: well, you can't have two Finance Directors, that's fair enough, but he can't be that sanguine about acting effectively as Fanny Craddock's book-keeper. Sheridan is being asked to act as Head of Research, or some such spurious title. In having to assimilate one developed management structure into an undeveloped one, it all looks like Peanut Head has made up some sort of organogram on the back of an envelope with a few fancy titles to make everyone seem important, but has omitted any detailed thought about the practicalities of the situation. No wonder he gets on with the Americans.

It is all highly unsatisfactory, and it is at this point that, if we had an ounce of self-respect, we would tell him to fuck right off. The deal's off. But we don't. We may agonise about the shape (or lack of it) in the merged business, but ultimately the lure of the filthy lucre is stronger than the reservations about structure, style, business continuity or Peanut Head's over-arching arrogance. Never mind opening the box (ref: "*Take Your Pick*", a 60's TV game show), we're taking the money. And once that is clear in our minds, Peanut Head has carte blanche to do whatever the hell he wants. The bastard.

Just around now, we learn we've won the Rothmans Winfield business, on the back of our Aussie road signs creative, and another half million is added to the forward billings. While we're all jolly pleased, for some reason the celebrations seem a bit muted. Could it be because the profits will all be going to someone else, not us? Or am I being unnecessarily cynical?

As Christmas approaches, there comes a point when all the outstanding issues have finally been resolved – or we've just decided to put our joint and several heads in the sand and ignore them, in favour of a fat wallet. All the contracts have been signed. Finally, two or three weeks previously, we've told the rest of our staff officially what's going on. There is no real surprise. With all the comings and goings, it doesn't take too much to put two and two together, and with snatches of phone conversations and the throw-away butt-end of conversations – well, they almost certainly have already got wind of the basic facts. I wouldn't say it goes down well. Change is rarely welcome, and radical change like this much less so. It is very much the end of an era, however much of a cliché that is, and everyone knows it. Of course in a growing and dynamic small business, radical change is what happens all the time; it's what makes it such a roller-coaster ride of an experience – the highs, the lows, the celebratory popping of champagne corks, and the inevitable (if hopefully rare) black Fridays.

The day we gather as a Board to celebrate the completed sale of the business, champagne in attendance, is the strangest atmosphere I've ever experienced. The lawyers have phoned to say the deal has officially and legally gone through; the Americans have phoned to say congratulations, welcome to the fold and, by the way, the money's in your bank accounts. We pop the corks and go through the ritual. And yet, and yet. The Cat and I have a substantial seven-figure number in our bank accounts, the others have substantial six-figure sums, but there is no sense of elation. Everyone seems quite flat. I think it's a combination of things: we're not just losing control of the business we've started, built up and run for nearly 12 years, we're also all moving to new jobs with, horror of horrors, a boss (who's an arrogant twat as well), in new premises, where we don't know the natives or how they do things round there. What celebration there is in the room is tempered by a strong dose of apprehension. Have we done the right thing? Are we going to regret at leisure? Should we, if we were going to sell the business, have conducted the sale in a different way and invited interest from other parties? Maybe we could have sold and continued with the business as it is, rather than being merged and disappeared. Because what the champagne cannot mask is that at this precise moment, Marketing Principles' short but eventful life has come to a juddering and permanent full-stop. It is no more; it has ceased to be; etc etc ad nauseam.

We go off on what would normally be a pub crawl of the city, but with champers instead of pints, starting at an underground bar at the Randolph Hotel called Torso, which is having its own brief life in the sun (or more correctly shadows) on the Oxford social scene. It's early doors, so it's not exactly buzzing with its usual late-evening, coke-snorting elite that it has started to attract (allegedly) and which probably eventually contributes to its downfall. Out come the corks once more, but you can tell: no one's heart is really in it. Six people who are all of a sudden seriously rich – and all rather depressed. In the end, we stop trying to force-feed the jubilation and admit defeat. Slowly we drift away, one by one, and go home. It's all very dispiriting. When you hear the phrase, "Money isn't everything," you might think, "No, but it doesn't half help" (especially if you're a business owner), but at last I think I understand the sentiment. A bit.

The only remaining thing to do is physically pack our bags and move, and like anywhere that you've lived for ten years, there is an enormous amount of accumulated crap. We've already been told that they don't want our old office furniture (slightly dodgy black-ash Habitat desk anyone?) and that we're all going onto a PC-based computer network (how shit is that?) so all our Apple Macs are effectively redundant. Apart from one or two of the studio machines which are top-of-the-range recent additions, a lot of the desk-top units that the account handlers use are a few years old, so hardly state-of-the-art, but nevertheless it is a terrible waste of technology. It is also, in my opinion, a really backward step, using a PC-based network. Anyone who has ever used an Apple Mac will proselytise endlessly about its innate superiority in virtually every respect, and in a creative environment particularly, it represents a retrograde step. Needless to say, the creative department which operates out of a separate building, will be continuing with Macs, so at least the expensive kit won't be trashed, but the rest of us are going to have to learn the convoluted alleged benefits of the double-click mouse, and forget that drag-and-drop ever existed. What a bummer.

As with many house moves, we've forgotten all about the

contents of the loft, where all our financial files are stored. Since the law says you have to keep records going back seven years, it's not as simple as just getting a skip and having a giant chuck-out (and putting it where in any case? We're in a courtyard off an alley off a pedestrianised city centre thoroughfare). It's choc-a-bloc with boxes of invoices and purchase ledgers. As you're putting them up there, a few at a time at the end of each financial year, you don't think forward to the moment when all the dozens and dozens of accumulated storage boxes are going to have to be brought down again, all at one go. You could fill a Luton box-van with the boxes of papers that descend.

Then there is the decorative stuff: the things we've bought along the way, to make the office seem a bit more like home. The pictures on the walls; the bound leather books for the board-room display cabinet; the house plants; the desk-lamps and lighting accessories, acquired to make the harsh overhead neon strips a bit less brutal; the arty artefacts that have accumulated (where do they come from originally? Can anyone remember?). Officially, we've sold the lot to our acquirers, and I'm fairly sure someone comes over and makes an inventory at some stage, but since they're obviously not going to use much, if any, of it, I decide there are a few things that need liberating. Let's call them souvenirs. The pictures of Oxford life; a framed print of a Cartier Bresson photo of Paris; a wooden parrot peeping through the house-pants, or occasionally perched in one of the bay-trees (what wit); the leather-bound Oxford dictionaries of this and companions of that (I'm particularly not letting that philistine, Peanut Head, have them). These will be relocated in advance of the furniture men's arrival to a location not unadjacent to my house, where they can still be found. I guess that technically that makes me a thief. Technically, however, I don't give a toss.

The day finally dawns when the removal vans arrive. All our

possessions are crated and boxed; the computers unplugged and dead to the world. We've left things all ready for collection on one Friday, and they're going to cart everything over to our new offices over the weekend. On Monday morning, we all travel to a new beginning. Packing up an office is not very different from moving house: the decisions about whether you really need to keep this or that item (answer: be ruthless – if you have to ask the question, it's toast); discoveries of forgotten items that jog old memories; all those end-of-an-era emotions. Except that, instead of there being two or three of you on the job, there are twenty or thirty (or more). It creates for an hour or three, a bit of a buzz, as everyone pulls in the same direction, driven for once by the same basic task. And then it's done, and there's nothing left but to cast your eyes around and walk out the door for the last time. It's an odd feeling – in limbo between one reality and the next.

In fact I go back in, after the removals men have done their stuff, to check that everything has gone as planned. Since I'm managing the process of marketing the offices, it behoves me to make sure the empty shell is a) empty and b) in as good a shape as it can be after a decade of occupation. I have to look at it through the eyes of a potential new lessee, rather than the misty eyes of the departing one. There's not much you can do about the carpet: dented where heavy furniture has left long-term imprints and ragged in one or two areas of high or heavy-duty traffic, it was never top quality at the outset. The walls will need repainting to air-brush out the marks of notice-boards, blu-tacked mementoes of this and that, and the finger marks which have gradually accrued round light-switches and doors.

It's all eerily silent and empty, like the day we arrived, only grubbier and with more history – apart from the studio (wouldn't you know), where there is a pile of board, paper and old unrequired artwork sitting un-neatly in the middle of the floor, the size of a decent bonfire, with paper strewn everywhere. They've packed their bags all right, but left half the (unwanted and unneeded) contents in a heap. What the hell am I going to do with it? Which is probably what they thought, and why they've left it like it is. There's no way this lot – over-sized board in preponderance – could go into the usual council refuse sacks, which is all we have available for the disposal of our detritus.

Luckily, casting my eye round the surrounding area outside, I spot a giant blue wheelie-bin, which the cellar bar uses for its bottles and stuff. It's early morning and there's no one about, so I spend half an hour humping the whole lot out through the courtyard and stuffing it into the mercifully nearly empty bin. By the time I'm through, the lid won't shut properly for the sticky-out board that's crammed it full. I feel slightly guilty at misappropriating someone else's facility in this way, but I can't think of any more practical way of sorting out the problem, that isn't going to take days of organisational effort. Let's call it the line of least resistance, and at least they can take comfort from the fact that it's not likely to recur for several years. If ever.

And so the dream is over. I take one last look round, clang shut the Norman Stanley Fletcher courtyard gate for the last time, and look forward with no relish whatsoever to a return to normal employment.

Eleven

Peanut Head and Fanny Craddock

STARTING A NEW JOB IS ALWAYS a bit tense and fraught with uncertainty. Turning up on your first day, with a zillion new people to meet, new ways of working, even just the new journey to work, all conspire to a sense of nervousness: some of us may be restless for change, but I suspect the majority of humans are happiest with the status quo, when they know (or think they know) what they are doing and why, and are generally operating within their comfort zone. Selling your business and merging it with another, whose boss is now effectively your boss, is very definitely outside anyone's comfort zone. It's brand spanking new territory and the feeling it engenders is not a good one.

Day one, of course, is taken up with the unpacking of crates and boxes, familiarisation with new routines (tea and coffee making for example), getting to know the office layout, who everyone is, what they (allegedly) do, where they do it and whom they do it for. Within their allotted work-space, everyone tries to create their own little house for one, where they can carry out the tasks they are given with a degree of equanimity and, hopefully, efficiency: it's called nesting, and we all do it. In a shared open-plan work-space, there is a natural buzz to all this interactivity, with new friendships and alliances beginning to be formed, and everyone casting their eyes over the new and unknown members of the opposite sex, with a view to … well, all the usual possibilities. There is undoubtedly more interest here for the sitting tenants on our band of incomers – certainly from the blokes' perspective – than vice versa: the Cat and I have somehow (alright, by very positive vetting at the interview stage) assembled a veritable bevy of fine-looking women who jointly and severally would turn heads in any company. Peanut Head's lot are frankly just not premiership material – barely Southern League. The head turning is all one way.

While all this bonding and team-building is going on at first-floor level – the Cat has a glass-fronted office of his own to overview the territory (and totty watch) – I am unpacking alone in my own office, tucked away at the far end of the ground floor. It has our old and extremely comfortable Habitat sofa, for lounging around and informal meetings, and a view over the courtyard with its garden furniture and swimming-pool, but having unpacked and nested as much as I can, I sit in splendid isolation, staring into space at the blank wall opposite my desk and wondering, "Now what?"

I have a fancy job title (Chief Executive) and a fancy salary, but no executive power and no clear job description, roles or responsibilities. What happens when two organisations merge is that, particularly at the highly visible top, there are duplications of job roles. In big corporate mergers, it is generally accepted that half the senior management involved are going to be (handsomely) paid off. In our case, Peanut Head has been less than honest about all of this – either that or he's been plain stupid, which is possible: he's not as clever (or any other attribute) as he thinks he is. Whatever, it's not just me: it's pretty clear that, in the new 'structure', several others will also find it difficult to justify their position and salary long-term, given the non-income-earning roles they now have.

In the meantime, we get on with the business, as if the only change has been one of office location. We've brought them a blue-chip brand and client list that they could only dream about getting through the door before our arrival: there's some nice work for Twinings Tea that has finally borne fruit from an initial meeting over two years ago on the Oriana; Holsten Pils continues to put large-budget projects our way; but they're more interested in the newspaper business with the FT and the Mirror, which is core direct marketing work, and much more in line with their own market offering. Look at the client list on their side of the business, and there's some petfood business with a decent blue-chip name which doesn't seem to add up to much in actual billings, a motor cycle insurance company we've never heard of (and unless you ride a motor-bike, neither will you) and a few other nonentities of the corporate world. They make a big deal of the work they're doing for the BBC, which is admittedly about as blue-chip as you can get; the only trouble is, it's hard to understand what it is they're actually doing. They have some consultancy going on which is paying big fees, but after having explained to me the nature of the project, I am none the wiser. I can't seem to pin down who is actually doing what, and with what end-objectives, to justify the large-ish sums of money that are flowing our way. We ourselves had a similar situation at Alfred Dunhill a couple of years back – we did do some work that won an ISP Gold at the awards ceremony for some really low-budget European work – but most of the fees for consultancy were simply not justified by the work levels or results, and eventually we got found out after an internal job reorganisation. I have a feeling the same will happen here.

There's also a database department, which has two or three people employed to help clients build and improve their CRM systems. They're always busy tapping keys when you walk in, and looking intently at gobbledygook on their screens, but I never manage to get a one-syllable comprehensive answer to the question about what they actually do or how they justify their salary. In fact I'd say that the whole edifice is built on paper-thin foundations, when it comes to substantive business – which I know is a bit rich coming from a sales promotion man, where you're only ever as good as your last campaign. Putting it bluntly, I'd say that, far from being a merger of equals, our billings represent a huge majority of the merged numbers, going forward. This is hard to justify in reality, because there doesn't appear to be the transparent accounting reporting which we are used to, based on actual invoices raised, for work actually done. Pierre of course will soon get a handle on that, and then we'll see what's what.

Except he won't, and neither will we. We've only been in the new place for a few weeks when Pauline announces that she's decided that Pierre, our trusty FD who has been responsible for keeping us stable and ship-shape (indeed afloat in the difficult times), is surplus to requirements, and she's "going to let him go." I've no idea whether this is genuinely her idea or Peanut Head's (though I know where my suspicions lie), but it brings home with a 40,000 volt jolt our total loss of executive power, and fully justifies our concerns about the trustworthiness of the new regime. Before the sale, we extracted a verbal commitment that all our senior staff – and particularly Board members – would have a continuing role to play in the new organisation. When confronted about it, Peanut Head simply shrugs it off as being Pauline's decision as MD (yeah, right) and in any case commercial reality: he's just not needed in the new set-up, and that's that.

Well, now we know what we're up against. The Cat and I have no power to protect our people if the big liar at the top decides to dispense with them, and furthermore we can't trust a single word he says. At a stroke, he's demonstrated why we won't ever be able to work with him in any meaningful way and justified all our misgivings. We have, though, as we have to keep reminding ourselves, got the money in the bank. Except that I still haven't: because my 50th birthday is at the end of February and because the government's tax arrangements give big tax advantages to those selling their businesses after that age (like the first half million tax free) – why? What's the logic? – I've had a clause inserted in the sale document to delay the sale of most of my shares until that time. So in reality I'm still waiting for the cash when Pierre is given his marching orders. Not that it could possibly be withheld legally, even if we have the mother of all fall-outs, but it's another small constraint in our (my: the Cat's got all his cash) ability or perhaps commitment to stand and fight our corner.

In retrospect, maybe it's Peanut Head's way of seeing how much we're prepared to do to protect our people. Although that may be crediting him with more intelligence than is justified by the facts. What we discover is that whatever he decides to do, he just does, whatever arguments there may be to the contrary, and if that leads to a trail of destruction as a result (which it frequently does), well just deal with it. Anyway, our failure to stand up and be counted at the first sign of trouble, regardless of where the decision really comes from, sends out all the wrong signals. I'm guessing that one or two of the other senior people (Nick for one, Stuart for another) are looking over their shoulders as a result.

As always though, things settle down again, and we get used to the idea that one of our number is no more. Like a sudden death, you familiarise yourself with the new reality. Not far down the track, though, there's another and much worse new reality, with the loss of our biggest client. We've just launched Winfield – the Aussie cigarette brand which we won in a competitive pitch at the back end of the year – and have recently won another pitch for the multi-million pound Peter Stuyvesant brand. Then, just two days after being given the brilliant news, the new Rothmans Marketing Director calls the Cat to have what he describes as "one of the most difficult conversations in his life." The campaign is being canned. This is bad enough, given the vast billings that are riding on it (in 'firm' in the forward billings), and it would certainly have ensured the continuing profitability of at least our side of the equation. Worse, much worse, is to follow, however, not too long afterwards (and in retrospect it is likely that the two things are inter-linked). The entire worldwide Rothmans business is acquired by British American Tobacco, and the new owners, shortly afterwards, announce that all the UK marketing of the Rothmans brands will be merged into its London office and that its existing roster of agencies will be handling all advertising and promotion forthwith. No discussions. No negotiations. Our services are simply no longer required. We've done nothing wrong (for once) and yet overnight we find a million pounds – or more – lopped off our forward billings.

This is a real hammer blow, and one we always feared the possibility of – not because we had any reason to fear, but because when any client represents more than a quarter of your total business, it makes you very vulnerable. At one point it had been an even greater percentage, over half, so we have been happy to see its dominance gradually reduce, as new blue-chip business has been won. Nevertheless, in our previous guise as Marketing Principles, this would almost certainly have precipitated a round of redundancies. You simply can't sustain 35 staff if a quarter of your turnover and profit suddenly walks out the door. It's the immutable rule of the service industry that the fine balance between the provision of resource (human) to deliver the services you provide and the cash value of those services has to be maintained. Staff numbers have to go up and down with the cash being generated, which is why accurate forward billings projections are so vital.

What will happen now? Who makes the job cuts anyway? The Cat, who as Client Services Obergruppenführer is responsible for client income – and presumably the provision of the human resource to sustain it? Or Peanut Head, who appears to take all the hiring and firing decisions? Or his puppet, Pauline? You'll notice I don't feature in the list. I may carry the Chief Executive title, but it is purely ceremonial. One thing's for sure: since it is no longer our business, and following the acrimony of Pierre's enforced departure, the Cat won't be making any hurried decisions on this score. The team has other business to work on, and our houses are no longer on the line if the business makes losses. Let's see what the overall business looks like before any hasty decisions are made.

You'd expect this to be item number one on the next board meeting agenda, but it doesn't seem to have registered quite the same seismic shock waves here as it would have done in the ancien regime. Of course the whole financial reporting is different and just a bit schizoid. Gone are the 25-page management accounts, "which wouldn't have disgraced ICI"; in is a measly financial summary, which is about as clear as mud, and forward billings. Then there are the figures which Fanny Craddock sends to the Americans, and which are not presented for scrutiny at board meetings, but which are shown to me and the Cat in some half-arsed attempt at 'team building.' Apart from the forward billings, which the Cat produces from figures submitted by his team heads, and which therefore represent reality, (and at present not a particularly healthy reality), nothing else seems to tally or add up. In particular, the numbers that Fanny Craddock sends to our stateside masters each month are a masterpiece of obfuscation: how they relate to the actual figures being achieved, only she knows, but it doesn't take long before we realise that the nickname we've given her may have been because of her looks and demeanour, but in fact is frighteningly prescient: she's cooking the books. As far as we can see, the business is in pretty poor shape, but over in Chicago and New York, everything looks hunky dory. That's because she's sending them fictional numbers that appear to show us hitting our targets. God knows how she's rationalising it all: maybe she's got a slush fund tucked away for a rainy day (where did that come from though?); or maybe she's hoping that it will all come right later in the year and she can re-adjust the fibs.

The Cat thinks that when the two businesses were merged, it somehow enabled her to mould all the figures to her own ends, to demonstrate that they themselves are on target for their own personal earn-outs. We both wonder whether the cash pile which was in our bank account is somehow being used to paper over the ever-widening cracks in the current business performance. Whatever, we're both as sure as we can be that m'learned friends would have a field day if Inspector Knacker were ever invited to take a look at things.

Whether or not this is an open conspiracy is difficult to judge. The Cat and I are effectively recruited into it, when Fanny Craddock presents us with some executive incentive scheme, which means we walk away even richer at the end of each year if we hit our targets. The fact that hitting these targets each quarter is highly implausible without her jiggery-pokery makes us accessories after the fact. Is this a clever bit of psychology or just a ham-fisted attempt to put some sticking plaster across our gobs? We discuss the options. We could go to the Americans – alright, Jaydon: he's the only one we know, but he is head honcho of the whole shebang – and blow the whistle. The trouble is, whenever he's over here on one of his monthly or bi-monthly presidential visits, he and Peanut Head give every impression of being as thick as thieves. Given that he's an accountant by trade, we make the assumption that if we can figure out what's going on with our limited access to the books and knowledge of detailed finance, he must know too, and that therefore he's a party to any sleight of hand in the way the figures are dressed up for corporate consumption. Whatever the truth, we elect to stay our hand and just get on with it. So what does getting on with it actually mean in practice for a man with a fancy job title and no job description? It's surprising how much 'work' you can create to fill the hours, if you choose to. I guess it's called justifying your existence, and it goes on in office environments all over the world. First up, there are the trade associations, which I've supported grudgingly until now, because I hate committee meetings generally (talk shops that achieve little: all the real activity takes place between two or three real movers and shakers elsewhere), but I know that participation gives both me and the business a higher profile. So going to Institute of Sales Promotion meetings, and volunteering to be on the judging panel of the annual awards, is one way of filling the hours. Even better is my elevation, if that is the right word, to being the ISP's representative at the EFSP – the European Federation of Sales Promotion – a flimsy organisation of eight or nine countries, which meets every couple of months in search of a raison d'être. I can't for the life of me see what it achieves, or indeed what it might ever achieve, but it gives me an excuse to swan around Europe at someone else's expense, attending talk shops from which little concrete action ever emerges, and eating well: you can be sure that whoever is hosting each get-together knows their onions when it comes to the best restaurants in town. I can't remember whether being asked to do it by the ISP had anything to do with me speaking reasonable French, but if it was, it's a complete irrelevance. The organisation is currently being run by a Frenchman called Jaques, so you'd expect his language to feature pretty strongly: there's no doubt that the French would expect the rest of the world to speak their language, just as we do, if they could get away with it, and you'll notice that their politicians refuse to make any public utterances in English, even though they undoubtedly could if they chose to, but Jaques doesn't even try to make an issue of it. He may (he does) speak English with the anticipated outrageous accent, but he knows that the business lingua franca is English, especially in the American-dominated advertising and market services industry, and all communication is therefore conducted for my convenience.

So I spend a pleasant two or three days in places like Lisbon or Dublin (there are also representatives from France – of course – Belgium, Holland, Spain, Germany, Italy, any more? Damned if I can remember, though there may have been a fledgling member from Austria too.) We spend hours trying to find ways to continue justifying our existence (there's another awards ceremony, natch) so we can go on junketing around Europe. It's all a complete waste of effort and time, but I've got fuck all else to do, so why not? I wonder if it still exists? Answers on the back of a postcard, etc.

Peanut Head himself is responsible for another way of filling in the hours between birth and death. As part of a huge multi-national conglomerate, Draft necessarily has some big advertising agency brothers and sisters, one of which is called Lintas. They have some fancy offices in Soho Square (surprise) and Peanut Head has determined they would make the perfect partners for joint ventures, whereby we get access to their client base and benefit from developing genuine 'through-the-line' campaigns (as they're called) – effectively bolting on direct marketing and sales promotion to their high-profile advertising campaigns. I've no idea how he's managed to get the authority to try to make this happen, but down there we go, and he's busy throwing his considerable weight around and trying to prove what a big man he is. You can see in an instant that the senior management, whose arms he is attempting to twist, loathe and detest him. The idea is to set up a Draft office in theirs, where resource and expertise can be readily accessed and to have someone always available for consultation, meetings, etc. And I am the chosen disciple to lead this crusade.

After a presentation to their Board – around two or three dozen senior personnel in practice: a board position in advertising land is just about massaging egos; there's no way any efficient decision-making or strategy could come out of it – I find myself with a fancy penthouse office next to a roof terrace, with views over the roof-tops of Soho and the Charing Cross Road. I'm not expected to be there full-time – just a day or two a week, or as required. Looking back of course, it's just Peanut Head's way of getting me out of his Oxford office as often as possible, but at the time I don't realise, or care much. I'm quite grateful to get out of there myself: the whole place has a horrible atmosphere and feeling about it, and the excuse to mosey on up to the West End a couple of days a week, in my own time and leisure, is not that unappealing. I've no interest in commuting full-time and won't be doing it, but this is as good a balance as you could wish for.

The only trouble is that it's a crap idea, for two reasons. One: Lintas is one of the few big London agencies that does more than pay lip-service to integrated marketing; they already have a small team of sales promotion people, and indeed last year won the top ISP Grand Prix Award for their Peperoni campaign (entitled, for those of you who care, "It's A Bit Of An Animal"), so they hardly need me to show them the way. And two: they're a big, brash advertising agency with huge attitude and an enormous chip on their corporate shoulder about wanky little direct marketing agencies telling them what to do or how it should be done. We might be part of Draft, which is enormous over in the States, but over here they know we're just some hick Oxfordshire unit trying feebly to punch above its weight. No one says as much of course. Well, they wouldn't, would they? It's not the British way. Just smile, be polite, friendly even; invite them to meetings (and especially meetings about meetings); but just make sure nothing concrete ever comes of it.

It's a re-run of my year trolling up the M1 to Advertising Principles in Leeds, so I recognise all the signs, but it's nicer offices and it's Soho, so what do I care? As with the Leeds affair, I get to meet a few clients, get close to a bit of business here or there – and it is always just a bit of business – but nothing ever comes of it. It's interesting being involved in European campaigns, even if just on the fringes, and I find myself going to meetings in Milan (Unilever) and Helsinki (Finlandia vodka) for planning meetings (don't ask). The latter in particular is interesting because it's a pitch for the business, involving every facet of marketing, from research through PR and sales promotion to pan-European advertising. Our experience with Smirnoff gives me ample excuse to talk knowledgeably about the vodka market, though only in the UK admittedly. Trouble is, they don't have a prayer of winning it (and don't) because the creative work is so lacking in any sparkle or originality. Naturally my opinion on this is neither sought nor welcome, and in further overtones of the Leeds episode, I find myself not even in the team presenting at the pitch, which tells you everything you need to know about the emphasis they're likely to put on the promotional element. It's an interesting idea too: drinking vodka off the bottom of a large ice sculpture of a helter skelter in trendy bars and clubs, as the centre-piece to sampling nights – aka the Finlandia Vodka Luge.

So plenty more time to swan around Europe, though without

the fancy dinners regrettably. Lintas's big problem is that half the agency is dependent on the Rover account, which it's had for ever, but which is threatening to move its business elsewhere. The creative work is frankly tired and uninspiring (still produced by creative teams on huge salaries with attitude of course), and there's a sense of foregathering gloom about the place.

The small promotion team is a nice enough collection of 20-somethings with no real idea but plenty of good intentions. They soon recognise Peanut Head for the arrogant arsehole he is, and despise Fanny Craddock even more, dubbing her with their own moniker of the White Witch, which I quite like. It all staggers on for six months or more before the experiment, having borne no fruit whatsoever, is called off, not long before Rover does indeed move its business, the whole agency goes into meltdown and is eventually folded into one of the other group agencies.

It's at about this time that I take on the (unpaid) job of producing a history of my village for the millennium – we're now in 1999 – and given that I'm not exactly stretched at work, I use some of the time on that particular project too. It's called "Brillennium" (the village is called Brill) and, looking back, the 178-page hard-back coffee-table book represents the only real achievement in the whole year for me personally.

Meanwhile the business staggers on, but all our worst fears are confirmed, as first Stewart and then Nick are eased out, "let go", call it what you will. There's hardly any shock or even reaction in all honesty, just a degree of resignation and a hint of wistfulness that the decision to leave an unhappy, if not yet quite sinking, ship hasn't been made for them too. The Cat, under pressure to cut costs on the basis of too many Chiefs and not enough Indians, does what he can to ease the pain with decent redundancy pack-ages.

The blondes continue their rivalry, though now on the same

floor, so it's a bit more difficult to be bitchy about each other. Liza has shown her true colours by overtly allying herself with Peanut Head and the new regime. What she's saying, and demonstrating, is, "The power to further my career isn't with you any more, it's with him." So she sucks up to him. The Weather Girl is made of different stuff of course, but there again, she and we have been working together for nigh on a decade, and you don't break down old loyalties so easily. It is at moments like this, when the going gets tough, that you find out who your friends are. Forget the good times, when the world and his wife beat a path to your door to slap you on the back and drink your wine. Check out and keep close the ones who are still at your side, with a spanner in one hand and a gun in the other, when the wheels are coming off the wagons and the Indians are massing on the horizon.

I certainly have a bad feeling in the pit of my stomach every morning that I get in the Jag and head off to the new offices (if I'm not swanning around Europe or Soho). Even when we were in difficulties as an independent agency, I still went to work in a positive frame of mind and a sense of determination. Now I feel drained, negative and strangely demoralised. It isn't the building or location, which most people would describe as idyllic, notwithstanding the crappy local pubs (and I mean crappy) and the poxy sandwich van that comes round daily – Prêt it ain't. We have a long hot summer, and sitting round the pool for tea and discussions about this or that would draw the comment, "lucky bastards" from most quarters. For me, I suppose it's a combination of loss of authority and no obvious way forward that makes the situation uncomfortable, if not quite intolerable.

During this period, Peanut Head organises a staff summer party in an attempt to pull the two sides of the new equation together. There are no warring factions, as such, but there is still a palpable feeling of them and us. Whether this will be broken down by a tennis tournament, poolside frolics and a lot of liquor is open to question, but no one cares too much about that. It's a day off, the sun shines (mercifully) and everyone has a chance to let their hair down. Not least, it's a chance to see some of the women in their swimming costumes. Most of the Draft lot look better with their clothes on, frankly, but there's one pneumatic blond whom we're all looking forward to viewing, and she doesn't disappoint. It's a pleasant enough event, but by early evening I've had enough and depart sober for only the second time in a decade from a company do. No appetite for a long drunken binge, and in any case I'm driving. Gone are the days when you could just stagger to a city centre taxi rank, slur "Brill" at the driver and slump in the back seat for half an hour of the whirling pits, putting it all on account. ABC Taxis must have loved us. Well, possibly not on reflection, but they took a lot of money off us. The Jag might virtually know its own way home after six months of the same route, but living in one village and working in another one twenty miles away, I simply can't afford to lose my licence, and anyway, by early evening, I've lost interest in the enforced jollities, and slip away.

As the longer days of Autumn start to bite, the outdoor attractions of tea and biscuits al fresco fade with the weather, and we're back to reality. The reality is the business is in poor shape and frankly doesn't need the still top-heavy management structure, if you can call it that. Pauline is already history, her seven-month reign as MD terminated shortly after the total eclipse of the sun in mid-August. Talk about omens. Ancient tribes might have ascribed all sorts of misfortunes to such an event, but her sending round a memo to all staff, allowing them to take 20 minutes away from their desks to witness the spectacle, probably had more impact. As the Cat puts it, ever so tongue in cheek, she really was a woman of the people. More to the point she was an expensive and wholly unnecessary overhead, who should never have been installed in the first place, along with her PA, Kitty, who also receives an unwanted P45.

The Cat himself is now installed unceremoniously as her replacement, though it's doubtful whether anyone notices any difference either in his daily activity plan or the results. It just demonstrates all too vividly that her original appointment was as flawed as it first appeared to be, when presented to us as a fait accompli the previous Autumn.

As the nights start to draw in, Jaydon comes over and brings with him some Canadian agency big-shot who, having himself been acquired, is now busy making himself at home on the slippery corporate ladder. We're not sure whether he's here in the role of familiarisation with all things British/European, or there's another agenda. The latter seems likely when he holds one-to-one interviews with all the senior management, including me. How are we feeling? What do we think of the way things are going? Etc etc. He obviously fancies himself as a bit of a human resources expert – except, when you don't know someone from Adam and he behaves like the usual agency toss-pot, you're hardly likely to open up to him and tell it like it is. So what he gets, from me at least, is a lot of bland platitudes about taking time for the new structure to settle down, and so on and so on. The Cat, I think, is a bit more strident and critical of things, because that's his way, but I'm pretty sure he falls short of calling Peanut Head and Fanny Craddock a couple of confidence tricksters who shouldn't be put in charge of a whelk stall, which is just one more in our joint litany of mistakes about how we should have handled things.

Jaydon takes a back seat during most of this, but there is one moment that sticks in the memory. He's been out with the Creative Head, Pete – another one-to-one, trying to find out what's going on? He won't get much out of Pete, mainly because there's not much to be got out. I bet Pete knows less about all the financial shenanigans than we do, and probably doesn't want to know. Anyway on their return in Pete's flash (but shite) TVR, he can't find the door handle to let himself out. He's a dapper little chap and he likes to be in control, but after ineffectually feeling around the door for the right lever, Pete leans across and does it for him. Whether there's an issue here with latent inadequacy, or what, far from saying thank you or something self-deprecating (though that would be far too British for an 'I'm in control' Yank), he simply quips, "Ya little fucker" and gets out, leaving Pete bewilderedly wondering what that was all about.

He's also knocking off some blond in the Draft ranks (not one of ours, in case you're wondering) while he's over here, despite being presumably married – happily or otherwise, we have no clue, though I guess you can draw your own conclusions. What's extraordinary is the behaviour, of both of them, in public. There's one evening when we're all under orders to attend some utterly meaningless direct marketing awards ceremony that Peanut Head's involved with (thus guaranteeing its awfulness), and he's engineered Jaydon as its key-note speaker. It is the direst of dire evenings, the awards are tenuous, spurious and no one knows or cares about them, but we sit around our sponsors' table looking self-important. There isn't even any of the drunken excess that characterises sales promotion events to relieve the tedium. And Jaydon gives the dullest, most irrelevant speech in the history of the universe: after ten minutes of it, I'm feeling a mixture of fidgety and embarrassed; at twenty, I'm about to start tipping petrol over myself and lighting matches. And still he drones on. But it's the entrance and exit that most excites comment. In he strolls, like the cat that's got the cream, with blond Anna on his arm, behaving for all the world like some First Lady, playing the part of lady bountiful. OK, she's reasonably fit and, given the opportunity, we probably would, but certainly not all flaunty in public like this. Plus she's our employee, so swanning around looking all superior, like she does, just makes us make a mental note about due retribution coming right her way one of the days. I imagine it's no more than an exercise in power fucking for Jaydon, but you never know.

Back, though, to our Canadian friend's visit, which is capped by dinner for the senior management at a hostelry in the little Oxforshire village of South Leigh, called Jerry Stonor's Masons Arms. It is an extraordinary little place – big and rambling, all a bit dusty and dingy inside, but concealed by dim lighting and candles, with fancy bottles of wine racked all round the walls. It's like a cross between a wine cellar and someone's slightly tatty country house dining-room. It is, to put it mildly, eccentric, as is Jerry, the eponymous host who owns and runs it. As you'd expect, Jerry is full of himself, which is probably why Peanut Head rates the place. Michael Winner eventually visits the place for one of "Winner's Dinners" and does a wonderful hatchet job on it, closing with the immortal phrase, "Jerry's problem is that someone once told him he was a bit of a character, and unfortunately he believed them." Marvellous. And spot on. It's ruinously expensive for what it is, but we're not paying, so who cares, and Mr Canadian shows how outré he is by finishing off the evening with glasses of absinthe. It's vile stuff and usually only comes into play when everyone's so pissed, they'll drink their own entrails, but we all go along with the charade that we're a happy enough team. Then we all drive home: there's no way we would survive the breathalyser if the filth are doing any spot checks, but once again we all get away with it.

It's about now that another little contretemps arises. It all starts with a call from our favourite lawyer at Biddle & Co (there is no irony intended here: his name is Martin Lane and he actually is our favourite lawyer, and as a result of this, and ensuing conversations, will remain so for life in all probability.) As reported in the last chapter, he's inserted a clause in the company sale document, which says that if they want to exercise their option to give us back the shell company with the office lease in it and £100,000 to cover possible short-term liabilities, they have to do so within six months of the sale. We're now into Autumn, and their useless local solicitor, whom Martin has run rings round throughout, has forgotten to do so. He's contacted Martin and asked if we'd mind doing it anyway. I bet his palms are sweaty and his anus is having to work extra hard not to shit himself.

In case you've forgotten (we surely haven't), our 25-year lease on the city centre offices still has the thick end of 13 years on it, and a cumulative potential liability on it, therefore, at current rates, of around half a million, were it to remain unoccupied for the duration. Unlikely as this scenario is, it still represents a sword of Damocles hanging over our heads, which the Cat in particular is not happy about. As it happens, we seem to have found a tenant for the place at least for the short term, but if they ever leave or default, the whole responsibility as head lessees would fall to us again. Until 2013.

I ask Martin to clarify what this means, and in particular, can they make us accommodate their request. His reply is succinct: no, they can't make us, but he'd just like to mention that we do have to work with these guys on a day-to-day basis. It takes the Cat and me about a nanosecond to consider our options. I tell him that his response to them should be that, having been asked his opinion by his clients, he couldn't possibly tell them in all honesty that it is in our best financial interests to accommodate their request, and that therefore we decline to play ball. Mighty sighs of relief at the lifting of the sword are tempered by an anticipated swirl of shit hitting the fan when Peanut Head finds out. We wait, with breath fully bated, but the storm never comes. In fact, he seems to make light of it, whether because he doesn't know or care about the implications, or because it's not his money. We may never know. The Cat still laughs about the way Biddle always called the hick solicitors, when they needed to speak with them, "towards the end of the day, when the elderly partners were dozing off after too much port and game pie." But at least it's over forty grand a year of weight off our shoulders.

And so we stagger on through this charade of a business. The feeling in the pit of my stomach as I approach the offices each morning is just the same. It's probably a feeling that many employees have, unhappy in their work or the circumstances surrounding it, but I've never had it before, and certainly not in the last twelve years, when I've been my own boss effectively. They talk of the problems of people becoming institutionalised, but I think you can become institutionally unsuited for employment (by others, that is), once you've had a lengthy spell running your own show.

The long winter evenings draw in, making the place more oppressive, but the Cat is busy organising the Christmas party, which (naturally) has to be bigger and better than anything we've done before – not counting our 10th anniversary outing to Paris presumably. Taking 50 or 60 people abroad probably would bankrupt us in the current state of affairs. So no popping down the Red Lion for a roast turkey dinner with crackers and paper hats, before going back to the office at 2.30 (2.45 if you're lucky) to get on with work – which is what happens in most offices. Talk about token gestures: you can see the owner/managers looking at their watches and begrudging their employees every last second. And they wonder why they struggle to recruit and keep good people.

We're going to Michel Sadone's place for lunch (Ma Belle, aka Mabel's, down an alley off the High where we're taking over the place for the afternoon. Then we're strolling over to the Cock and Camel, where we've got exclusive use of their downstairs bar for a disco. (You will look in vain for these establishments today: Ma Belle sold out some years ago, and the Cock and Bollocks, as we called it, is now wunderkind Jamie Oliver's latest venture.) So far, all very straight up and down. But to get us all from our "rural idyll" into the centre of town, the Cat has organised not an executive coach with video facilities and bar, not a fleet of taxis, but a fleet of chauffeur-driven stretch limos, complete with lashings of champagne. Given that the journey time is half an hour max, the convoy of half a dozen vehicles is going to do a little tour of local places of interest, such as Blenheim Palace, so we can have a good hour or more's piss-up in "style" (well, it is horribly nouveau, isn't it?) before the main event kicks off.

It all goes off as planned (though finding spaces to park six stretch limos in the High Street to decant their squiffy occupants is fun and excites comment from the casual passers-by, so job done, I guess). No one throws courgettes at the mirrors in the restaurant, which happened the last time we were here: Michel had been his usual phlegmatic Gallic self – "Ah told zem to stop throwing food at ze mirrors and zey stopped; so zat is OK." He has form with a few drinks inside him, so maybe that's why he is more sympathetic than most restaurateurs would be. This time it's all very civilised, and even the Cocky can't produce much, if any, bad behaviour. Interestingly enough, though, Peanut Head and Fanny Craddock don't participate at all. What does that say about their management style (I use the last word reluctantly)?

Since we're getting to the last few pages (well, you are if you're reading this as a physical book – if you're reading it electronically, tough), you've probably already guessed that this can't go on. And sure enough, it doesn't. The end, when it comes, still manages to surprise though. It's just a few days before Christmas and the Cat's been out to lunch with Peanut Head – nothing especially unusual in that: any excuse for a decent feed and a bit of a chinwag. But on their return, Peanut Head pops into my office, flops down on the settee opposite my desk and informs me he's got a bit of news: he's just fired him. The inevitable question ensues: why? There then follows some cock and bull story about how he's organised the Chrtistmas party and invited someone along who is not an employee (Julia, our loyal debtor chaser and accounts clerk, who'd left a few weeks before, having finally been unable to resolve her differences with Fanny Craddock – quelle surprise – and who, having worked for us for seven or eight years, deserved a send-off). Apart from not being grounds for dismissal, it is so patently just some hastily assembled pretext that it isn't even worth challenging or discussing. What it actually amounts to is, "I don't like him and I can't work with him". He almost certainly knows we call him Peanut Head, which won't go down well with his bloated ego. He's probably also figured out that staff loyalty (of our people for sure, and maybe even a few of his own) is more likely to adhere to the Cat, who knows how to manage people, than him – and who is in any case infinitely more popular. And he's certainly calculated the significant savings on his overhead without him – not to mention the likelihood, which he has undoubtedly calculated, being the devious cunt that he is, of me following him. All of this flashes through my brain in a second or two.

It is also probable that Liza and the 'part-time' advertising research woman, Maz (who will eventually end up, laughably, as the last senior bod standing) have connived in his departure in some way. Maz gets the MD title – a poisoned chalice, if ever there were one, unless you're very matey with Peanut Head, which she is, and Liza becomes Deputy MD, so all her scheming has seemingly paid off.

The Cat is effectively being escorted off the premises and I am invited to go with him – take the rest of the afternoon off – to talk things through with him (and basically consider my position). That latter bit is not actually articulated, but we both know that is what it means. And so we find ourselves, in mid-afternoon, in the bar of a north Oxford restaurant, discussing the meaning of life, and the prospect of existence without employment. In truth, without even weighing up the pros and cons or considering the options in any way, I have already gone with him psychologically. The very idea of being in that horrible building with those two vile individuals, and making even the pretence of working with (for) them, is utter anathema.

We can talk and discuss all we like, between the two of us and me with Cath (my long-suffering wife), but in my head I walked out the door simultaneously with the Cat. In actual fact, he is officially on 'gardening leave', which means Peanut Head is going to continue to pay him, while he tries to find a way of getting him out that won't result in a messy legal action. I, on the other hand, am going to take the Christmas break to consider my options. Peanut Head has said he wants me to stay, though why, I can't imagine. Possibly for some short-term stability with the staff, before he applies the same stiletto in the ribs to me. Possibly as a sop to the Americans, or so he doesn't look like a total incompetent (some hope). He is without doubt the nastiest, most unpleasant individual I've ever dealt with (you can probably tell) – a potent mixture of arrogance and ignorance, which is never a winning combination. To paraphrase Michael Winner, the trouble with Peanut Head is that at some point someone told him he was god's gift to the world, and unfortunately he believed them.

I spend Christmas contemplating the dawn of a new millennium without a job or obvious purpose in life. In all honesty, I don't spend very much time weighing up the options. My main concern is not my own future – it may be uncertain, employment-wise, but it isn't insecure financially, with the sale funds in the bank – but how to get that stiletto out of Peanut Head's hands and into his own ribs. I may be going down, but I am damned determined to take him with me. And this is where, with hindsight, I think I make a fatal error of judgement. I should have acted more boldly. Again.

When I go back in the New Year, I tell Peanut Head I am not interested in continuing without the Cat, that we come as a unit and I can't or won't function without him, and that in any case I have lost the appetite for it. I describe myself, I think, as a busted flush, and am far too anxious to negotiate a handsome pay-off, before attending to the stiletto in the ribs issue. What I should have done is fly to New York, confront Jaydon and all the rest of the Draft management with all the facts – not least the fraudulent figures they are still being fed, which show the agency doing a whole lot better than it actually is. What holds me back? Still the nagging doubt that none of it would come as shattering news to Jaydon, plus the assumption that the Americans must surely have known about and approved the Cat's demise, whatever trumped-up bollocks have been presented to them as justification. I also assume that the hand of the wanky Canadian is at work here in some way. Would, in fact, a trip to New York be any more than an expensive ego trip on my behalf?

We'll never know, because I don't make it. Instead I spend January and February in limbo – a gardening leave of my own, which is all very pleasant and to be recommended, reading lots of novels and pottering about, organising the local pantomime (irony of ironies), while composing the letter of death to Jaydon, comprehensively spilling all the beans on Peanut Head and Fanny Craddock's fraudulent incompetence and arrogant uselessness at being able to manage a team of increasingly demotivated people. It is two or three pages long and pulls no punches, but it won't be sent until the end of February, when I have a signed agreement giving me six months pay, including £30,000 for "loss of office" which comes tax free, and the XK8 – the visible symbol of success which I've become attached to (and in fact still drive). The Cat, ironically, is still on gardening leave and will remain so for months after I've officially gone, while collecting a fat monthly pay cheque for swanning around and drinking heavily. All right, just swanning around. Mainly.

The reason I have expressed uncertainty about whether I should have gone to New York to spill the beans is the effect my letter to Jaydon actually has. Whether he flies over specifically because of it or he is here anyway, I don't know, but he asks to meet in some posh hotel by Hyde Park frequented by rich Americans. Since I've obviously got that stiletto close to the rib area, the temptation to see if I can get it well and truly inserted is irresistible. The meeting is affable enough and I give Peanut Head and Fanny Craddock both barrels. In fact I probably give them five or six barrels. I do hope so. The impression I get, though, is that while Jaydon is definitely not aware of all of this, he already has some antipathy towards Fanny Craddock and doesn't fully trust her. My letter and interview merely confirm what he already suspects. So maybe he and Peanut Head are not as in cahoots as we thought. He does express disappointment that Peanut Head and I have not been able to work together, as he had hoped, which just shows how useless they were at the due diligence they did, concentrating solely on the money, and ignoring entirely the personality issues which always dog post-acquisition organisa-tions. Since it has been intimated to me that Peanut Head never expected me to stay on after they'd bought us (though he never articulated any such thought, but maybe that was behind getting me up to Lintas in London – hoping it would take off and he'd have me out of his hair), it also suggests that Jaydon and Peanut Head are not necessarily singing from the same hymn sheet.

The last word, I think, should be mine. Given that I express to Jaydon all the doubts we had from the start about Peanut Head's character and fitness for office – it is still my view that in a sensible world we should have been taking them over and running things – he asks why we did the deal in the first place. I suppose I am shocked that he needs to ask, since it should be obvious to anyone, I'd have thought. I look him squarely in the eye and tell him, "We took your money."

NOT QUITE THE END

Two or three months later, I hear on the grapevine that Fanny Craddock has been dismissed from her post, presumably by Jaydon, and that, without her protective smokescreen for cover, Peanut Head has also fallen on his sword and has negotiated an exit which allegedly covers him against any retrospective action for wrong-doing. I can only assume that, if true, the only reason that Jaydon would conform to such an agreement is because he himself doesn't want any naughtiness raked over: he may not be directly implicated, but the smell of shit is likely to cling to all those who should have known what was going on. He might get away with the charge of gross negligence, but he'd certainly go down on one of incompetence. Keeping Peanut Head's own incompetence and misdemeanours under wraps gives him a chance of never being charged himself.

At least I feel vindicated in sending the letter, which has presumably played some part in his eventual demise. It won't bring back my business (which incidentally Draft have entirely squandered in the interim) – and anyway I've a fat bank account in compensation for that – but it has helped get that stiletto nice and deep between the ribs, and given it a twist. So it may not be a happy ending, but there is without doubt a whiff of satisfaction that some sort of closure has been achieved.

DEFINITELY THE END (Apart from the Post Script)

Post Script

AFTER PLOUGHING THROUGH all this and correcting as much of my defective memory as he could (while issuing dire warnings about possible legal action from certain featured characters), the Cat thinks it would be a good idea to finish off with a few "lessons learned."

I'd rather hoped that this was happening as we've gone along, but on the presenter's premise that you need to tell 'em what you're going to tell 'em, tell 'em, then tell 'em what you've just told 'em, here are ten things to take away with you and put in your memory bank for future reference, should you be running your own business, or feel tempted to start one.

1. The most over-arching thing is a simple, but mighty large, concept: knowledge. As Jimbo so presciently put it way back in chapter one, when we all handed in our notice to go it alone, we knew fuck all about running a business, but assumed we could learn it all as we went along, from experience. Well we certainly did that, and made our fair share of schoolboy howlers along the way, as we did so.

If there's one thing I've learned as a result of advising other small businesses since the final chapter of Marketing Principles, it is that, just like us, most business owners can't or won't read books that will help them understand business better and run a tighter ship. Actually I get the impression that most business

314

owner/managers don't read books at all, full stop, never mind self-improvement ones. Perhaps that's because so many of them are middle-aged men who already know it all.

Anyway, if I'd known then what I know now, I'd have invested more time and energy into accumulating the knowledge that we later depended on "experts" for. (You know the definition of an expert: someone who, on any given subject, knows a couple more things than you do.) It may not have stopped the fraudsters or the splitters doing what they did, but it might have left us (me) in a better place to deal with it, or even nipping in the bud the worst effects.

2. Pick your business partners with care; don't just accept anyone who says they're interested in coming along for the ride. The more partners you have, the more likely you are to have differences of opinion – and eventually one of those differences will be fundamental to the business and/or you.

You don't have to socialise all (or indeed any) of the time out of the office; but if you don't feel all that comfortable with them and their partners when you do, it's a warning sign that when there are disagreements about direction or strategy, they may not be entirely resolvable.

Those who play together well, work together well. Generally. Though there can still be majestic fallings out. Witness the Cat and Stid. We all played together extremely well initially, as chapter five demonstrates all too graphically. But only in work connected situations, at least as far as I was concerned.

3. Running a business with more than two or three employees is all about the people and your ability to manage a team. It doesn't matter how good you are at whatever technical work you do; if you don't know how to pass on your knowledge to others, organise and run teams, give people clear job descriptions and objectives, and manage them sympathetically, your business is doomed to flat-line, or at best under-perform.

So if there's only one thing you're prepared to invest your time and energy in, make it people management skills, unless you're a natural. Few are.

It's your employees' ability to make money for you when you're not looking over their shoulder (or even in the same country) that will make your business more profitable and valuable.

4. Every year, re-jig your business plan (I'm making the possibly over-optimistic assumption that you have such a document, however slim a volume it is), so that you have some clear and achievable objectives for the next twelve months and the next five years. Written down. With sufficient detail about how you're going to go about achieving them. With a Plan B for when or if Plan A doesn't work. Failing to plan is planning to fail. A tiresome truism, but still true.

5. Learn to manage your time effectively, and if that means taking courses or reading books about time management, so be it. (My favourite is called, "Eat That Frog"; it's short and to the point.)

Understand the Pareto Law, which says that 80% of your worthwhile achievements will accrue from just 20% of the effort employed. And vice versa. So figuring out how to take the productive 20% – just understanding what that 20% actually is – and doing more of it, while cutting down the unproductive 80%, will make you more effective, profitable and fulfilled.

Business activity can roughly be divided into four: urgent and important; urgent but not important; not urgent and not important; and not urgent but important. These obviously equate to the Pareto Law too, but by understanding where all your activities fit into this simplistic scheme of things, and doing something about it, you might, just might increase your productivity many-fold.

And in case you're in any doubt, once you've sorted out the

urgent and important stuff, you should spend as much time as you possibly can on the "Not urgent but important" category.

6. Unless you're an accountant by trade or have a particular affinity for detail and numbers, get someone who is/does to manage your accounts – and particularly cash-flow – as soon as you can afford to do so.

It's fundamental to the business, but is either very time-consuming or is ignored – a perilous option. Find someone trustworthy and reliable to do it for you, and release your time to do the things you're best at, and the things which will help the business grow.

Virtually all the businesses I visit summarise their key issues in terms of Time, Team and Money. They don't have the time to do all the things they know they ought to be doing (see point 5, above); they can't find, train and keep the people they need to maintain business growth (point 3 above); and they're always short of cash – that life-blood of ... well, life, the universe and everything.

Making your business's accountancy and administrative systems and processes a fundamental part of its DNA, but separate from your tender mercies, will make the whole enterprise structurally robust.

7. You will eventually have to employ experts in one capacity or another, unless you're determined to stay small and insignificant (your prerogative).

The most important are accountants and lawyers. Not necessarily in that order, as you'll appreciate if you've been reading this book with the rapt attention it surely deserves.

Either way, do not be tempted to be a cheapskate and employ either on the basis of cost. Having an expensive accountant won't necessarily save you lots of tax; you have to select carefully and wisely, if that is a core criterion. You may decide that their reputation with the tax authorities for probity, which means you're likely to get fewer time-consuming visits from Her Madge's inspectors, is a worthwhile trade-off. Personally, I'd have liked ours to have offered more (or just some) tax avoidance options, but you may prefer a quiet – if more expensive – life.

When it comes to lawyers, though, I highly recommend paying top dollar and going to the best. It may seem ruinously expensive, but if you're going to get embroiled in matters legal, the key thing is to win. Pay the extortionate rates for city slicker lawyers and they'll run rings round the country hicks that most businesses rely on. It may cost you money, and lots of it, but you'll nearly always get a result.

8. Whatever else happens, try and have fun. When you're knocking out widgets, and the customers are thin on the ground and getting ever more awkward, this may seem like a tall order. But if there isn't the sound of laughter around the work place, chances are it's not a happy business. And if it isn't a happy business, it probably isn't a profitable one either, and certainly not as profitable as it could or should be.

9. Trust your instincts. If it doesn't feel right, then it probably isn't right – at least for you. I allowed one or two things to happen which instinctively didn't feel right, and regretted at leisure when things went pear-shaped later.

Better to have a fighty now and a full airing of misgivings, than to regret later not having tried to put your foot down.

But at the same time, keep the faith if (or should that be when) you hit turbulence. If you've planned the business adequately, are doing the right things and are doing things right (there is a difference), eventually things will come right.

10. If you ever get in the happy position of being able to sell your business for lots of lovely money:

i) Be sure you know precisely what you want out of the deal, apart from the money, once the deal is done.

ii) Check what your acquirer's post-acquisition strategy is, in detail. Some vague baloney about merging you with this or that business, where there is ample accommodation for you all, does not constitute a strategy or plan. It's the bullshit of someone with more money than brain cells, but a large ego to compensate.

iii) They may equate due diligence with matters financial; you, on the other hand, unless you are planning to walk away into the sunset as soon as that fat juicy cheque clears, should treat it as fundamentally a people issue. Can you work with these people? On what terms? And with what ongoing authority? What indeed is your job description (never mind title – total irrelevance) and what are your core objectives, post acquisition? What resources do you have at your disposal to achieve them, human and other? And if you will be reporting to anyone other than the head acquiree (god forbid), who are they, and what exactly are their objectives and job description? And do you at least respect them, even if you're never going to be buddies?

iv) Do not ever do a deal based on the acquirer's share value, which as any advertising blurb will tell you can go down as well as up, and frequently does. Sure, you might get lucky. There are examples where the share value has doubled or trebled in the next couple of years, and everybody's happy. And there are others where values have halved or quartered. Do you want your hard-earned wealth to be at the mercy of other people's executive decision-making and competence? People over whom you have no influence or authority? No, thought not.

When Marketing Principles was acquired, IPG bought a vibrant, thriving and profitable company, and then systematically deconstructed it until nothing was left. Given we were only one of dozens of similar acquisitions around the world over a two- or three-year period, all of whom presumably had a similar lack of realistic post-acquisition strategy, it's hardly a surprise that the IPG share price, which at the time of the sale was around $35, had sunk to below $10 just a few years later.

v) Most people only ever get one chance to sell their "baby". It's an emotional wrench to let go, however big the cheque being dangled in front of your disbelieving eyes. Just be very sure that the cheque will in fact be adequate compensation for your loss of office, authority and raison d'être.

Looking back over these ten lessons, and applying them to what we did at Marketing Principles, I suppose I'd give us maybe five out of ten. If you're on a similar journey, I hope that some of our mistakes help you score more highly (and make more money).

The Cat disagrees with my over-harsh self-assessment and would have given us seven. So let's split the difference and call it six.